DECEIT ON THE ROAD TO WAR

A volume in the series

CORNELL STUDIES IN SECURITY AFFAIRS

edited by Robert J. Art, Robert Jervis, and Stephen M. Walt

A list of titles in this series is available at www.cornellpress.cornell.edu.

Deceit on the Road to War

Presidents, Politics, and American Democracy

John M. Schuessler

Cornell University Press

Ithaca and London

The views expressed herein are those of the author and do not reflect the official policy or position of the U.S. government or the Department of Defense.

First published 2015 by Cornell University Press
Printed in the United States of America

Library of Congress Cataloging-in-Publication Data
Schuessler, John M., 1977– author.
  Deceit on the road to war : presidents, politics and American democracy / John M. Schuessler.
      pages cm. — (Cornell studies in security affairs)
   Includes bibliographical references and index.
   ISBN 978-0-8014-5359-5 (cloth : alk. paper)
  1. Politics and war—United States—History. 2. Deception—Political aspects—United States—History. 3. Political leadership—United States—History. 4. World War, 1939–1945—Deception—United States. 5. Vietnam War, 1961–1975—Deception—United States. 6. Iraq War, 2003–2011—Deception—United States. I. Title.
   JK558.S44   2015
   355.02'720973—dc23   2015004882

Cornell University Press strives to use environmentally responsible suppliers and materials to the fullest extent possible in the publishing of its books. Such materials include vegetable-based, low-VOC inks and acid-free papers that are recycled, totally chlorine-free, or partly composed of nonwood fibers. For further information, visit our website at www.cornellpress.cornell.edu.

Cloth printing   10 9 8 7 6 5 4 3 2 1

To Sarah, Ella, and Reed

CONTENTS

ACKNOWLEDGMENTS

I have incurred numerous debts during the writing of this book. First and foremost, I thank John Mearsheimer. John was "present at the creation," when this project first started to take shape, and has been an invaluable source of guidance and support throughout. I could not ask for a better mentor. Charlie Glaser has also had a profound impact on me, serving as a role model for what a scholar should be.

I owe a debt of gratitude to all those at the University of Chicago who helped to shape my thinking about international politics. Special thanks go to Dan Drezner, Stathis Kalyvas, Charles Lipson, Bob Pape, Duncan Snidal, and Alex Wendt. Leaving the deepest mark were the graduate students I overlapped with: Jon Caverley, Alex Downes, Todd Hall, Anne Harrington, Jenna Jordan, Adria Lawrence, Chris McIntosh, Nuno Monteiro, Michelle Murray, Emily Nacol, Taka Nishi, Negeen Pegahi, Sebastian Rosato, Frank Smith, Lora Viola, and Joel Westra. Michelle and Sebastian, in particular, have been close friends and reliable sounding boards through the years. Last but not least, Kathy Anderson, Heidi Parker, and Mimi Walsh were unfailingly generous when I needed administrative assistance.

Beyond the confines of Hyde Park, I benefited immensely from a year at the Belfer Center for Science and International Affairs at Harvard University. The Belfer Center provided an ideal environment in which to write and, more important, introduced me to a new group of friends and colleagues. Special thanks go to Steve Miller, Susan Lynch, Sean Lynn-Jones, and Steve Walt for their work with the International Security Program, and to Nick Biziouras, Mike Glosny, Mike Horowitz, and Paul MacDonald for their continuing friendship and advice. The Eisenhower Institute provided me with additional financial support during the year.

I have been fortunate to land rewarding jobs with the Committee on International Relations (CIR) at the University of Chicago and with the Air War College. Special thanks go to Duncan Snidal for providing me with the first opportunity and to the students in the CIR program for helping me to grow as a teacher. At the Air War College, I have benefited from the leadership of the dean, Mark Conversino, as well as from day-to-day interactions with an excellent group of faculty and students. Special thanks go to Jeff Record, who has contributed immensely to my understanding of the World War II, Vietnam, and Iraq cases.

I could not have completed the final draft of the book without the assistance of several generous people. Austin Carson, Kelly Greenhill, Josh Rovner, Elizabeth Saunders, Marc Trachtenberg, and Xiaoming Zhang patiently indulged me as I worked through the implications of their work for my own. The book is stronger in key places for their efforts. Also instrumental was a book workshop hosted by the Notre Dame International Security Program. Special thanks go to Sebastian Rosato for organizing the workshop, to the participants for their extensive feedback, and to Jon Caverley for making the drive from Chicago to join the group. Finally, I could not have asked for a more professional process at Cornell. Comments from reviewers—one of whom turned out to be Bob Jervis—improved the book from front to back. Roger Haydon lent his expert touch at every turn. And Sara Ferguson and Julie Nemer did their parts as production editor and copyeditor, respectively, to polish up the manuscript.

On a personal note, I thank the family and friends who have supported me through the years. Special thanks go to my Notre Dame crew; the extended Reed and Schuessler families, especially my Uncle John, who introduced me to the Chicago Bulls, and my Aunt Moe, who provided a welcoming place to study during grad school; my parents, Terry and Jane Schuessler, who provided me with every opportunity and instilled a deep love of learning; my brother and sister, Mark and Kathryn; and, most important, my wife, Sarah, and my kids, Ella and Reed. This book is dedicated to them.

Deceit on the Road to War

INTRODUCTION

Democracy and Deception

There is widespread agreement inside and outside the academy that democracies are exceptional in their foreign relations. Although this argument comes in many different forms, a common point of departure is that democracies are institutionally constrained in ways that nondemocracies are not when it comes to going to war. Democratic leaders, according to this liberal institutional logic, must generate broad support for war and must do so through an open process of persuasion.[1] They are thus unlikely to seek war unless the benefits clearly outweigh the costs. An important implication is that democracies generally pursue more prudent and successful foreign policies than nondemocracies, winning most of the wars that they start, for example.[2]

Although influential, the liberal institutional logic suffers from an empirical shortcoming: democratic leaders are regularly able to overcome the institutional constraints that they face through the use of deception. This becomes clear when we survey the history of U.S. foreign relations. There is considerable evidence, for example, that the administration of George W. Bush inflated the threat posed by Saddam Hussein to justify the invasion of Iraq in 2003.[3] Bush, however, is hardly the first president to hype and stretch the truth to sell a war. His immediate predecessor, Bill Clinton, justified intervening in Kosovo on the grounds that it was necessary to stop the Milosevic regime in Serbia from committing ethnic cleansing and even genocide against the Kosovar Albanians. Yet, although Milosevic's counterinsurgency campaign in Kosovo was indisputably brutal, it did not approach the level of genocide, claiming between 1,000 and 2,000 Albanian lives before the North Atlantic Treaty Organization (NATO) commenced its bombing campaign, Operation Allied Force, on March 24, 1999.[4] Clinton based his claims of genocide on unconfirmed reports of 10,000 dead promoted by, among others, the Kosovo Liberation Army (KLA), which had deliberately provoked Serb reprisals and had an obvious interest in drawing NATO into the conflict.[5] If anything, outside intervention worsened the plight of the Albanians, with Serb forces ramping up their campaign of ethnic cleansing in response to the bombing.[6] The fact that NATO decision makers did not expect Milosevic to resort to ethnic cleansing on the scale that he did when they kicked off Operation Allied Force undercuts the notion that they intervened to preempt large-scale atrocities.[7] Rather, concerns about the credibility of the alliance appear to have been preeminent.[8]

Likewise, the historical record is clear that the administration of Lyndon Johnson escalated the Vietnam War by stealth so as to subvert domestic debate.[9] Johnson, however, is hardly the first president to be evasive with the public about a coming war or the U.S. role in bringing it about. The popular narrative surrounding World War II is that the United States desired only to be left alone but was forced to fight in the face of Axis aggression. When we take a closer look at how events unfolded, it becomes apparent that World War II was hardly forced on the United States. Well before the Japanese attack on Pearl Harbor, Franklin Roosevelt had come to the conclusion that the United States would have to play a more active role in defeating Nazi Germany and its allies. At the same time, he understood that domestic support for a declaration of war would not be forthcoming in the absence of a major provocation. In this light, both the "undeclared war" in the Atlantic and the oil embargo on Japan should be understood as intended, at least partly, to manufacture an incident that could be used to justify hostilities. Although controversial, a compelling case can be made that Roosevelt welcomed U.S. entry into the war by summer 1941 and manufactured events accordingly.[10]

The pattern of deception evident in U.S. foreign relations cuts to the core of the liberal institutional logic. The democratic process may act as a constraint on leaders' ability to go to war, but deception provides a way around that constraint. Indeed, we can go further. Exactly because "democratic decisions for war are determined and constrained by public consent," as the liberal institutional logic says, democratic leaders have powerful incentives to manufacture that consent through whatever means necessary.[11] It should not be surprising, in other words, that democratic leaders regularly resort to deception to maximize domestic support for war.[12]

We need only begin with assumptions that should be familiar from the liberal institutionalist literature. Democratic leaders want to secure broad support for war, support that cannot be taken for granted at either the mass or elite levels. On rare occasions, we find unified support for war, for example when the homeland has been attacked or victory promises to be nearly costless, but those are the exceptions that prove the rule. As a general matter, the benefits of war are usually ambiguous enough and the potential costs substantial enough that leaders have to grapple with some level of domestic opposition, even if only latent.

Where the liberal institutional logic breaks down is on the issue of deception. Proponents argue that the democratic process should serve as a deterrent to deception.[13] This deterrent is partial at best, however, as leaders retain considerable ability to manipulate domestic audiences without being fully exposed. Most important, they can exploit information and propaganda advantages to frame issues in misleading ways, cherry-pick supporting evidence, suppress damaging revelations, and otherwise skew the public debate in advantageous directions.[14] These tactics should be particularly effective in the prewar period when the information gap between leaders and the public is greatest and the latter's perception of reality is most elastic.[15]

In practice, leaders resort to varying degrees and types of deception to sell wars. As a general rule, however, the more contentious the domestic politics surrounding a war, the more leaders will have to engage in *blame-shifting*. In cases where expected costs are high, for example, or success is uncertain, leaders can anticipate serious resistance to going to war. They will not be inclined to welcome domestic debate under these conditions. Rather, they will do their best to conceal the fact that they are actively considering war while seeking out provocations that shift the blame for hostilities onto the adversary. If the public becomes convinced that the other side has forced the issue, it will be more tolerant of the high costs and initial setbacks that can attend war against a capable opponent.

The more permissive the domestic political environment, in turn, the more deception will take the form of *overselling*. In the event that expected costs are low, for example, or an easy victory seems assured, public discontent will be latent and will center on the fact that war seems unnecessary. In this case, leaders will oversell the threat to convince the public that the stakes are high enough to justify the use of force. Any threat inflation will go uncontested as expectations of a one-sided victory dilute whatever incentives the political opposition might have to force a contentious debate.

When resorting to deception, leaders take a calculated risk that the outcome of war will be favorable, with the public adopting a forgiving attitude after victory is secured. In the event that the outcome is unfavorable, leaders will suffer a political cost, less for misleading the public than for launching a failed war.

These propositions are borne out in three in-depth case studies: World War II, the Vietnam War, and the Iraq War. In each case study, I examine the role that deception played in blunting domestic opposition to a coming war, enabling leaders to circumvent the constraints posed by the democratic process.

The World War II case is the most striking of the three, as it is characterized by the highest levels of prewar opposition as well as the most sophisticated forms of deception. Franklin Roosevelt wanted to bring a unified country into the European war but faced an energized anti-interventionist movement, an obstructionist Congress, and a public that supported aiding the Allies but opposed declaring war. Mindful of domestic opinion, Roosevelt engaged in blameshifting. He maneuvered the country in the direction of war, seeking out pretexts in the Atlantic and Pacific while allowing the public to believe that the United States was being pushed into the conflict. He was finally able to ask for a declaration of war when matters came to a head with Japan in December 1941. With domestic opinion galvanized by Pearl Harbor and the Allies winning a decisive victory over the Axis in 1945, Roosevelt was spared much in the way of damaging scrutiny.

The second case study is the Vietnam War. In 1964–1965, Lyndon Johnson faced a milder version of the domestic political predicament that had confronted Roosevelt prior to World War II. He felt he had no choice but to expand the U.S. presence in Vietnam to contain communism. At the same time, he understood that whatever domestic support he enjoyed was brittle and could quickly evaporate in the event the costs and risks of war were highlighted. Following Roosevelt's lead, Johnson engaged in a creeping form of blameshifting, exploiting a series of pretexts to justify the bombing of North Vietnam and the insertion of ground forces into South Vietnam. All the while, he denied that a major change in policy was in the offing, subverting debate. Johnson's deceptions backfired when the war degenerated into a quagmire.

The third case study is the Iraq War. Unlike Roosevelt and Johnson, George W. Bush faced a relatively permissive domestic political environment on the eve of war. With the public in a vengeful mood after the 9/11 attacks and Democrats in Congress not wanting to be seen as weak on national security, Bush had a relatively free hand in 2002–2003, although not so free as to allow for total candor. Accordingly, overselling played the leading role in his securing domestic support for the Iraq War.[16] Misrepresenting the available intelligence, Bush and members of his administration suggested repeatedly that Saddam Hussein was an undeterrable madman, in league with al Qaeda, and on the verge of acquiring nuclear weapons. The overall effect was to obscure the preventive nature of the war by depicting Iraq as a clear and present danger when in fact it was a weak and isolated pariah. Bush was able to indulge in such blatant overselling, I argue, because of the widespread expectation that victory over Iraq would come cheaply and easily, which undermined the effective functioning of the marketplace of ideas by diluting whatever incentives Democrats might have had to expose even obvious instances of threat inflation. Bush was held to account for his misleading portrayal of the threat only when the deteriorating situation on the ground in Iraq renewed interest in the origins of the war and the arguments that had been used to justify it.

Implications for International Relations

Collectively, the case studies presented here suggest that deception is a natural outgrowth of the democratic process when war is on the horizon, which has implications for several important debates in the field of international relations.

First, are democracies as constrained in their ability to go to war as the liberal institutional logic would have us believe? The answer appears to be no, less because the domestic political constraints that democratic leaders face are inoperative or weak than because they can be overcome through the use of deception. It is difficult to dispute empirically that democracies have formed a separate peace with each other or that they have won an impressive percentage of their wars, but whether this has been due to the constraining effect of democratic institutions should be open to question.

Second, and related, how effectively does the marketplace of ideas function in the run-up to war? In theory, mature democracies are supposed to be characterized by free and open debates in which leaders are called to account for making false or misleading claims, ensuring that the decision to go to war is publicly vetted and underpinned by the best available information.[17] On the one hand, it would be going too far to say that the marketplace of ideas poses no constraint on the ability of leaders to manufacture consent for war. Democratic leaders have to contend with the prospect of public scrutiny, which forces them to be creative and subtle in their tactics, eschewing the crudest forms of deception used by their autocratic counterparts. Indeed, if the marketplace of ideas were not effective at all at fomenting debate, leaders would have little reason to deceive in the first place. On the other hand, the marketplace of ideas rarely lives up to its full potential as a deterrent to deception. This is partly because opposition parties have political incentives to jump on the pro-war bandwagon when a war is expected to be popular or successful, depriving the marketplace of ideas of dissenting viewpoints.[18] As important, leaders benefit from considerable information and propaganda advantages when engaging in debate with their critics, advantages that tilt the rhetorical playing field in their direction.[19] Leaders cannot say whatever they please, of course, but they retain the ability to set the terms of the debate, which is often enough to open up the political space needed for war.

Finally, what is the impact of deception on foreign policy? There is a long-running debate between liberals and realists on the relationship between democracy and a prudent foreign policy.[20] Public opinion, from the liberal perspective, is rational and exerts a moderating influence on leaders. Deception is to be frowned on because it erodes the constraints that keep leaders honest, increasing the risk of policy failure.[21] Realists, in contrast, have traditionally distrusted the public, seeing it as hostile to balance-of-power thinking.[22] Democracy, from the realist perspective, is less a moderating influence than a distorting one, with deception justified when public opinion deviates from what is in the national interest.

Which perspective is borne out by the evidence? The safest conclusion is that the effects of deception on foreign policy are conditional, depending on whether war is justified in a particular case. A distinction should be drawn, for example, between World War II, in which vital interests were threatened, and Vietnam and Iraq, in which they were not. The lesson to be learned from the U.S. experience is not that dishonesty should be avoided at all costs but that one must learn to discriminate between deception that advances the national interest and deception that harms the national interest. Of course, this is easier to do in hindsight and necessarily involves value judgments about the conditions under which war is justified. But, at the very least, deception cannot be ruled out a priori as contrary to the national interest.

1

EXPLAINING DEMOCRATIC DECEPTION

This chapter answers a number of important questions about deception. First, what is deception? How should it be defined? Second, why do democratic leaders resort to deception, and what forms does that deception take? Third, when does deception pay off for leaders, and when does it backfire? Fourth, which debates in international relations are implicated by the deception issue? Finally, how should a theory of democratic deception be tested, and what research design and methodology are appropriate?

Defining Deception

I define *deception* as deliberate attempts on the part of leaders to mislead the public about the thrust of official thinking, in this case about the decision to go to war as well as the reasons to go to war. This definition is consistent with those found in the scholarly literature, but I have made it more specific to fit the research problem at hand. Sissela Bok, in her

well-regarded book on lying, a form of deception, says, "When we under-
take to deceive others intentionally, we communicate messages meant
to mislead them, meant to make them believe what we ourselves do not
believe."[1] John Mearsheimer defines *deception* in similar terms: it is "where
an individual purposely takes steps that are designed to prevent others
from knowing the full truth—as that individual understands it—about a
particular matter." Deception, in this sense, can be contrasted with *truth-
telling*, when "an individual does his best to state the facts and tell a story in
a straightforward and honest way."[2]

A few points of emphasis are in order. First, deception has to be deliberate. In other words, for a statement to be deceptive, leaders must intend for
that statement to mislead.[3] If the intention is lacking, then the statement is
not deceptive. For example, any number of misleading claims can be used
to justify hawkish policies. Among them are the "myths of empire" that
Jack Snyder identifies as primary drivers of great power overexpansion.[4]
However misleading the myths of empire may be, they are deceptive only
if leaders intend them to mislead. Otherwise, they are erroneous or biased,
but not deceptive. As Bok puts it, "truth and truthfulness are not identical,
any more than falsity and falsehood."[5]

Second, leaders appear to be more likely to deceive their own publics
than other leaders. Interstate lying, as Mearsheimer finds, is surprisingly
rare.[6] On occasion, leaders do deceive one another to gain strategic advantage. They may, for example, exaggerate their willingness to fight to deter
or coerce an adversary. Alternatively, they might downplay their hostile
intentions toward another state to disguise an attack on it.[7] Although there
is potential overlap between deception targeted at other states and that targeted at domestic audiences, I limit my focus here to the latter.

Third, I am interested in strategic deception, or deception done in the
service of what leaders consider the national interest. Strategic deception
can be contrasted with selfish deception, or deception done in the service
of parochial goals such as protecting bureaucratic turf or avoiding personal
embarrassment.[8] However prevalent such deception might be, it is not the
focus of this study.

Finally, lying, when a leader makes a knowingly false statement, is
the most blatant form of deception, but for that reason, it is also the least
common. Democratic leaders have to reckon with the fact that their
deceptions may be uncovered in the course of domestic debate.[9] Lying,

therefore, should be less prevalent than other, subtler forms of deception such as spinning, when a leader uses exaggerated rhetoric, and concealment, when a leader withholds vital information.[10] Spinning and concealment are pervasive in politics, so it is tempting to draw a sharp distinction between them and lying when it comes to defining deception. This would be a mistake, however. The deception campaigns featured in this book are characterized by a great deal of spinning and concealment but little outright lying; the cumulative effect is no less misleading. The key is to identify patterns of deceptive behavior, in which leaders are less truthful with the public than they could have been, since the line between deception and something more benign, such as persuasion, can be blurry in individual instances. The bottom line is that deception can be pervasive even while lying is rare.

Explaining Democratic Deception

Why do democratic leaders resort to deception? A reasonable starting assumption, which should be familiar from the liberal institutionalist literature, is that leaders want to secure as much domestic support for war as possible, both to provide political cover and to increase the odds that the public will see the war through to victory.[11] With unified support as the goal, democratic leaders will be sensitive to stirrings of domestic opposition as they edge toward war and will go to some lengths to preempt it lest it intensify. The central argument follows: democratic leaders resort to deception to maximize domestic support for war.[12] Exactly because "democratic decisions for war are determined and constrained by public consent,"[13] democratic leaders have powerful incentives to manufacture that consent through whatever means necessary.

Opposition to War

Although democratic leaders place a high value on domestic support for war, they cannot take it for granted. On rare occasions, we find unified support for war, for example when the homeland has been attacked or victory promises to be nearly costless, but those are the exceptions that prove the rule. As a general matter, the benefits of war are usually ambiguous enough and the potential costs substantial enough that leaders have to grapple with some level of domestic opposition, even if only latent.

The public, for starters, is rarely as firm in its support for war as leaders would like. Partly, this reflects differences in information levels and time horizons. Most people are not national security experts attuned to potential threats.[14] Quite understandably, they have more pressing claims on their attention and cannot be expected to share the same sense of urgency about the external situation as those charged with running the foreign policy apparatus. "Given limited information and high discount rates," as Thomas Christensen has argued, "the public will judge the importance of international challenges by how immediately and clearly they seem to compromise national security"[15] By this standard, public consent for war should be most forthcoming when an adversary appears ready to launch an attack on the homeland or an important ally and least forthcoming when no such attack is on the horizon. For example, in the event that an adversary is geographically distant or does not have much in the way of an offensive capability, the public should be reluctant to pick a fight with it. Normative considerations should reinforce this tendency because force is generally viewed to be legitimate only as a last resort and only for defensive purposes.[16]

When threats are diffuse or indeterminate, potential costs will loom large. A long-standing assumption is that the public is more sensitive to the costs of war than its leaders because it is the public that directly bears those costs.[17] How well supported is this assumption? A recurrent finding in the public opinion literature is that mass support for war declines as casualties accumulate.[18] This is not to suggest that the process is inexorable or that context does not matter. In their work on casualty sensitivity, Christopher Gelpi, Peter Feaver, and Jason Reifler find that the public is best described as "defeat phobic"; that is, beliefs about a war's trajectory matter most in determining the public's willingness to tolerate casualties. When the public is confident that victory is within reach, casualties will have little effect on popular support. But when the public comes to believe that a war could end in stalemate or defeat, its tolerance for casualties will diminish considerably. Gelpi, Feaver, and Reifler marshal a wealth of evidence to support their claims, reanalyzing polling data from a number of conflicts dating back to the Korean War and conducting original surveys designed explicitly to tap into public attitudes on casualties.[19] The implication of their work is that the public is going to be reluctant to pay the human cost of war when victory is uncertain, especially when that cost promises to be high.

A defeat-phobic public, in turn, provides an opening for the political opposition to foment debate. Opposition parties, as Kenneth Schultz argues, publicly contest government policies to present voters with an alternative. In his words, "Opposition parties by their nature seek to highlight and exploit the government's failings in order to convince voters that they would be better off with a change."[20] There is no benefit, however, in presenting an alternative to a policy that is popular or widely regarded as successful. The implication is that opposition parties will line up in support behind a war—or at the very least not be vocal in their criticisms—whenever a successful outcome seems assured, to rob the issue of whatever political salience it might have. When there is a risk that a war could be a costly failure, on the other hand, opposition parties will register their dissent so that they can harness antiwar sentiment at the next election.[21] The political opposition, in other words, reflects and amplifies the public's defeat phobia.

Beyond the political opposition, democratic leaders must be wary of other segments of the elite that could aggravate their problems with the public. As John Zaller has argued, the more contentious the debate at the elite level, the more polarized the public will become as an issue gets politicized.[22] The media enable this process by indexing elite debate; when there is controversy surrounding an issue among elites, this controversy will be reflected in the media.[23] The media is especially attuned to in-fighting among elites who are close to the center of power.[24] For this reason, leaders will be acutely sensitive to signs of dissent among elites who have independent influence—powerful legislators, high-ranking bureaucrats, and senior military officers—and will work hard to make sure their misgivings do not spill over into the public domain.[25]

Three Scenarios

To summarize, democratic leaders want to secure as much domestic support for war as possible, but they can hardly count on unified backing. Instead, they expect to grapple with some level of opposition, both at the mass and elite levels, unless the benefits of war clearly outweigh the costs.

As a general rule, the less substantial and imminent the threat and the less assured a quick and decisive victory, the more contentious a war will be.[26] Three scenarios serve to illustrate the point, all drawn from the literature on great power politics.

The first is preventive war. As Jack Levy defines it, "The preventive motivation for war arises from the perception that one's military power and potential are declining relative to that of a rising adversary, and from the fear of the consequences of that decline."[27] The stronger the preventive motivation, the more willing leaders will be to gamble on a war that holds out some hope of forestalling decline. The public, however, will be reluctant to absorb the costs of a major war when the threat is more potential than actual. What results is a gulf, identified by Randall Schweller, between what realpolitik requires of leaders and what the public is willing to sanction.[28] Schweller's original finding, that democracies do not wage preventive wars, has since been qualified.[29] The logic of his argument remains compelling, however, and suggests that democratic leaders should have some difficulty securing public consent for war in the event that it is preventively motivated.

The second scenario is balancing, or allying with others against a hegemonic threat. If a state has aggressive intentions and enough offensive capability to overturn the balance of power, we would expect its potential victims to band together and, if necessary, to defeat the aggressor in war.[30] As it turns out, even these defensive measures can be controversial, leading to underbalancing if leaders are unable to generate a political consensus for stronger action.[31] Offshore balancing is particularly controversial. It entails intervening in a distant region to forestall the rise of a powerful adversary when local states prove unequal to the task.[32] The political problem confronting leaders is that, in the event that war becomes necessary, the fighting can only be costly and protracted as the offshore balancer attempts to rollback a potential hegemon at the peak of its strength. The public can thus be expected to insist on evidence of direct provocation before it consents to a fight to the finish on the adversary's turf. This is likely part of the explanation for offshore balancers such as Great Britain and the United States historically being prone to buckpassing and intervening only at the last moment.[33]

The third, and final, scenario is intervention. Great powers have regularly intervened in areas of little intrinsic value because of fears that their geopolitical position would erode otherwise.[34] The justification has been provided by the domino theory, which warns that small setbacks in the periphery can snowball into a chain of defeats that threatens the core.[35] Leaders have feared, especially, that if they project an image of weakness then their credibility will be damaged, discouraging allies and emboldening adversaries.[36] The political problem they confront is that, however dire the consequences that may follow from falling dominoes, those consequences are hypothetical and eventually compare unfavorably with the high costs of sustaining a protracted intervention.[37] Given the indirect nature of the threat, leaders should have a difficult time justifying major sacrifices on behalf of peripheral interests.

Deception as a Solution to Leaders' Political Problems

How might leaders go about manufacturing consent for war when such consent is not readily forthcoming? Contrary to liberal institutionalists, who argue that the democratic process should serve as a deterrent to deception, I argue that leaders retain considerable ability to manipulate domestic audiences without being fully exposed.[38] Most important, they can exploit information and propaganda advantages to frame issues in misleading ways, cherry-pick supporting evidence, suppress damaging revelations, and otherwise skew the public debate in advantageous directions.[39] These tactics should be particularly effective in the prewar period, when the information gap between leaders and the public is greatest and the latter's perception of reality is most elastic.[40]

In practice, leaders resort to varying degrees and types of deception to sell wars. As a general rule, however, the more contentious the domestic politics surrounding a war, the more leaders will have to engage in blame-shifting.[41] The more permissive the domestic political environment, in turn, the more deception will take the form of overselling.[42]

In cases in which expected costs are high or success is uncertain, leaders can anticipate stiff resistance to going to war. Rather than making a direct appeal to the public under such unfavorable conditions, leaders will try to preempt debate by shifting blame for hostilities onto the adversary. The trick is to prepare domestic opinion for a possible, and even probable, war while providing firm assurances that war will come only as a last resort and only when the other side forces the issue. This entails two types of deception.

First, leaders must conceal that they are actively considering war.[43] This can entail a number of political and military distortions. For example, if diplomatic commitments have been made that threaten to entangle the state in a brewing conflict, leaders may downplay those commitments or deny that they are binding. Leaders can also negotiate in bad faith, professing a willingness to resolve matters peacefully while conducting talks with the adversary in such a way that they are likely to break down. This is what Evan Braden Montgomery calls "counterfeit diplomacy," in which leaders adopt less forceful measures than they believe are necessary but that they hope or expect will fail.[44] One example of this is initiating talks with an adversary despite a preference for war in the expectation that the talks will fail; in the meantime, the onus for confrontation will have been placed on the other side. To add credibility to the effort, leaders may even renounce the use of force, however disingenuously. In the military realm, leaders will focus on mobilizing in ways that do not betray aggressive intent. This may involve escalating incrementally, deploying forces in a piecemeal fashion so as not to arouse suspicion. In the event that larger, and more dramatic, buildups are required, leaders will offer justifications that the forces are necessary for defensive purposes or for coercive diplomacy but are not evidence of a war footing. Throughout, they will shroud their war planning in secrecy.

Second, leaders must wait for a suitable pretext, usually some hostile act on the part of the adversary, that they can point to as a rationale for war. These "justification of hostility crises," as Richard Ned Lebow calls them, "are unique in that leaders of the initiating state make a decision for war *before* the crisis commences."[45] In his words, "Justification of hostility crises serve to mobilize domestic and foreign support for an impending war and deprive an adversary of such support. They almost invariably attempt to do so by shifting responsibility for war to the adversary."[46] Justification of hostility crises follow a standard script, with leaders exploiting a provocation, real or imagined, to arouse public opinion. The provocation "is held out to the public as compelling evidence of the adversary's aggressive intentions" and "portrayed as a serious enough challenge to the nation's commitments, credibility, or honor to demand a forceful response."[47] Leaders engineering such crises claim to be reacting to events rather than driving them. In extreme cases, leaders may even try to provoke the adversary into striking first, although this strategy is difficult to achieve when the other side is intent on avoiding war.[48]

Either way, the goal is to head off a rancorous debate by exploiting a crisis and the rally-round-the-flag effect that accompanies it.[49] Public consent is sure to be more forthcoming under emergency conditions than if leaders had declared war outright. Moreover, if the public becomes convinced that the other side has forced the issue, it will be more tolerant of the high costs and initial setbacks that can attend war against a capable opponent.

The second form of deception is overselling. In the event that expected costs are low or an easy victory seems assured, leaders will face mixed incentives. On the one hand, they will have less to fear from going public and so should be more forthcoming about their belligerent intentions.[50] The public may be lukewarm about war but will not be strenuously opposed, which will dilute any incentives the political opposition may have to force a contentious debate.[51] To the extent that the political opposition does lodge objections, these should be largely procedural in nature and focused more on *when* and *how* to go to war than on *whether* to do so. Leaders will welcome such a debate because it promises to be one-sided.

On the other hand, leaders will have an incentive to oversell the threat so as to convince the public that the stakes are high enough to justify war. This may entail exaggerating an adversary's aggressiveness or offensive capabilities. The key point is that leaders can inflate the threat secure in the knowledge that their claims will not be rigorously vetted in the marketplace of ideas. The marketplace of ideas depends crucially on the political opposition to trigger broader public debate, so if key opposition figures elect to hold their tongues, misleading official claims will go unchallenged. In the lead-up to the Iraq War, for example, influential Democrats chose to bandwagon with the Bush administration, short-cutting the debate that should have been had on the rationales given for the invasion.[52] With the marketplace of ideas not fully activated, whatever threat inflation leaders engage in will be relatively blatant and will serve to underscore, rather than obscure, their determination to go to war. Overselling, counterintuitively, is enabled by the fact that the public is already somewhat predisposed toward war, if not enthusiastic about it.

Deception as a Calculated Risk

Leaders, in short, resort to deception to maximize domestic support for war. The questions remain: When does deception pay off and when does it backfire? What assurances do leaders have that they are not trading a

short-term political problem for a long-term one? Eric Alterman, a jour-
nalist who has written a book on presidential lying, argues that deception
is invariably counterproductive. The main problem is blowback. In Alterman's words, "The pragmatic problem with official lies is their amoeba-
like penchant for self-replication. The more a leader lies to his people, the
more he *must* lie to his people. Eventually the lies take on a life of their own
and tend to overpower the liar."[53] His advice for leaders is straightforward:
dishonesty should be avoided at all costs.[54]

Are there any exceptions to this rule? I argue that much depends on the
outcome of the war. If a decisive victory is secured, leaders will escape punishment for whatever dishonesty attended the outbreak of war. Indeed,
the public will retrospectively credit its leaders for their far-sightedness
and punish the political opposition for being on the wrong side of the
argument. Success excuses lying, or at least makes it tolerable, as John
Mearsheimer puts it.[55] This prospect is what emboldens leaders to resort to
deception in the first place. Deception will backfire only in the event that
a war goes badly, especially if it degenerates into a costly stalemate. Under
these conditions, public discontent will provide an opening for critics to
revisit the origins of the war and the deceptive tactics that were used to sell
it. Leaders will lose credibility as their dishonesty is exposed. In this case,
the public will punish its leaders less for being misleading than for launching a failed war.

Deception, then, constitutes a calculated risk; it ensures domestic support for war in the short term at the risk of backlash later. Why are leaders
willing to assume this risk? An important part of the answer is that they
ultimately expect to prevail on the battlefield. The larger calculation made
is that, however risky deception may be, inaction is even more so given the
stakes involved.

Democracy and Deception in International Relations

The intersection of democracy and deception implicates several important debates in the field of international relations. The first has to do with
the constraining effects of democratic institutions. From Immanuel Kant
onward, liberals have argued that democracies are uniquely capable of creating a separate peace among themselves.[56] The empirical record seems

to bear this out—democracies rarely go to war or engage in militarized disputes with one another.[57] Proponents of the democratic peace advance two explanations for democracies' being unlikely to fight each other.[58] The first, the normative logic, says that democracies tend to trust and respect each other, ensuring that conflicts of interest among them are resolved amicably.[59] The second, the institutional logic, says that democracies are institutionally constrained from going to war unless the benefits clearly outweigh the costs. This means that democracies will generally be reluctant to fight but will be able to credibly signal their resolve in the event that they are prepared to go to war.[60] Both increase the likelihood that conflicts among democracies will be settled peacefully.

Although the institutional logic comes in different forms, a common point of departure is that democratic leaders are more constrained by public opinion than their nondemocratic counterparts. Elected leaders are accountable to their publics by way of the ballot box, and those publics are sensitive to the costs of war. Kant famously lays out the logic in *Perpetual Peace* and is worth quoting at length because of the subsequent influence he has had on democratic peace theory:

> If (as must inevitably be the case, given this form of constitution) the consent of the citizenry is required in order to determine whether or not there will be war, it is natural that they consider all its calamities before committing themselves to so risky a game. (Among these are doing the fighting themselves, paying the costs of war from their own resources, having to repair at great sacrifice the war's devastation, and, finally, the ultimate evil that would make peace itself better, never being able—because of new and constant wars—to expunge the burden of debt.) By contrast, under a nonrepublican constitution, where subjects are not citizens, the easiest thing in the world to do is to declare war. Here the ruler is not a fellow citizen, but the nation's owner, and war does not affect his table, his hunt, his places of pleasure, his court festivals, and so on. Thus, he can decide to go to war for the most meaningless of reasons, as if it were a kind of pleasure party, and he can blithely leave its justification (which decency requires) to his diplomatic corps, who are always prepared for such exercises.[61]

Public opinion, in other words, induces caution in democratic foreign policy, ensuring that wars are fought only for popular, liberal purposes.[62]

Bruce Russett, building on Kant's insight, argues that institutional constraints should make it difficult for democratic leaders to take their countries to war. "Democracies," according to Russett, "are constrained in going to war by the need to ensure broad popular support," support that "can be built by rhetoric and exhortation, but not readily compelled." Not only may it take a long time for democratic leaders to mobilize their publics for war, but the process will necessarily be public. Simply put, "the greater the scale, cost, and risk of using violence, the more effort must be devoted to preparations in public, and of the public."[63] Institutional constraints, in this way, ensure that democratic leaders can only go to war after a complex mobilization process, reducing the odds that two democracies will find themselves at war with each other.

Drawing on democratic peace theory, scholars have pursued a related line of inquiry: Why do democracies tend to win their wars, especially those they initiate? In *Democracies at War*, the most important contribution to this debate, Dan Reiter and Allan Stam examine a data set of interstate wars from 1816 to 1990 and find that democracies win 93 percent of the wars they initiate, compared to 60 percent for dictatorships and 58 percent for mixed regimes. Although less successful than democratic initiators, democratic targets are also more likely to win than other types of targets, prevailing 63 percent of the time compared to 34 percent for dictatorships and 40 percent for oligarchs.[64] Reiter and Stam conduct a battery of statistical tests to control for other possible explanations for states' winning wars, including military-industrial capabilities, troop quality, military strategy, terrain, distance, and alliances. Even when controlling for these factors, Reiter and Stam find that democracies are more likely to win their wars than nondemocracies, whether they are initiators or targets.[65]

Reiter and Stam provide two explanations for democracies' winning their wars: a "selection effect" advantage that applies to initiators and a "warfighting" advantage that applies to both initiators and targets.[66] The selection effect, which is of particular interest, says that democracies will start wars only when their chances of winning are very high. The logic is rooted in institutional constraints. First, democratic leaders have powerful incentives not to start losing wars, given the threat of electoral punishment hanging over their heads.[67] Second, mature democracies are characterized by a robust marketplace of ideas, which ensures that leaders have the information they need to accurately estimate the probability of victory. "Democratic governments," in Reiter and Stam's words, "benefit from more and higher quality information, meaning that they are more likely to make better policy choices and therefore initiate only winnable wars."[68]

Crucially, proponents of the selection effect, and of the institutional logic more broadly, assume that leaders' ability to manipulate public opinion is highly constrained in democratic systems. Democratic political institutions deter deception and, if necessary, expose it, ensuring that the information that does reach the public is sound.[69] If the public could be reliably manipulated, any constraining effect it had on democratic foreign policy would obviously be weakened. As Reiter and Stam put it, "an important assumption of this perspective is that consent cannot be easily manufactured by democratic leaders. If democratic leaders could manipulate public opinion into supporting military ventures, then of course public opinion would provide little constraint on democratic foreign policy, as it could be actively molded to support the foreign policy aims of the leadership."[70] Alternative explanations for the democratic peace and for democratic victory, ones less dependent on the constraining effects of democratic institutions, would then be in order.

An offshoot of the first debate revolves around the failure of the marketplace of ideas in the case of the Iraq War. In theory, mature democracies are supposed to be less vulnerable to bad ideas than nondemocracies. The causal logic is straightforward. Democratic leaders must publicly defend important decisions such as whether to go to war; when they do so, opposition parties, the press, and independent experts can scrutinize their claims as part of a process of collective deliberation.[71] "Fully developed democracies," as Jack Snyder puts it, "have institutions that break down or limit information monopolies."[72] In the event that leaders are misleading the public, the marketplace of ideas can expose them, undermining whatever support they might have generated and deterring them from making specious claims in the first place.[73]

By now, there is widespread agreement that the marketplace of ideas failed in the run-up to the Iraq War. George W. Bush and members of his administration inflated the threat posed by Saddam Hussein to justify going to war, and those in the best position to expose the weakness of their claims, such as Democrats in Congress, failed to do so. A number of explanations have been offered for why prewar debate was so skewed. Chaim Kaufmann, notably, has emphasized executive powers. Five factors appear to have been critical.[74] First, the Bush administration was able to shift the terms of debate from regional aggression to terrorist attack, splitting whatever consensus there had been against forcible regime change. Second, the administration used its control of the intelligence apparatus to present a selective, and menacing, view of the threat. Third, the White House enjoys a privileged position in foreign policy debates, which allowed the administration to concentrate attention on its claims while marginalizing those of critics. Fourth, countervailing institutions—the political opposition and the press—failed to perform their policing function. Leading Democrats, for example, criticized the administration from the right lest they appear weak on national security. Finally, the shock surrounding the 9/11 attacks meant that the public was more receptive to threat inflation than it might otherwise have been.

The executive powers argument, in turn, has not gone unchallenged. The president's ability to set the terms of debate and to lead public opinion is limited in important respects, some argue.[75] In the specific case of Iraq, sufficient information was publicly available to discredit the administration's more alarming threat claims. The real puzzle, then, is why Bush encountered so little resistance in the marketplace of ideas, especially from Democrats, when his threat inflation was so transparent. Ronald Krebs and Jennifer Lobasz emphasize the framing of the Iraq War as part of the war on terror. This framing served to silence the Democratic opposition by depriving it of socially sustainable arguments against the war. By the fall of 2002, there was general agreement that a war on terror should be fought and that Saddam Hussein was a terrorist. By connecting the dots between the two, Bush narrowed the scope for debate, ensuring that Democrats could contest his claims only at the margins. The Democrats, in effect, were victims of "rhetorical coercion."[76] Alternatively, Jane Cramer has argued that norms of "militarized patriotism," left over from the Cold War, silenced the Democrats. Despite the fact that a majority of the Senate harbored misgivings about the war, bipartisan opposition collapsed because of the political risks entailed in appearing soft on national security and challenging the executive branch in a time of crisis.[77]

Each of the explanations for the failure of the marketplace of ideas in the Iraq case has merit. The executive branch certainly occupies a

privileged position in foreign policy debates, a position that Bush leveraged to conflate the Iraq War with the war on terror. This rhetorical
move backed Democrats into a corner, precluding them from mounting any kind of concerted opposition to the war. Also relevant, but
underemphasized in the debate, is the political context; the widespread
expectation that regime change would be cheap and easy diluted any
incentive Democrats had to expose even obvious instances of threat
inflation (see Chapter 4). For the purposes of this book, the key take-
away is that the marketplace of ideas can deter the use of deception
only up to a point. Outright lies may be rare, but leaders retain enough
of an ability to spin and conceal that the rhetorical playing field is
tilted in their favor. This is not to suggest that deception "always and
everywhere succeeds and that the opposition is always and everywhere
silent."[78] Rather, it amounts to the claim that the marketplace of ideas
is not so effective in its policing function that deception is not a viable
option for leaders.

The final debate of interest, which has implications for the paradigmatic divide between liberals and realists, concerns the impact of
deception on foreign policy. For liberals, democracy holds the key to
prudent foreign policy. In the words of Reiter and Stam, "When a country's informed citizens broadly participate in the debate surrounding
the formation and execution of political choices, superior public policy
results."[79] Deception as a practice is thus hard to justify because it is
antidemocratic to the core.[80] Specifically, deception interferes with the
free flow of information, creating substantial risks. In the short term,
it can inhibit the evaluation of options. When leaders use deception to
subvert debate, "the range of perspectives represented is narrowed, the
number of options examined is reduced, and all the implications of a
given course of action may not be considered."[81] Misguided policies can
result. In the long term, deception has a tendency to blowback onto
the leaders who use it.[82] They become entrapped in their own rhetoric and cannot acknowledge or correct past mistakes. Most important,
deception, when exposed, erodes public trust in government, forfeiting
a crucial political resource that leaders need to conduct an effective foreign policy.[83] Given these risks, dishonesty should generally be avoided,
liberals argue.[84]

Unlike liberals, realists have traditionally distrusted the public, seeing it as hostile to balance-of-power thinking.[85] Hans Morgenthau, characteristically, does not mince words on the subject:

> Thinking required for the successful conduct of foreign policy can be diametrically opposed to the rhetoric and action by which the masses and their representatives are likely to be moved. The peculiar qualities of the statesman's mind are not always likely to find a favorable response in the popular mind. The statesman must think in terms of the national interest, conceived as power among other powers. The popular mind, unaware of the fine distinctions of the statesman's thinking, reasons more often than not in the simple moralistic and legalistic terms of absolute good and absolute evil. The statesman must take the long view, proceeding slowly and by detours, paying with small losses for great advantage; he must be able to temporize, to compromise, to bide his time. The popular mind wants quick results; it will sacrifice tomorrow's real benefit for today's apparent advantage.[86]

The bottom line, according to Morgenthau, is that "a foreign policy that is passionately and overwhelmingly supported by public opinion cannot be assumed for that reason alone to be good foreign policy. On the contrary, the harmony between foreign policy and public opinion may well have been achieved at the price of surrendering the principles of good foreign policy to the unsound preferences of public opinion."[87]

From a realist perspective, blanket injunctions against deception are premature. Whatever their other differences, realists tend to be skeptical of democratic exceptionalism.[88] The democratic peace is better described as an imperial peace based on U.S. power; and if democracies tend to win their wars, it is because they happen to be wealthy and powerful, not inherently cautious or militarily effective.[89] When realists do discuss the inner workings of democracy, it is to draw attention to the ways in which "disruptions from below" deflect leaders from foreign policies that are rooted in the national interest.[90] Democracy is less a moderating influence than a distorting one, according to this line of argument.

Not surprisingly, given their ambivalence toward democracy, realists have been more forgiving of deception than liberals. Morgenthau, for example, in his classic book *In Defense of the National Interest*, contends, "A tragic choice often confronts those responsible for the conduct of foreign affairs. They must either sacrifice what they consider good policy upon the altar of public opinion, or by devious means gain popular support for policies whose true nature they conceal from the public."[91] John Mearsheimer strikes a similar chord in his book on lying in international politics. One of his key findings is that "it occasionally makes good sense for leaders to lie to their own people."[92] The litmus test for realists is whether deception advances or harms the national interest. In other words, the effects of deception on foreign policy are conditional.

Uncovering Democratic Deception

Given the stakes, it is important that any theory of democratic deception be tested carefully. To this end, I have opted for a case study approach.[93] Case studies have two advantages when it comes to the study of deception. First, deception is difficult to uncover. For obvious reasons, leaders rarely admit to deception. Indeed, they have strong incentives to conceal deceptive behavior. The result is that direct, "smoking-gun" evidence of deception is usually lacking.[94] Under these circumstances, the next-best strategy is to accumulate indirect evidence, such as inconsistencies between leaders' public and private statements.[95] Even when such inconsistencies are rampant, it is difficult to completely rule out the possibility that leaders' public statements are sincere, at least up to a point. Deception, that is, can be difficult to distinguish from self-deception.[96] Given the methodological challenges associated with uncovering deception, a case study approach is most appropriate. It allows deception to be accurately coded in a small number of cases, as opposed to loosely coded in a large number of cases. Second, case studies have advantages when it comes to exploring causal mechanisms.[97] John Gerring lays out the logic: "Case studies, if well constructed, allow one to peer into the box of causality to the intermediate causes lying between some cause and its purported effect."[98] In the present instance, case studies allow for the use of process-tracing to assess whether it was the need to maximize domestic support that drove leaders to deceive or some other factor.[99]

The historical analysis that anchors each case study hews closely to the method outlined by Marc Trachtenberg in *The Craft of International History*, which involves critically analyzing the secondary literature and supplementing with primary sources whenever the need arises.[100] "The basic technique," as Trachtenberg describes it, "is to take some major theoretical claim, bring it down to earth by thinking about what it would mean in specific historical contexts, and then study those historical episodes with those basic conceptual issues in mind."[101] To this end, several questions are asked of each case: When and why did leaders settle on war? How much domestic opposition did they anticipate? Did they resort to deception in response? What forms did that deception take? And what were the effects of deception? By way of this method of structured, focused comparison, we can draw inferences about the causes and consequences of deception.[102]

To facilitate case selection, I began with a universe that included all interstate wars fought by the United States since it became a great power in 1898.[103] The rationale was to maximize the chances that the institutional constraints featured in the literature would have a chance to operate. By general agreement, the United States has been a mature democracy throughout this period, one with an open political process and relatively weak executive branch.[104] As Colin Dueck argues, "The challenge of mobilizing public and legislative support for costly new initiatives in the United States is as great as in any democratic country."[105] Since it became a great power, moreover, its leaders have had considerable choice in whether and when to go to war. The United States has faced no serious threats on its borders, so there has almost always been ample space and time for debate. In short, *if* democracy functions to deter deception or alternatively to spur it on, then that should be evident in a selection of cases from the history of the United States as a great power.

To capture finer-grained variation within this universe, I then selected cases that were marked by different levels of domestic opposition to war, with the expectation that more opposition would be associated with blameshifting and less opposition with overselling.[106] As I demonstrate in the coming chapters, that expectation is largely borne out. The first case, World War II, is characterized by the highest levels of prewar opposition as well as the most sophisticated forms of blameshifting. Roosevelt is the only leader featured in this book to face an energized anti-interventionist movement, an obstructionist Congress, and a public that could not fully reconcile itself to war. He is also the only leader to be so devious as to pursue a back door into conflict. World War II, in other words, is best coded as a high-opposition, high-deception case. The Vietnam War, in contrast, is best coded as a medium-opposition, medium-deception case. Johnson did not have to grapple with the intense opposition that Roosevelt did, but he understood that there was little enthusiasm for a land war in Asia and that any support he enjoyed for his policies would not survive a protracted debate on the costs and risks of taking on a larger role in Vietnam. Johnson thus engaged in a creeping form of blameshifting, exploiting a series of pretexts to justify the bombing of North Vietnam and the insertion of ground forces into South Vietnam. All the while, he denied that a major change in policy was in the offing.[107] The Iraq War, the third case, stands out as having the most permissive domestic political environment on the eve of war, partly because of the recent 9/11 attacks and partly because of the expectation that toppling Saddam Hussein would be cheap and easy. Accordingly, overselling played the lead role in securing domestic support for the Iraq War, with the Bush administration blatantly inflating the threat posed by Iraqi weapons of mass destruction (WMDs) and ties to terrorism while doing little to conceal its intention to engage in regime change. It is the low-opposition, low-deception case in the book.

2

SHIFTING BLAME TO THE AXIS

FDR's Undeclared War

In the realm of national mythology, Americans remember World War II as "the good war."[1] According to the standard narrative, the United States desired only to be left alone but was forced to fight in the face of Axis aggression. But when we take a closer look at the historical record, it becomes clear that World War II was hardly forced on the United States. Well before the Japanese attack on Pearl Harbor on December 7, 1941, President Franklin Roosevelt came to the conclusion that the United States would have to play a more active role in defeating Nazi Germany and its allies. At the same time, he understood that domestic support for a declaration of war would not be forthcoming in the absence of a major provocation.[2] In this light, both the "undeclared war" in the Atlantic and the oil embargo on Japan should be understood as intended, at least partly, to manufacture an incident that could be used as a pretext for war.[3]

In this chapter, I first make the case that Roosevelt had powerful strategic reasons to enter the European war by summer 1941 while addressing the debate among historians about whether he sought full-scale intervention prior to Pearl Harbor. I then discuss the domestic political obstacles that Roosevelt had to contend with as he contemplated war and lay out in detail the deceptions that he used to shift blame to the Axis side, including using the Pacific war as a back door into the European war. Finally, I discuss the consequences of Roosevelt's deceptions.

Balancing against the Axis

During World War II, the United States pursued a grand strategy of off-shore balancing, intervening in Europe and Asia to contain potential hegemons in those regions.[4] The primary challenge to U.S. interests was Nazi Germany, which threatened to overrun the European continent. The Nazis came perilously close to doing so with the fall of France in June 1940. U.S. policymakers feared that if Adolf Hitler were able to dominate Europe he would pose an intolerable military, economic, and ideological threat to the Western Hemisphere. To check the Nazis, the United States extended assistance to Great Britain, most significantly in the form of Lend-Lease aid. As Great Britain's position grew precarious in summer 1941, however, Roosevelt reluctantly concluded that stronger measures were required and began to seek out opportunities to bring the United States into the European war. In Asia, the United States faced a secondary but still serious threat from Japan, which was embroiled in a protracted war with China and menaced Russia to the north and the British supply line to the south. As the Japanese expanded into the southwest Pacific, U.S. policymakers moved to contain them. The official policy was to deter the Japanese while not provoking them, so as not to divert scarce resources from the primary theater in Europe.

The Nazi Threat in Europe

By the end of 1938, after the Munich Crisis, Roosevelt was convinced that Hitler wanted nothing less than world domination and that, after subduing the European continent, he was sure to turn his sights on the United States.[5] Because of the nature of contemporary warfare, with aircraft capable of attacking at great speeds over long distances, Roosevelt felt that the United States could no longer afford to retreat within its borders and rely on its oceanic barriers for safety.[6] Instead, he envisaged the European democracies as the U.S. front line. As long as France and Great Britain resisted Nazi advances, the United States was afforded a degree of protection from the Nazi threat. If France and Great Britain were to succumb to Nazi rule, however, Germany would pose an intolerable threat to the Western Hemisphere. Roosevelt's primary fear was that Hitler would exploit political unrest in Latin America to install pro-Nazi regimes, which would provide staging areas for direct attacks on the United States.[7] As David Reynolds summarizes the president's thinking, "Above all, F.D.R. feared that Germany might combine its subversion in Latin America with a direct invasion of the Western Hemisphere, perhaps after neutralizing the British and French fleets and securing European possessions in West Africa or the Caribbean. He was particularly conscious of the relative narrowness of the South Atlantic and of the potential for long-distance aerial attack on the U.S. from West Africa, via bases in South or Central America."[8]

To check the Nazi threat to the Western Hemisphere, Roosevelt's preference was to pass the buck to the European democracies, which would serve as a front line for the United States. His assumption was that in the event that war broke out there would be an uneasy military stalemate on the ground, with France and Great Britain ultimately prevailing over Germany by way of blockade and bombing.[9] Instead, in June 1940 France fell with stunning rapidity, succumbing to the German blitzkrieg in little over a month. Thereafter, the survival of Great Britain became of paramount importance. As Roosevelt warned in a fireside chat at the close of the year, "If Great Britain goes down, the Axis powers will control the continents of Europe, Asia, Africa, Australasia, and the high seas—and they will be in a position to bring enormous military and naval resources against this hemisphere. It is no exaggeration to say that all of us, in all the Americas, would be living at the point of a gun—a gun loaded with explosive bullets, economic as well as military.[10]" To avert this outcome, it was vital that the United States extend whatever assistance was necessary to sustain Great Britain in its fight against the Nazis, even if that meant courting war.

By fall 1940, Roosevelt's military advisers were thinking along similar lines.[11] Indeed, some were willing to go further. In November 1940, Admiral Harold Stark, the chief of naval operations, circulated one of the more explicit statements of the offshore balancing logic that was to motivate

U.S. entry into the war a year later, commonly known as the Plan Dog memorandum. In it, Stark warned that "the present situation of the British Empire is not encouraging" and that "should Britain lose the war, the military consequences to the United States would be serious." He further cautioned that Britain's mere survival would be insufficient. Rather, "to win, she must finally be able to effect the complete, or, at least, the partial collapse of the German Reich." This would require a land offensive against the Axis powers, with U.S. help: "For making a successful land offensive, British manpower is insufficient. Offensive troops from other nations will be required." Specifically, "the United States, in addition to sending naval assistance, would also need to send large air and land forces to Europe or Africa, or both." At the same time, Stark understood that "account must be taken of the possible unwillingness of the people of the United States to support land operations of this character."[12]

At the time, Roosevelt was not ready to concede, at least publicly, that British victory would require formal U.S. entry into the war or an invasion of Europe, so he avoided any direct approval of the Plan Dog memorandum.[13] He subscribed to its basic thinking, however, so military planning proceeded under the assumption that, in the event of war, the United States would pursue a Germany-first approach in conjunction with Great Britain while maintaining a defensive posture against Japan. This assumption underpinned the joint planning done by Anglo-American officers in spring 1941 and is reflected even more clearly in the Victory Program. The Victory Program, prepared at Roosevelt's request after the German invasion of Russia in late June 1941, outlined production requirements in the event of a global war.[14] Echoing Plan Dog, it reiterated that "if our European enemies are to be defeated, it will be necessary for the United States to enter the war, and to employ a part of its armed forces offensively in the Eastern Atlantic and in Europe or Africa." Moreover, it stressed that "naval and air forces seldom, if ever, win important wars" and that "it should be recognized as an almost invariable rule that only land armies can finally win wars."[15] The logic, as Mark Stoler argues, was unassailable: "if British survival and German defeat were essential to U.S. security and if this required ground operations beyond British capabilities or competence, then Washington would have to create and deploy the enormous army needed for such operations."[16] Vitally, it would have to do so by July 1943, at which point Germany would have consolidated its gains.[17]

U.S. Entry into the War?

As evidenced by Plan Dog and the Victory Program, Roosevelt's military planners were in agreement that a German defeat would require U.S. entry into the war, including an invasion of Europe. Historians, however, remain divided on the issue of whether Roosevelt himself sought more than to contain Hitler by proxy. As one review of the literature concludes, "After a half century of research, it must be noted that there is still no scholarly consensus as to whether the president sought full-scale intervention in the European war."[18] David Reynolds, for example, suggests that Roosevelt's "desire in 1941 was that America's contribution to the war would be in arms not armies—acting as the arsenal of democracy and the guardian of the oceans but not involved in another major land war in Europe."[19] Roosevelt had good reasons for avoiding formal entry into the war, according to Reynolds: public opinion would demand that rearmament take priority over Lend-Lease aid, with potentially disastrous consequences for the Allies; and war with Germany would inevitably mean war with Japan, given the Tripartite Pact.[20] Mark Stoler, along similar lines, has argued that Roosevelt "had no intention of creating or sending to Europe a large army" because he viewed the British and Russian armies as substitutes for U.S. ground forces.[21] As late as September 1941, Stoler notes, Roosevelt deferred army expansion so as to release supplies for Great Britain and Russia.

Roosevelt undeniably had deep misgivings about entering the war. He was especially reluctant to concede that it would be necessary to mobilize a mass army. He was known to say privately that it would be politically impossible to send another American Expeditionary Force to Europe. Moreover, he seems to have genuinely believed that strategic bombing had displaced land warfare in importance.[22] At the same time, his military advisers had made it clear to him that fighting Hitler by proxy could be only a temporary expedient and that an invasion of Europe would ultimately be necessary to defeat Nazi Germany. And that invasion could not wait too long because, in the event that Germany defeated Russia and turned to mobilizing the resources of the Eurasian landmass, it would quickly become invulnerable. In the words of the Victory Program:

> Time is of the essence and the longer we delay effective offensive operations against the Axis, the more difficult will become the attainment of victory. It is mandatory that we reach an early appreciation of our stupendous task, and gain the whole-hearted support of the entire country in the production of trained men, ships, munitions, and ample reserves. Otherwise, we will be confronted in the not distant future by a Germany strongly entrenched economically, supported by newly acquired sources of vital supplies and industries, with her military forces operating on interior lines, and in a position of hegemony in Europe which will be comparatively easy to defend and maintain.[23]

Robert Dallek, who has written the most comprehensive account of Roosevelt's foreign policy, concludes that Roosevelt wished to take the United States into the war by the time of the Atlantic Conference in August 1941.[24] It is worth noting that through the fall of 1941 even those who were relatively optimistic about the prospects of Russia were not sure that it could hold out against the German onslaught through summer 1942, which meant that the window of opportunity to intervene was closing.[25] Steven Casey concurs with this logic, speculating that, had Roosevelt been free to act in fall 1941, "he would probably have favored a balanced response to the Nazi danger, based primarily on the use of U.S. land power."[26] Because of pressing domestic constraints, however, he was reluctant to push too openly for a formal declaration of war or the creation of an American Expeditionary Force.[27] Instead, he maneuvered the country in the direction of war while allowing the public to believe that the United States was being pushed into the conflict. Even those scholars, such as Waldo Heinrichs, who remain skeptical that Roosevelt was seeking war before Pearl Harbor, concede the credibility of this position, noting that "it is hard to believe that he did not understand that sooner or later, one way or the other," the course of action he was pursuing "would lead to war."[28]

Containing Japan

If Roosevelt intended to balance against Germany, even if that meant war, what were the implications for U.S. policy toward Japan? First, it meant a clear recognition that the Japanese threat was of secondary importance and that the United States should not court war in the Pacific while it deepened its involvement in the Atlantic.[29] Roosevelt himself, as Casey points out, "strongly believed that Nazi Germany posed the most powerful threat to U.S. interests" and that "wherever possible, the conflict in Asia had to be contained and dampened so that scarce U.S. resources would not be diverted away from Europe."[30] This was a sentiment that was shared by the military. War planners agreed that in any war against the Axis the United States should pursue a Germany-first approach while maintaining a defensive posture against Japan.[31] The Plan Dog memorandum called for "a positive effort to avoid war with Japan" as a preliminary to war in Europe.[32]

At the same time, there was widespread agreement that the United States should make some effort to contain Japan, which by July 1941 appeared poised to attack north, into Russia, or south, into Southeast Asia. Either scenario was troubling, the former because it would jeopardize Russian prospects against Germany and the latter because it would disrupt the British supply line in the southwest Pacific. As Joseph Grew, ambassador to Japan, explained to Yosuke Matsuoka, the Japanese foreign minister, in May 1941, it "would be utter folly for us, having adopted a policy of supporting Great Britain, to supply Great Britain by the Atlantic while complacently watching the downfall of Britain through the severance of the British lifeline from the East."[33] Heinrichs summarizes the overall approach of the administration: "Whether Japan went north or south it threatened to upset the improving balance of forces. This careening expansionism must be stopped. Japan must be boxed in, contained, immobilized."[34] To this end, the U.S. fleet was redeployed to Hawaii, the Philippines was reinforced with land and air forces, and, most important, increasingly stringent economic sanctions were placed on Japan. The dilemma was how to deter Japanese aggression without provoking a war in the process.[35] One of the enduring puzzles of the period is why the United States failed in this regard and ended up at war with Japan in December 1941. (I return to this subject later.)

Anti-Interventionism

Even as the Axis threat intensified, Roosevelt had to contend with domestic opposition to expanded U.S. involvement in the war. Most prominently, a diverse anti-interventionist movement, with significant representation in

Congress, mobilized to challenge the president's initiatives. This movement fed off a deeply ambivalent public, which came to support aid to the Allies but was strongly opposed to a declaration of war.

"The Many Mansions of Anti-Interventionism"

The anti-interventionists of 1940–1941 were a highly diverse coalition. Their ranks included former presidents (Herbert Hoover), influential members of Congress (Hamilton Fish and Robert Taft), newspaper magnates (William Randolph Hearst and Colonel Robert McCormick), celebrities (Charles Lindbergh), radio personalities (Charles Coughlin), prominent business and labor labors (General Robert Wood and John Lewis), and even members of the Roosevelt administration (Adolf Berle and Joseph Kennedy). As Justus Doenecke has characterized the movement, "the house of anti-interventionism contained many mansions."[36] The organization that came to embody these diverse tendencies was the America First Committee (AFC), which established itself during the 1940 presidential election as the primary anti-interventionist organization in the United States, in opposition to such interventionist groups as the Committee to Defend America by Aiding the Allies.[37] With its financial base in the Chicago business community, the AFC had considerable grassroots appeal in the Midwest. By the time it disbanded on December 11, 1941, with the German declaration of war on the United States, the group had 450 local chapters and at least 250,000 members. The AFC posed enough of a political threat to the Roosevelt administration that its spokesmen were routinely attacked as Nazi sympathizers. As Michaela Hoenicke Moore relates, "FDR and his supporters did not hold back in using the label of Nazism to disparage their political opponents. Apart from a right-wing radical fringe . . . the majority of isolationist-minded, Republican-voting Americans believed in democracy. Nevertheless, the Roosevelt administration succeeded after the outbreak of the European war in discrediting the organized part of the isolationist movement by denying the loyalty, patriotism, and integrity of individual spokesmen, portraying them as pro-Nazi or arguing that they were playing into the hands of the enemy."[38]

Although as a group the anti-interventionists were certainly hostile to Roosevelt's foreign policy, this was not because they were pro-Nazi but because they thought the traditional philosophy of hemisphere defense was still viable. In its inaugural press release of September 4, 1940, the AFC stressed four basic principles:

1. "The United States must build an impregnable defense for America."
2. "No foreign power, nor group of powers, can successfully attack a *prepared* America."
3. "American democracy can be preserved only by keeping out of the European war."
4. "'Aid short of war' weakens national defense at home and threatens to involve America in war abroad."[39]

The anti-interventionists were especially adamant about the last point, with one isolationist senator, Burton K. Wheeler of Montana, referring to the Lend-Lease program of aid to Britain as "the New Deal's triple A foreign policy; it will plow under every fourth American boy."[40]

To bolster their case, the anti-interventionists hammered home a number of points in speeches and writings: that the Axis posed neither a military nor an economic threat to the United States, that Russia would emerge as the primary beneficiary of the conflict, that Great Britain was an imperial power and unfit ally, that aid to the Allies would come at the expense of national defense, that overseas involvement would lead to domestic ruin, and that a negotiated peace could be secured.[41] It is worth elaborating, in particular, on the anti-interventionist claim that Nazi Germany posed no real threat to the Western Hemisphere because this was in direct opposition to a central plank of the Roosevelt administration case for intervening in the European war.[42] Charles Lindbergh, because of his standing as an authority on aviation, was especially effective in discounting some of the more worrisome scenarios. Testifying against the Lend-Lease Act in January 1941, Lindbergh reassured the House Committee on Foreign Affairs that a U.S. air force of "about 10,000 thoroughly modern planes," working in conjunction with the U.S. Navy, "would make it practically impossible for a foreign navy to do serious damage or to land an expeditionary force of any size on our coasts." Although admitting the feasibility of bombing raids, Lindberg insisted that the costs of a full-scale air invasion would so outweigh the benefits that it was no surprise that "not a single squadron of transoceanic bombing planes exists anywhere in the world today." Aviation, in his judgment, had "added to America's security against Europe," not detracted from it, as the interventionists claimed.[43] Hanson Baldwin, the military correspondent for the *New York Times*, thought enough of Lindbergh's testimony that he wrote in *Fortune* in March 1941, "Colonel Charles Lindbergh obviously was right when he declared that this country could not be invaded or seriously assaulted by air, so long as no Eurasian air power possessed bases in this hemisphere."[44]

Despite Lindbergh's best efforts, the anti-interventionists lost the great debate over Lend-Lease and continued to cede ground as war approached. The sheer force of events was encouraging most Americans to adopt a moderate interventionist stance.[45] This did not mean, however, that the AFC and its affiliates did not complicate Roosevelt's task with Congress and the public. Roosevelt recognized that "if he came out in favor of full belligerency he would undoubtedly face a stubborn and well-organized minority determined to undermine domestic unity at a time when harmony was vital for a successful war effort."[46]

Congress and the Neutrality Acts

At the beginning of his presidency, Roosevelt enjoyed his share of legislative triumphs, most famously with the New Deal. Congress, however, proved less cooperative when it came to measures that might embroil the country in another European war. By the mid-1930s, as Dallek reminds us, "Americans generally believed that involvement in World War I had been a mistake, that Wilson's freedom to take unneutral steps had pushed the country into the fighting, and that only strict limitations on presidential discretion could keep this from happening again."[47] The result was a series of Neutrality acts. The first, passed in August 1935, imposed an embargo on the sale of arms to belligerents. The second, passed in February 1936, added a ban on loans. The final Neutrality Act, passed in May 1937, restricted travel and shipping. The intent was "to minimize the economic entanglements and naval incidents that had supposedly drawn America into the Great War."[48]

Initially, Roosevelt was not opposed to the idea of a neutrality act, as long as it permitted him a degree of executive discretion in discriminating between aggressors and victims. The legislation that came out of Congress strongly tied the president's hands, however, and as the situation in Europe deteriorated in 1938–1939, he began to chafe at the constraints it imposed.

Roosevelt wanted to be able to sell armaments to France and Great Britain, and later to finance and transport them, but he faced an uphill battle in Congress when it came to revision of the legislation. This is not to say that he met only with failure. With the outbreak of war in Europe in fall 1939, Congress repealed the arms embargo and placed trade with belligerents on a cash-and-carry basis.[49] Right up until Pearl Harbor, however, Roosevelt remained reluctant to ask for full repeal of the Neutrality Act. He understood that there were limits to congressional interventionism. Indeed, as late as November 1941, Congress only narrowly revised the legislation to allow armed merchant ships to carry their cargoes all the way to Britain.[50] Close votes such as these convinced Roosevelt that winning a declaration of war would be impossible in the absence of a substantial provocation from abroad.[51]

The Public: Anti-Axis and Antiwar

In its ambivalence toward intervention in the European war, Congress reflected public opinion. On the one hand, overwhelming majorities detested the Nazi regime. At the outset of the war in Europe, 83 percent of Americans wanted the Allies to win, according to an October 1939 *Fortune* poll; a mere 1 percent favored Hitler and the Nazis.[52] This did not translate, initially, into a willingness to come to the aid of the European democracies. Once France fell, however, more and more Americans came to favor a moderate interventionist stance that included military preparedness and doing everything possible to help Great Britain, short of war.[53] In every poll conducted after November 1940, a majority of the public supported the policy of helping Great Britain and defeating Germany.[54] By 1941, almost two-thirds (66.1 percent) chose aid to Great Britain over staying out of war; twice—in March and October 1941—that number passed the 70 percent mark.[55] On the other hand, Americans "remained adamantly opposed to a direct, unlimited, and formal involvement in the conflict."[56] Polls taken from 1938 to late 1941 show that an overwhelming majority of the public opposed direct U.S. involvement on the side of the Allies, with no more than one-third ever supporting a declaration of war.[57] Roosevelt's perpetual problem, as described by the British ambassador in October 1941, was "to steer a course between the two factors represented by: (1) The wish of 70 percent of Americans to keep out of war" and

"(2) The wish of 70 percent of Americans to do everything to break Hitler, even if it means war."[58]

This dichotomy in opinion was also evident in attitudes toward the Pacific war. By 1941, anti-Japanese sentiment was rampant, fed by moral revulsion at Japanese atrocities in China as well as the Axis association with the Nazis.[59] Americans needed little convincing that stiff action should be taken to halt and contain Japanese aggression. As early as June 1939, Gallup polls showed that 72 percent of the American people favored an embargo on war materials shipped to Japan.[60] At the same time, the public's desire for action in Asia did not run very deep.[61] "Most Americans," according to Steven Gillon, "clung to widely held notions of Japan as a third-rate military power that was no match for the United States."[62] This fed the belief that a hard line could be taken with Japan with few adverse consequences. As an aide reported to Roosevelt after surveying the press in July 1941, "The prevailing editorial judgment is that four years of warfare has exhausted the Japanese, undermined their economy, and revealed them as a second-rate power . . . A great many commentators cherish the conviction that the American Pacific fleet would polish off Japanese sea power between daybreak and breakfast—with the Atlantic fleet tied behind its back, at that."[63] Gallup polls asking whether the United States would win a war with Japan demonstrated a similar complacency, with up to 92 percent of respondents saying yes.[64] The key point is that Roosevelt could afford to take a hard line with Japan without fearing a public backlash, exactly what he needed to open up a back door into the European war.[65]

Roosevelt's Undeclared War

Roosevelt was famously sensitive to the domestic mood. He firmly believed that an effective policy abroad first required a consensus at home.[66] Given the persistence of anti-interventionism, such a consensus was bound to be elusive in the case of a declaration of war. Roosevelt thus maneuvered the country in the direction of war while allowing the public to believe that the United States was being pushed into the conflict. As Ian Kershaw observes, "his policy in these crucial months was determined in good measure by the need to prepare the public for something it did not want and which he had solemnly promised to avoid: sending American troops to fight in another war in Europe."[67] Roosevelt's strategy entailed two types of deception: (1) efforts to obscure the belligerent drift of U.S. policy, at least through summer 1941 and (2) a search for pretexts in the Atlantic and Pacific that would allow him to shift blame to the Axis side.

The Guise of Nonbelligerency

Roosevelt went to some lengths to obscure the belligerent drift of U.S. policy, which was especially important before public opinion solidified behind the moderate interventionist stance of aid to Britain in summer 1941. He did this in three ways. First, he kept up the pretense that the United States was a neutral power even as he waged a proxy war on behalf of the Allies. This pattern is evident as far back as the debate over revision of the Neutrality Act in fall 1939.[68] In that debate, the Roosevelt administration presented cash-and-carry as a peace measure even though it was primarily intended to benefit France and Great Britain, which had the cash to pay for arms and the ships to carry them.[69] The administration, as Robert Divine argues, "carried on the elaborate pretense that the sale of arms to the Allies was but the accidental by-product of a program designed solely to keep the United States clear of war."[70] In a speech to Congress on September 21, 1939, asking for repeal of the arms embargo and its replacement with cash-and-carry, Roosevelt reassured skeptics, "To those who say that this program would involve a step toward war on our part, I reply that it offers far greater safeguards than we now possess or have ever possessed, to protect American lives and property from danger. It is a positive program for giving safety. This means less likelihood of incidents and controversies which tend to draw us into conflict, as they unhappily did in the last World War. There lies the road to peace!"[71] Critics, such as Senator Arthur Vandenberg, were not fooled, warning that in the long run the United States could not "become an arsenal for one belligerent without becoming a target for another."[72]

The gap between rhetoric and reality remained wide through summer 1941 as the United States moved to bolster the British. During that period, Roosevelt defended such unneutral acts as Destroyers-for-Bases, Lend-Lease, and intervention in the Battle of the Atlantic as straightforward measures of self-defense, necessary for keeping the war away from the Western Hemisphere. To prepare the ground for the Destroyers-for-Bases deal, Roosevelt put much more emphasis on the acquisition of Atlantic bases than the release of destroyers to Great Britain. At a press conference on August 16, 1940, he even implied that there was no connection between the two.[73] As far as Lend-Lease was concerned, Democratic leaders titled the enabling legislation "An Act to Promote the Defense of the United States"; and during hearings in the Senate, friendly witnesses claimed that the bill was actually designed to keep the United States out of war, in response to warnings by anti-interventionists that it would accomplish the opposite.[74] Expanded naval patrolling, which had the effect of aiding the British in the Battle of the Atlantic, was said to be entailed by a series of Western Hemisphere Defense Plans, with the concept of the hemisphere suitably stretched to include the North Atlantic area.[75] The emphasis on hemispheric security was not entirely disingenuous, at least on Roosevelt's part. As Heinrichs argues, "While Roosevelt unquestionably considered the Atlantic vital as a bridge to Britain and ultimately the conquest of Germany, he also regarded it as vital for protecting the safety and existence of the United States in case of British defeat."[76] The key point is that a common-law alliance was developing with Great Britain, and Roosevelt could only be so forthcoming about it given the risk of war with Germany at a time when anti-interventionist sentiment still held some sway.[77]

Second, Roosevelt pledged to keep the country out of the fighting, even as official thinking started to come around to the conclusion that entry into the war might eventually be required. The most prominent examples come from late in the 1940 election campaign, when Roosevelt's opponent, Wendell Willkie, began to charge him with warmongering to dent his lead in the polls. "On the basis of his past performance with pledges to the people," Willkie said of Roosevelt on October 23, 1940, "if you re-elect him you may expect war in April 1941."[78] To rebut these charges, Roosevelt felt compelled to predict that the country would not become involved in fighting of any kind. Most famously, he promised at a campaign stop in Boston on October 30, 1940, "I have said this before, but I shall say it again and again and again: Your boys are not going to be sent into any foreign wars."[79] Deliberately, he left out the qualifying phrase in the Democratic platform, "except in case of attack."[80] Nor did Roosevelt's pledges end with the election. In a fireside chat on December 29, 1940, the president reassured the public, "There is no demand for sending an American Expeditionary

Force outside our own borders. There is no intention by any member of your Government to send such a force. You can, therefore, nail any talk about sending armies to Europe as deliberate untruth. Our national policy is not directed toward war. Its sole purpose is to keep war away from our country and our people."[81] Roosevelt may have shared some of these sentiments, but he also must have understood that such unqualified assurances of peace were at odds with the central tendency of U.S. policy.

Finally, Roosevelt was careful to shroud military planning in secrecy. He not only kept internal exercises such as Plan Dog and the Victory Program under wraps, but he also authorized secret talks between U.S. planners and their British counterparts, which were held from the end of January to the end of March 1941.[82] Known as the American-British Conversations (ABC), the talks revolved around contingency plans in case the United States entered the war. They culminated in agreement "that Germany was the primary threat to the security of both countries, that the defeat of Germany and Italy was the priority, that the Atlantic lifeline between Britain and the U.S.A. must be secured and that a purely defensive, deterrent policy should be maintained against Japan."[83] The participants even produced a war plan to that effect—RAINBOW-5—in case the United States entered the conflict.[84] Robert Sherwood, a White House speechwriter and biographer of Roosevelt, has written that these staff talks "provided the highest degree of strategic preparedness that the United States or probably any another non-aggressor nation has ever had before entry into war."[85]

Such detailed planning belied Roosevelt's assurances that the United States would remain out of the fighting. The overlap with the Lend-Lease debate in Congress was especially sensitive, given the gap between what the administration was saying in public and what it was planning in private. As James Leutze summarizes the situation:

> The debate over the Lend-Lease Bill provided a counterpoint for the ABC Conference. . . . While the debate over the bill proceeded in Congress and in the press, the ABC Conference was being conducted in camera at the Navy Department. Time after time the administration contended that Lend-Lease was essential to keep England fighting and America out of the war. On the floor of Congress and in press conferences, commitments and plans to convoy or send American troops out of the hemisphere were denied repeatedly by administration spokesmen. But at the other end of

Pennsylvania Avenue the military representatives of that same administration were conducting the first prewar staff conferences in American history and laying plans for convoying, building bases in the British Isles, and replacing British Tommy's in Iceland with American GI's.[86]

The political sensitivities attached to the talks explain why the Roosevelt administration went to such lengths to keep them secret. Admiral Stark warned participants that leaks to the press "might well be disastrous." British planners dressed in civilian clothes and were officially described as technical advisers to the British Purchasing Commission.[87] In Leutze's judgment, there was reason for caution: "The president's credibility would have been seriously undermined had it been learned that a few blocks from the Capitol British and American officers were making plans for a coalition war."[88] Sherwood concurs: "It is an ironic fact that in all probability no great damage would have been done" had the details of the ABC agreements "fallen into the hands of the Germans and the Japanese; whereas, had they fallen into the hands of the Congress and the press, American preparation for war might have been well nigh wrecked and ruined."[89]

Looking for an Incident in the Atlantic

As the ABC talks were coming to a close, Germany moved aggressively to further isolate Great Britain. In April 1941, Nazi armies advanced through the Balkans, overrunning Yugoslavia and Greece. Compounding the loss was the decision by Great Britain to divert troops there, which served only to weaken its defenses in North Africa. Once Libya fell, the road to the Suez Canal lay open. Even more serious was the German war on British shipping and communications, the main object of which was to cut the people and factories of Britain off from crucial overseas sources of food and raw materials so as to starve them into submission.[90] With U-boats and surface raiders on the prowl in the Atlantic, Great Britain was losing ships at the rate of more than 500,000 tons a month, and because its shipyards were under air attack, it could replace at best 30 percent of the losses. If the trends continued, Great Britain would import 14 percent less than its required minimum for the year.[91] Desperate, Winston Churchill, the British prime minister, sent a telegram to Roosevelt on May 4, 1941 asking for a U.S. declaration of war, the first time he had done so since June 1940.[92]

With Great Britain's position growing precarious, Roosevelt concluded that the United States would ultimately have to join the fighting, but he was reluctant to ask for a declaration of war in the absence of a provocation from abroad. As Dallek summarizes the president's thinking in May 1941:

> While he believed that the public would strongly line up behind intervention if a major incident demonstrated the need to fight, he did not feel that he could evoke this response simply by what he said or did. . . . In his view, if a substantial minority in the country felt that he, rather than a meaningful threat to national security, compelled involvement in the conflict, it would be difficult to assure wartime unity in the United States, especially in the face of any temporary defeat. In short, if he were to avoid painful wartime divisions, the nation would have to enter with a minimum of doubt and dissent, and the way to achieve this was not through educational talks to the public or strong Executive action, but through developments abroad which aroused the country to fight.[93]

The problem was how to court such developments when Hitler was going out of his way to avoid a confrontation with the United States. With German forces massing for the invasion of Russia, Hitler was hardly ready to invite U.S. belligerency. In fact, he repeatedly gave instructions to the German Navy to avoid contact with U.S. ships, lest Roosevelt be provided with a pretext to declare war.[94] Hitler's instincts, in this case, were sound; Roosevelt saw a potential opportunity in the "undeclared war" that was about to be waged in the Atlantic.

Roosevelt first edged into the Battle of the Atlantic on March 15, 1941, when he ordered the Atlantic fleet to prepare for active duty. Roosevelt's principal concern was to ensure that Lend-Lease supplies arrived safely in Great Britain. Over the course of the summer, however, as reinforcements arrived from the Pacific and the Atlantic fleet grew in strength, the United States adopted an increasingly confrontational posture toward Germany. In April 1941, Roosevelt extended the U.S. defense zone across the Atlantic to include Greenland and the Azores. This allowed the navy to patrol the western Atlantic and broadcast the location of German ships to the British.[95] In July 1941, a contingent of marines arrived in Iceland, "the turntable of the Atlantic," to help with its defense. Roosevelt envisioned Iceland as an eventual transshipment point for Atlantic convoys. In August 1941, the president met with Churchill at Argentia, Newfoundland, to establish the political basis for waging war if it should come to that, culminating in the Atlantic Charter. In September 1941, the navy began escorting convoys as far as Iceland, with orders to "shoot on sight" in the event that they encountered Axis warships. By this time, the United States was at war with Germany in the western Atlantic in all but name. As Stark put it on September 22, 1941, "So far as the Atlantic is concerned, we are all but, if not actually in it."[96]

In his public appearances, Roosevelt defended intervention in the Battle of the Atlantic in hemispheric security terms. In a radio address announcing the proclamation of an unlimited national emergency on May 27, 1941, the president warned listeners that "unless the advance of Hitlerism is forcibly checked now, the Western Hemisphere will be within range of the Nazi weapons of destruction." Because "it would be suicide to wait until they are in our front yard," Roosevelt pledged to "actively resist wherever necessary, and with all our resources, every attempt by Hitler to extend his Nazi domination to the Western Hemisphere."[97] However sincere his concerns for hemispheric security, there is evidence that Roosevelt harbored a more provocative end in mind when it came to intervening in the Battle of the Atlantic. Namely, might it be possible to force an incident that would justify war with Germany? Roosevelt's conversations with Churchill at the Atlantic Conference, held in early August 1941, are especially revealing in this regard. According to Churchill's recollection of the talks, Roosevelt volunteered that "he was skating on pretty thin ice in his relations with Congress" and that "if he were to put the issue of peace and war to Congress, they would debate it for three months." Instead, Roosevelt indicated that "he would wage war, but not declare it, and that he would become more and more provocative. If the Germans did not like it, they could attack American forces." As Churchill understood it, "Everything was to be done to force an 'incident'" once the American navy began escorting convoys.[98] This was hardly an isolated remark. In the presence of advisers, Roosevelt made several allusions to provoking an incident in the Atlantic, leading Henry Stimson, his secretary of war, to speculate, "The President shows evidence of waiting for the accidental shot of some irresponsible captain on either side to be the occasion of his going to war."[99]

In September 1941, Roosevelt used just such an incident to announce that the U.S. navy would commence escort operations in the North Atlantic, a policy that had been adopted in secret in late July 1941.[100] The details are as follows. On September 4, a U.S. destroyer, the *Greer*, exchanged fire with a German submarine, U-652, in the North Atlantic at a point within the overlap between the German combat area and the U.S. defense zone. U-652 fired on the *Greer* only after being pursued for several hours and evading depth charges from a British plane, which had alerted the *Greer* to the submarine's presence. The navy reported to the president on September 9, "Submarine was not seen by *Greer* hence there is no positive evidence that the submarine knew nationality of ship at which it was firing."[101] In a fireside chat delivered on September 11, Roosevelt deliberately distorted the details of the incident.[102] He claimed that the *Greer*'s "identity as an American ship was unmistakable" and that "the German submarine fired first upon this American destroyer without warning, and with deliberate design to sink her." Such an act "was piracy—piracy legally and morally." Roosevelt went on to outline a "Nazi design to abolish the freedom of the seas" as a prelude to domination of the United States and the Western Hemisphere. Reminding his audience that he had "sought no shooting war with Hitler," Roosevelt insisted nonetheless that "when you see a rattlesnake poised to strike, you do not wait until he has struck before you crush him." He then announced that the U.S. navy would protect all merchant ships engaged in commerce in the North Atlantic and that Axis ships would enter U.S. waters "at their own peril." The navy began escorting convoys six days later, with 62 percent of those polled by Gallup approving of the "shoot on sight" order.[103]

The *Greer* incident certainly facilitated intervention in the Battle of the Atlantic, but it was hardly the *casus belli* that Roosevelt had promised Churchill at Argentia. With the German Navy under strict orders to avoid contact with U.S. ships, there were few major incidents in fall 1941.[104] As for the incidents that did occur, it became clear that naval skirmishes would not suffice to generate the kind of consensus for war that Roosevelt wanted. In the second half of October 1941, German U-boats torpedoed the destroyers USS *Kearny* and USS *Reuben James*, with the loss of over one hundred crew in the latter case. Congress remained as divided as ever, barely passing revisions to the Neutrality Act arming U.S. merchant ships and allowing them to enter combat zones. Roosevelt reluctantly concluded that it would take a more dramatic event than any sinking in the Atlantic to draw the United States into the war, telling the press on November 3, 1941, "We don't want a declared war with Germany because we are acting in defense—self-defense—every action. And to break off diplomatic relations—why, that wouldn't do any good."[105] The fact had to be faced: "unless the United States were to be attacked, a declaration of war—even in the unlikely event that it could be pushed through Congress—would undoubtedly produce a bitterly divided country."[106] As is well known, only Pearl Harbor eased this political dilemma for Roosevelt.

Pearl Harbor: Back Door to War?

Conspiracy theories persist that suggest that Roosevelt deliberately allowed the Pearl Harbor attack to happen to bring a unified country into the war. Among serious scholars, such arguments have been discredited, however. According to David Kennedy, "Despite decades of investigation, no credible evidence has ever been adduced to support the charge that Roosevelt deliberately exposed the fleet at Pearl Harbor to attack in order to precipitate war."[107] Jeffrey Record has a similar take: "The recurring historical revisionism that accuses Roosevelt of having prior knowledge of the attack on Pearl Harbor remains unaccompanied by a shred of convincing evidence."[108] The scholarly consensus, rather, is that the Roosevelt administration did not anticipate a Japanese attack on Pearl Harbor, preoccupied as it was with developments in Southeast Asia. "Although there remain many dark corners to the Pearl Harbor story," David Reynolds concludes, "the evidence points to confusion and complacency, not conspiracy, in Washington."[109]

Although the most notorious conspiracy theories have been found wanting, the notion that Roosevelt allowed matters to come to a head with Japan so that the United States could have a back door into the European war remains defensible. The argument has recently been revived by Marc Trachtenberg, for example.[110] Official policy, he notes, was to deter the Japanese while not provoking them, so as not to divert scarce resources from the primary theater in Europe. Given these limited aims, it is puzzling that

Roosevelt adopted such a hard line in late summer and fall 1941, imposing an oil embargo and then insisting that the Japanese withdraw from
China before supplies would be resumed. When negotiations predictably
unraveled and Japanese action was imminent, Roosevelt talked openly of
maneuvering Japan into firing the first shot rather than redoubling efforts
for a diplomatic compromise. In these ways, Pearl Harbor was neither a
complete surprise to Roosevelt nor entirely unwelcome.

In late June 1941, Japanese leaders debated how they could best exploit
Hitler's invasion of Russia. On July 2, 1941, they decided to move forward
with the Southern Advance, which promised control of the resources
of Southeast Asia and the encirclement of China. Japanese troops made
their first moves in this direction on July 24, 1941, occupying southern
Indochina. At the time, Japanese leaders did not expect a war with the
United States to result.[111] To their surprise, the Roosevelt administration
responded by imposing a de facto oil embargo. Rather than banning oil
exports to Japan, Roosevelt issued an order freezing Japanese assets and
then invited the Japanese government to apply for exchange permits
from the Treasury Department to free up dollars for purchases of limited
amounts of oil and gasoline.[112] After several attempts to arrange payment
for oil were rebuffed, it became clear to the Japanese that the embargo
was complete; and with the British and Dutch imposing their own asset
freezes, the economic access of Japan to the outside world was largely cut
off. Disingenuously, Roosevelt justified the trade restrictions by peddling
the false notion that "the United States could not spare California oil for
Japan because it was scarce in New York."[113]

The United States, for all intents and purposes, had imposed an
embargo without saying so.[114] As was widely recognized, this was a provocative move because Japan imported 90 percent of its oil, 75–80 percent
of which came from the United States, and could not continue its war in
China indefinitely without outside supplies.[115] Roosevelt himself understood that an embargo could well lead to a Japanese attack on the Dutch
East Indies to secure the oil fields there, which in turn would lead to war
with Great Britain and the United States.[116] On July 24, 1941, two days
before he signed the order freezing Japanese assets, Roosevelt told the
Japanese ambassador that "for more than two years the United States had
been permitting oil to be exported from the United States to Japan. He said
that this had been done because of the realization on the part of the United

States that if these oil supplies had been shut off or restricted the Japanese government and people would have been furnished with an incentive or a pretext for moving down upon the Netherlands East Indies in order to assure themselves of a greater oil supply than that which, under present conditions, they were able to obtain." "If Japan attempted to seize oil supplies by force in the Netherlands East Indies," he continued, "the Dutch would, without the shadow of a doubt, resist, the British would immediately come to their assistance, war would then result between Japan, the British and the Dutch, and, in view of our own policy of assisting Great Britain, *an exceedingly serious situation would immediately result.*"[117] The next day, Roosevelt took a similar line with a group of civil defense enthusiasts, explaining to them, "It was very essential from our own selfish point of view of defense to prevent a war from starting in the South Pacific. So our foreign policy was—trying to stop a war from breaking out down there. . . . Now, if we cut the oil off, they [the Japanese] probably would have gone down to the Dutch East Indies a year ago, and you would have had war. Therefore, there was—you might call—a method in letting this oil go to Japan, with the hope—and it has worked for two years—of keeping war out of the South Pacific."[118]

It is generally assumed that Roosevelt did not want an open break with Japan at this time, so some observers have concluded that mid-level officials hijacked the policy process and engineered an embargo against his wishes.[119] At the Cabinet meeting on July 24, 1941, during which the freezing order was discussed, Roosevelt intimated that "he was inclined to go ahead with the order in a regular way and grant licenses for the shipment of petroleum as the applications are presented to the Treasury." The point was not "to draw the noose tight" but "to slip the noose around Japan's neck and give it a jerk now and then."[120] Roosevelt, in other words, "intended the freeze to be not the first blow in a program of economic warfare but a final warning, designed to bring Japan to its senses, not its knees."[121] His mistake, however, was in turning over implementation of the asset freeze to an interdepartmental Foreign Funds Control Committee (FFCC), chaired by assistant secretary of state Dean Acheson. Acheson and fellow hawks from the State and Treasury departments took advantage of their positions on the FFCC to give Japan the administrative run-around and to ensure that no dollars were released to pay for oil imports. Acheson himself believed that it was safe to impose a total embargo because "no rational

Japanese could believe that an attack on us could result in anything but disaster for his country."[122]

What evidence is there that the oil embargo met with Roosevelt's approval and was not just the work of hawkish, middle-level bureaucrats? As it turns out, Acheson was reporting to undersecretary of state Sumner Welles, who was very close to Roosevelt at the time. At a meeting of the FFCC on July 29, 1941, Acheson said that he had seen Welles, who felt that "for the next week or so the happiest solution" would be "to take no action on Japanese applications" until Roosevelt had a chance to review the situation with Churchill at their upcoming meeting in Argentia. "Given the close association of Welles and Roosevelt, the fact that Welles was currently Acting Secretary of State, and the vital importance of the issue, it seems inconceivable that Welles did not secure the president's approval for this course of action, or inaction," Heinrichs concludes.[123] Acheson, in other words, was hardly acting without high-level sanction when he held up the exchange permits.

The conversations at the Atlantic Conference are also revealing. On August 11, 1941, Churchill said that "it would be essential to maintain the full pressure of economic measures which the U.S. Government had already adopted in regard to Japan." Roosevelt responded "that he had every intention of maintaining economic measures in full force." In meetings with his British counterpart, Welles was even more explicit, assuring him that the application of the freezing order against Japan was "very strict" and that in the case of oil "no licenses were being granted expect for crude oil up to an amount corresponding with that exported in 1935. This quantity had already been reached and therefore no more crude oil would be allowed except sufficient to take Japanese ships from American ports home to Japan."[124] Welles, at least, was hardly in the dark about the complete nature of the embargo, and neither, it appears, was Roosevelt.[125] This might explain why, when Roosevelt was notified in early September 1941 that all oil exports to Japan had been suspended, he did not reverse the decision, even though a relaxation of sanctions would have been perfectly consistent with a policy of giving the Japanese a very strong "jerk" without actually driving them to war.[126] It is hard to escape the conclusion, which Trachtenberg reaches, that Roosevelt "deliberately opted for a policy which he knew would in all probability lead to war with Japan."[127]

If that was Roosevelt's intent, the embargo had the desired effect. It accelerated preparations for a general war that Japanese leaders had hoped to avoid. Faced with the prospect that their oil reserves would run out in less than two years, Japanese policymakers decided that they had no choice but to seize the Dutch East Indies by force, even if that entailed war with Great Britain and the United States.[128] Japan, many of them felt, was "like a fish in a pond from which the water was gradually being drained away."[129] A moderate faction led by Prince Konoe, the prime minister, still held out hope for a diplomatic settlement that would restore normal trade relations. To secure an agreement, the moderates were willing to forgo further expansion, to withdraw from territory Japan had occupied as part of the Southern Advance, and even to work toward an accommodation on the China issue. Great hopes were placed on a meeting between Konoe and Roosevelt, at which the two leaders could reach an understanding that would avert war. At an Imperial Conference on September 6, 1941, the emperor threw his weight behind the diplomatic effort, rebuking the army and navy for their single-minded focus on preparing for war by reading a poem composed by his grandfather, the Meiji emperor: "All the seas, in every quarter, are as brothers to one another. Why, then, do the winds and waves of strife rage so turbulently throughout the world?"[130] The emperor could exert only so much influence, given his role as a ratifier of policies that had already been reached by consensus, but his intervention was sufficient to slow down the momentum for war and provide some room for diplomacy.[131] Until late November 1941, "the Japanese government bent all its efforts toward securing some kind of agreement with the United States which would relax the economic pressure now grown intolerable, without sacrificing all of Japan's gains."[132]

Dashing any hopes the moderates might have had for a softening of the U.S. position, Cordell Hull, the secretary of state, held firm in his demand that Japan withdraw all its troops from China, a demand that the Japanese army found hard to accept after four years of intense fighting there.[133] General Tojo Hideki, the army minister, voiced his dilemma in a meeting with his navy counterpart on October 7, 1941: "We have lost 200,000 souls in the China Incident, and I cannot bear to give it all up just like that."[134] Hull's insistence that Japan accept defeat in China was more consistent with a policy of rollback than containment.[135] It was certainly at odds with the thrust of U.S. strategy, which was to remain on the defensive in Asia until Nazi Germany was defeated. "America," as Paul Schroeder argues, "went on the diplomatic offensive after July 1941. Her aims were no longer simply those of holding the line against Japanese advances and of inducing Japan to draw away from an alliance [the Axis] which the United States considered menacing. The chief objective of American policy now was to push Japan back, to compel her to withdraw from her conquests. . . . The objective that had previously been the least important and pressing in American policy, the liberation of China, now became the crucial consideration."[136] The United States, in effect, went to war over China rather than Southeast Asia, "a volte-face of enormous strategic consequence."[137]

Roosevelt's military advisers were opposed to the hard line that he and Hull were taking with the Japanese. From their perspective, the White House and the State Department seemed to be "insanely willing" to provoke a second war in the Pacific when hostilities were escalating in the Atlantic.[138] In August 1941, Welles had to remind Roosevelt that "in the opinion of both the War and Navy Departments of the United States the chief objective in the Pacific for the time being should be the avoidance of war with Japan inasmuch as war between the United States and Japan at this time would not only tie up the major portion of if not the entire American fleet but would likewise create a very serious strain upon our military establishment and upon our productive activities at the very moment when these should be concentrated upon the Atlantic."[139] Rather than bring matters to a head with Japan, the military wanted Roosevelt to gain time through clever diplomacy, so that the reinforcement of the Philippines could be completed.[140] It was hoped that a force of new, long-range B-17 bombers based in the Philippines not only would serve to defend the islands but would deter Japan from further aggression in the southwest Pacific.[141] A Japanese withdrawal from China would also be strategically counterproductive because the Japanese troops in China were troops unavailable for military operations elsewhere.[142]

Rather than play for time as the military was recommending, Roosevelt largely gave up on diplomacy as fall progressed. In October 1941, prodded by Hull, he shut the door on the idea of a summit with Konoe because a comprehensive settlement could not be reached beforehand, ostensibly the purpose of the meeting. He did so against the advice of Ambassador Grew, who urged in the strongest terms that Roosevelt accept

Konoe's invitation. Only in such a setting would Konoe be able to make "far-reaching concessions" that could then be presented to the Japanese military as a fait accompli, with the emperor's support.[143] "The good," Grew wrote, "which may flow from a meeting between Prince Konoe and President Roosevelt is incalculable."[144] The alternative was the replacement of the current government with a military dictatorship and a steady drift to war. Despairing, Grew warned in early November 1941 that it was only a matter of time before Japan's leaders resorted to "an all out, do-or-die attempt, actually risking national hara-kiri, to make Japan impervious to economic embargoes abroad rather than to yield to foreign pressure."[145]

Konoe resigned, as Grew had predicted, on October 16, 1941, when his efforts to achieve a face-to-face meeting with Roosevelt came to naught. The door had not yet closed, however, on diplomacy. In an unprecedented move, the emperor asked the new prime minister, Tojo, to "wipe the slate clean" and make a final push to avert war; his government would not be bound by previous decisions that had set a deadline of mid-October 1941 for diplomacy to be successful.[146] At issue was whether the two sides could agree to a *modus vivendi* that would postpone hostilities and buy time for a compromise agreement to be worked out. The Japanese version, "Plan B," envisioned a return to the status quo ante as of July 1941, with Japan withdrawing its troops from southern Indochina in exchange for the lifting of the oil embargo. The Japanese also asked that the United States suspend aid to China once an armistice was reached.[147] Initially, Roosevelt seemed intrigued by the idea of a *modus vivendi*, handing Hull an outline of one around November 17, 1941. The proposal involved a limited resumption of economic relations and an offer to bring Japan and China together for peace talks. In return, Japan would send no more troops south or north and agree not to invoke the Tripartite Pact in the event of a German-U.S. war.[148] Roosevelt abandoned the search for a *modus vivendi*, however, just as the two sides were moving within negotiating range of each other. He was no doubt influenced by Hull, who decided "to kick the whole thing over" when the Chinese reacted violently to what they feared would be a sellout. The British response was also lukewarm, with Churchill asking, "What about Chiang Kai-shek? Is he not having a very thin diet? Our anxiety is about China. If they collapse, our joint dangers would enormously increase."[149]

Roosevelt and Hull understood that, with the demise of the *modus vivendi,* diplomacy had come to an end.[150] Their calculation was that it was more important to keep the anti-Axis coalition intact than to maintain peace with Japan. On December 1, 1941, Roosevelt assured the British ambassador that, in case of a Japanese attack on British or Dutch territory in Southeast Asia, "we should obviously be all together." In further conversations on December 3, the president was more explicit, confirming that when he talked about "support" for the British and Dutch he meant "armed support."[151] The chief remaining concern was domestic opinion and how to rally the public in the event Japan confined its aggression to European colonial possessions, as seemed likely. As Jeffrey Record has asked, "What if the Japanese had attacked only Malaya, Singapore, and the Dutch East Indies, leaving the Philippines and Hawaii alone? Could Roosevelt have persuaded Congress to go to war on behalf of European colonies in Asia?"[152] To help with this problem, American diplomats had reintroduced the issue of the Tripartite Pact into the final round of talks with the Japanese. The revival of the pact issue, according to Paul Schroeder, was a propaganda device meant to help sell the anticipated war with Japan to the American people. The thinking was that "there could be no more direct and effective way to justify going to war with Japan over her drive southward than to show that Japan was tied to Hitler and participating in his plan for world conquest."[153]

Japanese planes attacked Pearl Harbor on December 7, 1941, seemingly confirming the warnings about an Axis conspiracy. The reality, however, was far different. Japan had fought only after being backed into a corner by the U.S. diplomatic and economic offensive. Yoshimichi Hara, who as president of the Imperial Privy Council spoke for the emperor, captured Japanese thinking on the eve of war: "If we were to give in, we would give up in one stroke not only our gains in the Sino-Japanese and Russo-Japanese wars, but also the benefits of the Manchurian Incident. This we cannot do. We are loath to compel our people to suffer even greater hardships, on top of what they have endured during the four years since the China Incident. But it is clear that the existence of our country is being threatened, that the great achievements of the Emperor Meiji would all come to naught, and that there is nothing else we can do."[154] Fatefully, because the Japanese assumed the United States and Great Britain were strategically indivisible, they felt they had no choice but to strike the first blow at Pearl Harbor to protect the flank of the main advance against Malaya, Singapore, the Philippines, and the Dutch East Indies. The objective of the attack was to knock out the U.S. Pacific fleet for at least six months so that Japan could conquer Southeast Asia without interference from the U.S. navy.[155] The Japanese strategy for victory, such as it was, was to secure enough of a stronghold in the central and southwestern Pacific that the United States would be forced into a "murderous, island-by-island slog" that would eventually exhaust the political will of the American people.[156]

Anticipating the main thrust into Southeast Asia, Roosevelt was shocked that the Japanese had taken the fleet by surprise at Hawaii. He was also relieved, however, that they had not limited their attacks to British and Dutch possessions, potentially depriving him of the popular backing needed to declare war. Harry Hopkins, a top Roosevelt adviser, says this explicitly when recounting the events of the day:

> I recall talking to the President many times in the past year and it always disturbed him because he really thought that the tactics of the Japanese would be to avoid a conflict with us; that they would not attack either the Philippines or Hawaii but would move on Thailand, French Indo-China, make further inroads on China itself and possibly attack the Malay Straits. . . . This would have left the President with the very difficult problem of protecting our interests. . . . Hence his great relief at the method that Japan used. In spite of the disaster at Pearl Harbor and the blitz-warfare with the Japanese during the first few weeks, it completely solidified the American people and made the war upon Japan inevitable.[157]

By December 1941, Roosevelt and his advisers wanted such a war because it promised entry into a European conflict that demanded U.S. intervention. Again, Hopkins makes this explicit when describing the mood at the White House following the Pearl Harbor attack: "The conference met in not too tense an atmosphere because I think that all of us believed that in the last analysis the enemy was Hitler and that he could never be defeated without force of arms; that sooner or later we were bound to be in the war and that Japan had given us an opportunity."[158]

What reason did Hopkins have to believe that Japanese military action would facilitate U.S. entry into the European war? It is important to point out in this context that it had been assumed since early 1941 that, in the event of a conflict with Japan, the United States would go to war with Germany and Italy at once.[159] As it happens, Roosevelt was not forced to declare war first because he had intelligence in hand suggesting that Hitler would declare war on the United States in the event of a Japanese attack.[160] And he was inclined to wait to secure the extra margin of political support that would come from responding to a German declaration of war.[161] Even if Hitler had not obliged, however, Roosevelt would have been able to channel the popular anger surrounding the Pearl Harbor attack into a vote for war against Germany. Most Americans saw Germany as the dominant partner in the Axis, goading Japan into doing its bidding in the Pacific. Indeed, there was rampant speculation that German forces had participated in the raid on Hawaii. In the days following the attack, Pearl Harbor was widely blamed on Hitler. According to a Gallup poll taken on December 10, 1941, 90 percent of respondents favored an immediate declaration of war on Germany, even though Hitler did not issue his own declaration until the next day.[162]

For their part, Roosevelt and his advisers simply took it for granted that war with Germany was imminent. Hull, recounting a dinner at the White House on December 7, 1941, says, "We assumed that it was inevitable that Germany would declare war on us. The intercepted Japanese messages passing back and forth between Berlin and Tokyo had given us to understand that there was a definite undertaking on this point between the two Governments. We therefore decided to wait and let Hitler and Mussolini issue their declarations first. Meantime we would take no chances and would act, for example in the Atlantic, on the assumption that we were at war with the European section of the Axis as well."[163] It is telling, in this regard, that Roosevelt chose to use a fireside chat on December 9, 1941, to tie the Pearl Harbor attacks to the war in Europe, preparing the public for what was to come. "Your Government," Roosevelt disclosed, "knows that for weeks Germany has been telling Japan that if Japan did not attack the United States, Japan would not share in dividing the spoils with Germany when peace came. . . . We know also that Germany and Japan are conducting their military and naval operations in accordance with a joint plan. That plan considers all peoples and Nations which are not helping the Axis powers as common enemies of each and every one of the Axis powers." "We expect to eliminate the danger from Japan," he concluded, "but it would serve us ill if we accomplished that and found that the rest of the world was dominated by Hitler and Mussolini."[164]

As we have seen, a nuanced reading of the evidence suggests that, if there was a strategy underpinning Roosevelt's actions in the latter half of 1941, it was almost certainly that of the "back door." Since taking office, Roosevelt had been unwilling to take a hard line with Japan over its territorial ambitions in Asia but allowed matters to come to a head when the situation in Europe was demanding U.S. intervention. He did so even though the thrust of official thinking suggested that he appease Japan and even though he had provided public assurances that war was not at hand. One of the few logical explanations is that he was taking advantage of the East Asian situation to bring the United States into the European war, a war that the public had been reluctant to embrace.

Cautious Crusade?

My central argument in this chapter has been that deception was necessary to facilitate U.S. entry into World War II. Roosevelt understood that a declaration of war was bound to be divisive. Thus, he maneuvered the United States in the direction of hostilities while allowing the public to believe that the country was being pushed into the conflict. In the process, he concealed the belligerent drift of U.S. policy and sought out pretexts that would justify war, both in the Atlantic and in the Pacific. When all was said and done, he had successfully shifted blame onto the Axis.

What role did oversell play in this process? First, Roosevelt carefully calibrated his propaganda so as not to get too far ahead of public opinion. His crusade against the Axis was a cautious one in this respect.[165] This is not to say that Roosevelt was incapable of rhetorical excess on those occasions when he did make use of the bully pulpit. As has already been noted, he amplified the Nazi threat to the Western Hemisphere when announcing major policy departures such as Lend-Lease and the escort of convoys, placing particular emphasis on the dangers posed by air power and fascist subversion in Latin America. Infamously, in a Navy Day Address on October 27, 1941, he brandished a "secret map" that purportedly revealed Hitler's plans to divide South America into five vassal states, a map that turned out to have been forged by British intelligence.[166]

Although it is not known with any certainty whether Roosevelt was aware that the "secret map" was a forgery, it is safe to conclude that he was not above exaggerating U.S. vulnerability to advance his larger foreign policy agenda.[167] Anti-interventionists such as Lindbergh never tired of pointing out that air power augmented U.S. defenses as much as it rendered them obsolete, and it is generally agreed that the anxieties concerning political and military threats to Latin America were overblown.[168] Hemispheric security was the primary justification for intervening in the European war, however, so it is not surprising that Roosevelt tended to describe the threat in worst-case terms. The important point is that only a brazen provocation by the Axis would suffice to open the political space necessary for a declaration of war, and only more aggressive policies in the Atlantic and Pacific would suffice to bring on such a provocation.

Deception Pays Off, with a Cost

In the wake of the Pearl Harbor attack, Roosevelt got the result he wanted—overwhelming support for entry into the war against the Axis.[169] Even anti-interventionists dropped their opposition to U.S. involvement, with Lindbergh releasing a statement saying, "Our country has been attacked by force of arms and by force of arms we must retaliate."[170] Roosevelt's sensitivity to domestic opinion and his use of dramatic events overseas to win backing for intervention were among the great presidential achievements of the twentieth century, as Dallek argues.[171] For all his talk of wanting an incident, Roosevelt was remarkably cautious during this period, waiting for the right provocation before asking for a declaration of war. If he had pressed the issue prematurely, the result would have been a backlash from Congress and the public. Aided by a resounding victory and the fact that World War II has come to be seen as the "good war," Roosevelt has been insulated from the kind of scrutiny that might have shed a harsher light on his prewar dissembling. If anything, historians have been quick to forgive his lack of candor with the public. Dallek, for example, has said, "In light of the national unwillingness to face up fully to the international dangers confronting the country, it is difficult to fault Roosevelt for building a consensus by devious means."[172] We could even argue, as Warren Kimball has, that Americans understood that war was coming but did not want to be confronted with that fact, that "in a sense, they wanted to be lied to."[173]

None of this is to say that Roosevelt's maneuvering and indirection were without consequence. Most important, the United States had to fight a second war in the Pacific because Roosevelt could not bring himself to declare war on Germany as an act of policy.[174] Indeed, Pearl Harbor yielded a groundswell of support for revenge against Japan, which interfered with the administration's Germany-first strategy. Roosevelt worked throughout the war to counter such sentiment, downplaying Japanese intentions and capabilities. Such concerns contributed to his decision to invade North Africa in November 1942: Roosevelt wanted to get U.S. troops into action as quickly as possible against the Nazis to preempt demands for more effort in the Pacific.[175]

More indirectly, Roosevelt's use of executive power paved the way for the imperial presidency of the Vietnam era, enabling Lyndon Johnson to wage a massive undeclared war in Southeast Asia. Senator J. William Fulbright (D-Arkansas), one of Johnson's most perceptive critics, made the connection at the time, saying in 1971, "FDR's deviousness in a good cause made it easier for LBJ to practice the same kind of deviousness in a bad cause."[176] What this particular legacy suggests is that deception always comes with a cost, even when otherwise most justified.

3

Shifting Blame to the Communists

LBJ and the Vietnam War

Orthodox and revisionist accounts of the Vietnam War differ on a number of important questions. The orthodox interpretation is that the United States made a mistake in fighting the Vietnam War. There were no vital interests at stake, and the war itself was unwinnable. South Vietnam was simply too bankrupt politically and militarily to be salvageable. The revisionists counter that the Vietnam War was a necessary war. U.S. credibility was on the line. Moreover, defeat was by no means inevitable. If only political leaders had pursued a war-winning strategy and seen it through to victory, then a noncommunist South Vietnam could have survived intact.[1]

Stark differences remain over whether the Vietnam War was necessary or winnable, but few would argue that President Lyndon Johnson was open or honest with the public as he escalated the war in 1964–1965. A number of historians have noted Johnson's "policy of minimum candor."[2] According to George Herring, Johnson "took the nation into war in Vietnam by indirection and dissimulation."[3] David Kaiser, in agreement, writes, "Knowing that it was embarking upon a much longer and larger conflict than the American people seemed ready to support," the Johnson administration "decided disastrously to conceal its probable scope and duration for as long as possible, while pretending that negotiations might bring the conflict to an end at any moment."[4] Fredrik Logevall concurs, explaining how Johnson and his aides "worked hard in the first half of 1965 to keep the American people in the dark about Vietnam, to foster apathy, to conceal for as long as possible the Americanization of the war."[5]

What led Johnson to resort to deception in this manner, to escalate the war by stealth? The short answer is that he faced a milder version of the domestic political predicament that had confronted Roosevelt prior to World War II. Johnson felt that he had no choice but to expand the U.S. presence in Vietnam to contain communism. At the same time, he understood that whatever domestic support he enjoyed was brittle and could quickly evaporate in the event that the costs and risks of war were highlighted. Following Roosevelt's lead, Johnson engaged in a creeping form of blameshifting, exploiting a series of pretexts to justify the bombing of North Vietnam and the insertion of ground forces into South Vietnam. All the while, he denied that a major change in policy was in the offing, subverting debate. Johnson's deceptions backfired when the war degenerated into a quagmire.

In this chapter, I first briefly outline the history of U.S. involvement in Vietnam, with a special emphasis on the Cold War concerns that provided the rationale for intervening there. I then describe the domestic political climate that Johnson faced as he Americanized the war in 1964–1965 and detail the deceptions that Johnson used to shift blame for hostilities onto the communist side. Last, I discuss the fallout that attended the U.S. defeat in Vietnam, especially the "credibility gap" that drove Johnson from office.

The Road to War in Vietnam

The United States first took a serious interest in Vietnam during World War II, as Ho Chi Minh's resistance movement, the Vietminh, rebelled against the Japanese occupation. Whereas Franklin Roosevelt provided token assistance to the Vietminh and even voiced support for Vietnamese independence, his successor, Harry Truman, acquiesced in the return of the colony to France, not wanting to upset the nascent Cold War coalition forming against the Soviet Union. When the First Indochina War broke out between France and the Vietminh in November 1946, Truman adopted a position of benign neutrality. Like many Americans, he had a strong distaste for French colonialism, but this was outweighed by misgivings about the communist leanings of the Vietminh. By 1950, Truman was actively supporting the French war effort with economic and military aid. The Korean War reinforced the sense among administration officials that the United States could not afford to risk the loss of Southeast Asia to communism, important as the region was for the economic recovery of Europe and Japan and the military defense of the Far East.

Animated by the same national security imperatives, Truman's successor, Dwight Eisenhower, continued to aid the French and even considered taking military action in spring 1954 to relieve the besieged garrison at Dienbienphu. After Eisenhower failed to rally international and domestic support for "united action" against the siege forces, the garrison fell, and the French withdrew under the cover of the Geneva Accords, which partitioned the country into a communist North Vietnam and noncommunist South Vietnam. The partition was intended to be temporary, but the Eisenhower administration chose to ignore the provisions of the accords that called for reunification by way of national elections, fearing that the Vietminh would exploit their organizational advantages to turn out more votes. Instead, Eisenhower supported Ngo Dinh Diem in his efforts to consolidate power in South Vietnam, part of a larger strategy to build up pro-American, anticommunist regimes in Southeast Asia.[6]

While Diem was able to survive several challenges to his rule, his control over South Vietnam remained incomplete. Most important, a communist insurgency, popularly called the Viet Cong, took root in the countryside in the late 1950s, engaging in a rash of assassinations and kidnappings. At the direction of Hanoi, the National Liberation Front, an ostensibly independent organization, was stood up in December 1960 to provide political cover for the insurgency, and large swathes of rural South Vietnam quickly came under its influence. Despite enjoying generous U.S. backing, Diem was not able to suppress the Viet Cong or to rally public opinion to his side. Rather, his autocratic style alienated key bases of support, such as the urban educated class and the Buddhists; and whatever gains he made in pacifying the countryside proved ephemeral.[7] By fall 1961, John F. Kennedy, who had assumed office at the beginning of the year, was fending off calls from advisers that he insert ground troops, telling his National Security Council (NSC) during a November 15 meeting that he could "make a rather strong case against intervening in an area 10,000 miles away against 16,000 guerrillas with a native army of 200,000, where millions have been spent for years with no success."[8] Kennedy agreed, however, to dramatically expand the advisory presence in South Vietnam to bolster the counterinsurgency effort against the Viet Cong.[9] At the time of his death in November 1963, there were 16,000 U.S. military personnel in South Vietnam, many fighting alongside their South Vietnamese counterparts, despite assurances that they were there in an advisory capacity only.[10]

Taken as a whole, the evidence is fairly clear that Kennedy wanted to limit the U.S. commitment to something short of introducing ground troops, and a decent case can be made that he would have opted for some form of disengagement had he survived to serve a second term.[11] On October 2, 1963, less than two months before his assassination, Kennedy accepted a recommendation from Robert McNamara, his secretary of defense, and General Maxwell Taylor, the chairman of the Joint Chiefs of Staff, that he recall 1,000 troops by the end of the year, with the remainder of the advisory presence to be phased out by the end of 1965, provided that the military situation continued to improve.[12] At the same time, Kennedy feared conservative critics enough that he refused to consider a full withdrawal prior to the 1964 election, confiding to Mike Mansfield (D-Montana), Senate majority leader, in mid-December 1962 that "If I tried to pull out completely now from Vietnam, we would have another Joe McCarthy Red scare on our hands."[13] Kennedy also expressly ruled out negotiations, despite prodding from several quarters that he explore neutralization options.[14] The practical effect of Kennedy's middle course was to deepen U.S. involvement in the war. Especially consequential was the complicity of his administration in the overthrow of Diem in November 1963, which ushered in a prolonged period of political instability and military drift and increased the pressure on Lyndon Johnson, Kennedy's successor, to resort to drastic measures to avert the collapse of South Vietnam.[15]

However difficult the situation he inherited, it was Johnson who ultimately Americanized the Vietnam War. Although he harbored grave reservations about expanding the conflict, Johnson resigned himself to the inevitability of a wider war as political instability wracked Saigon, the Viet Cong gained in strength, and the South Vietnamese showed evidence of succumbing to war-weariness. Pausing long enough to secure reelection, Johnson made the critical decisions at the end of 1964 and the beginning of 1965, sanctioning first an air war against North Vietnam and then a ground war in South Vietnam. His strategy was essentially one of attrition, inflicting enough punishment on communist forces that they would reach a "breaking point" and abandon their attempt at reunification by force.[16] Although Johnson recognized that victory was by no means assured and that a costly stalemate would be difficult to avoid, he felt he had no choice but to escalate the war.[17]

Falling Dominoes

If Johnson was pessimistic about the prospects for victory in Vietnam, why did he nonetheless expand the war there? The short answer is that the president, along with leading members of his administration, feared the consequences of withdrawal more than the risks of escalation. Under-pinning these fears was the *domino theory*, which held that decisive action had to be taken to prevent the fall of even peripheral areas to communism because otherwise a chain of events would be set in motion that would lead to the erosion of the Cold War position of the United States.[18]

First articulated by Eisenhower in April 1954, the domino theory had assumed "the force of doctrine" by 1964, "becoming a de facto feature of the political debate over Vietnam."[19] The theory itself came in two versions: territorial and psychological.[20] The *territorial* domino theory focused on the geographical expansion of communism over Southeast Asia. The fear was that the loss of South Vietnam would endanger neighboring govern-ments in the region, rendering them vulnerable to overt aggression, exter-nally sponsored revolution, or neutralization.[21] National Security Action Memorandum (NSAM) 288, an important statement of administration policy authored by secretary of defense Robert McNamara in March 1964, was written with the territorial domino theory in mind.[22] In its statement of U.S. objectives in South Vietnam, NSAM 288 warned:

> We seek an independent non-Communist South Vietnam. . . . Unless we can achieve this objective in South Vietnam, almost all of Southeast Asia

will probably fall under Communist dominance (all of Vietnam, Laos, and Cambodia), accommodate to Communism so as to remove effective U.S. and anti-Communist influence (Burma), or fall under the domination of forces not now explicitly Communist but likely then to become so (Indonesia taking over Malaysia). Thailand might hold for a period with our help, but would be under grave pressure. Even the Philippines would become shaky, and the threat to India to the west, Australia and New Zealand to the south, and Taiwan, Korea, and Japan to the north and east would be greatly increased.[23]

The *psychological* domino theory predicted even farther-reaching effects, positing that U.S. credibility would suffer in the event that regional dominos fell, causing allies to waver and adversaries to challenge vital interests.[24] Dean Rusk, Johnson's secretary of state, laid out the worst-case scenario for him in a July 1, 1965, memo: "The integrity of the U.S. commitment is the principal pillar of peace throughout the world. If that commitment becomes unreliable, the communist world would draw conclusions that would lead to our ruin and almost certainly to a catastrophic war."[25] To avert such a disaster, Rusk was willing to escalate U.S. involvement in an area that was of little intrinsic strategic value.

Of the two versions of the domino theory, it was the psychological one that preoccupied decision makers more.[26] John McNaughton, assistant secretary of defense for international security affairs, famously quantified U.S. objectives in Vietnam in a paper dated March 10, 1965: "70%—To avoid a humiliating US defeat (to our reputation as guarantor). 20%—To keep South Vietnam (and then) adjacent territory from Chinese hands. 10%—To permit the people of South Vietnam to enjoy a better, freer way of life."[27] The thinking was that by fighting in Vietnam the United States would demonstrate to the world that it was a "good doctor" that was willing "to keep promises, be tough, take risks, get bloodied, and hurt the enemy badly," all to save a terminal patient.[28] Protecting U.S. credibility, in other words, did not require that the United States prevail in Vietnam. To the contrary, a failed intervention would be better than no intervention at all. In the words of McGeorge Bundy, Johnson's national security adviser, the cardinal goal of the Vietnam intervention was "*Not* to be a Paper Tiger."[29]

The Domestic Politics of the Vietnam War: 1964–1965

The domestic political climate that Johnson faced as he Americanized the war in 1964–1965 can best be characterized as permissive yet fragile. Although there was certainly a vocal minority calling for stronger action in Vietnam, this did not amount to a groundswell of support for intervening in another land war in Asia. Among elites, prominent dissenters included leading Democrats in the Senate such as Mansfield, William Fulbright (D-Arkansas), and Richard Russell (D-Georgia); shapers of elite opinion such as the editorial page of the *New York Times* and columnist Walter Lippmann; and even senior members of the administration such as George Ball, the undersecretary of state, and Hubert Humphrey, the vice president. The public, for its part, was largely inattentive to the issue. Among those who were paying attention, opinion was split between doves, who wanted to negotiate a withdrawal from Vietnam, and hawks, who wanted to go all-out to win the war. Many Americans expressed support for dovish and hawkish measures simultaneously, an indicator of the reigning uncertainty about how to proceed. In the end, Johnson would certainly have paid a political price for a communist takeover in Vietnam, but this did not translate into robust support for the Americanization of the war.[30] Escalation was bound to be controversial.

The Cold War Consensus Breaks Down

The anti-communist Cold War consensus did not extend to the Americanization of the Vietnam War.[31] On one side was a vocal minority of hawks, who spoke out in favor of taking whatever measures were necessary to win in Vietnam. This group included the syndicated columnist Joseph Alsop as well as Republican notables such as Representative Gerald Ford (R-Michigan), who became House minority leader in the wake of the 1964 election; Senator Barry Goldwater (R-Arizona), a staunch conservative and the party nominee for president in 1964; and Richard Nixon, who, in the words of Andrew Johns, functioned as an "agent provocateur" during the Kennedy and Johnson administrations, urging an expansion of the war and "looming as the personification of the fear of the Right that so heavily influenced both presidents."[32] Ironically, the strongest support Johnson received for his Vietnam policies came from the conservative wing of the Republican Party.[33] This irked Johnson to no end; as he complained to Everett Dirksen (R-Illinois), the Senate minority leader, in late February 1965, "I'm getting kicked around by my own party in the Senate and getting my support from your side of the aisle."[34]

On the other side was a larger but more circumspect collection of doves who harbored reservations about the wisdom of intervention. Of these, perhaps the most influential was Walter Lippmann. Lippmann's syndicated column appeared in well over a hundred U.S. newspapers and was required reading for the foreign policy establishment. "To Lyndon Johnson, certainly, no one was as important," according to Logevall.[35] As one indicator of his influence, Lippmann played a direct role in fomenting what little Senate debate there was on the war; it was at a party hosted by Lippmann that Frank Church (D-Idaho), George McGovern (D-South Dakota), and Gale McGee (D-Wyoming) agreed that Vietnam should be discussed on the floor of the Senate.[36] The "Vietnam Debate" officially got underway on February 17, 1965, with a speech by Church. The speech was based on an article Church had written for the *New York Times Magazine* with the provocative title "We Are in Too Deep in Asia and Africa." The article had elicited a letter of praise from Lippmann.[37]

George Ball, the second-ranking official at the State Department, also looms large during this period. Beginning in fall 1964, Ball authored a series of memos warning of the risks associated with escalation and urging consideration of a negotiated settlement to the conflict. Ball cited arguments commonly made by doves to support his recommendations: that the government of South Vietnam was chronically weak; that a stepped-up military effort, especially one targeting North Vietnam, was unlikely to stabilize the political situation in South Vietnam and in fact would only undermine it further; that the end result would be, at best, a costly stalemate and, at worst, a war with China; and that, regardless, a communist takeover in South Vietnam would not irreparably harm U.S. interests. Ball's efforts culminated in a paper he wrote in late June 1965 as the Johnson administration was making final preparations for taking over the ground war in South Vietnam. In it, Ball called for "cutting our losses in South Vietnam," concluding, "In my view, a deep commitment of United States forces in a land war in South Vietnam would be a catastrophic error. If ever there was an occasion for a tactical withdrawal, this is it."[38]

The intensity of his views notwithstanding, Ball, like other politically connected doves, was hesitant to speak out. In public, he toed the official line, talking tough on the war. He hardly went to great lengths to build support for his position within the foreign policy establishment, either, or even ensure that his dissent received the serious consideration it deserved in high-level decision-making circles. In early October 1964, Ball composed a lengthy memorandum outlining his reasons for opposing the bombing of North Vietnam, only to see it shelved by Bundy, McNamara, and Rusk. Rather than taking the memo directly to Johnson, who had requested it, Ball sat on it until late February 1965, by which time the president had already signed off on the Rolling Thunder bombing campaign.[39] Logevall has gone so far as to argue that Ball knowingly played the role of "house dove," or devil's advocate, putting his loyalty to the administration and his ambitions to be secretary of state ahead of the national interest.[40] As for Lippmann, he took at face value White House claims that it contemplated no major expansion of the war, which explains why his columns tended to take a hard line against escalation even while assuring readers that Johnson himself favored a peaceful solution. Lippmann made an open break with the administration only in spring 1965 (and was promptly ostracized for it).[41]

Especially notable was the lack of dissent in the Senate. As we now know, the senators with the greatest institutional responsibility for the war were actually opposed to it, yet they were unwilling to go public with their views.[42] This group included Fulbright, the chairman of the Foreign Relations Committee; Mansfield, the majority leader (and a former professor of Asian history); and Russell, the chairman of the Armed Services Committee. Mansfield repeatedly urged Johnson, in private correspondence, to accept the neutralization of Vietnam.[43] Russell, for his part, advised Johnson, a close friend, "If I was going to get out, I'd get the same crowd that got rid of old Diem to get rid of these people and get some fellow in there that said he wished to hell we would get out. That would give us a good excuse for getting out."[44] Gary Stone underscores just how critical it was that these prominent Democrats shied away from open dissent:

> Had such influential senators in early 1965 stated publicly and forcefully the views they expressed privately or in muted tones, it is likely that they would have emboldened many of their more timid moderate and liberal

colleagues to give voice to their own doubts. This is to say nothing of the president's natural enemies in the Senate, the Republicans and the newly elected Robert Kennedy (D-NY), forces likely to join the attack once they saw that the president had been wounded. Indeed, it is inconceivable that an open call to rebellion issued by Mansfield, Fulbright, and Russell in early 1965 would not have been heeded by at least a substantial minority of the Senate, a minority whose open opposition to escalation would have greatly accelerated the spread of public opposition to the war and inhibited presidential action.[45]

Johnson, of course, understood the stakes and went to great lengths to persuade his fellow Democrats to keep their opinions to themselves. Special attention was lavished on Fulbright; when, in January 1965, momentum built for a full Senate debate on the war, Johnson dispatched Rusk to meet with the chairman of the Foreign Relations Committee, who let himself become convinced that now was not the time for the Senate to hold public hearings and engage in full discussion.[46] As Fulbright wrote to an associate late in the month, "it is not exactly within my power to influence the course of events in South Vietnam, other than to express a personal opinion, as the matter is run by the Executive Branch."[47] After the "Vietnam Debate" had gotten underway, in mid-February 1965, the White House launched a "diplomatic offensive" on Capitol Hill, hosting a series of receptions at which Johnson could personally lobby legislators for their support. Overall, the pressure campaign produced mixed results.[48] On the one hand, it bottled up dissent. In mid-March 1965, Mansfield went so far as to commend Johnson for "trying to keep the lid on a dangerous volcano in Southeast Asia."[49] On the other hand, the combination of flattery and intimidation did little to win hearts and minds. Johnson, who was nothing if not politically savvy, surely recognized that whatever establishment support he enjoyed was paper-thin.

The Public: Not Dovish, but Not Hawkish Either

If elites were divided on the subject of Vietnam, the public was largely apathetic.[50] Logevall describes the general mood at the end of 1964: "In Middle America, ignorance and disengagement were the rule—it was doubtful that more than 20 percent of Americans could have placed Vietnam on a map, or provided concrete details about the ally on whose behalf the United States had intervened. Of those who paid attention, most were confused, not wanting to see a humiliating defeat for their country but seeing little sense in a land war on behalf of a weak government in a small country in a remote corner of the globe."[51] Polling done in late 1964 and early 1965 reflects the mass public's ambivalence about the war. Of the respondents to a Council on Foreign Relations poll released in mid-December 1964, 25 percent did not know there was fighting in Vietnam. Of those who did know, only 24 percent were "definitely in favor" of using ground forces to prevent a communist victory whereas close to half favored withdrawal. A University of Michigan study, also released in mid-December 1964, showed similar results: 37 percent of those polled were "strongly opposed" to getting out of Vietnam immediately (as opposed to 18 percent who were "definitely" in favor of withdrawal), but only 24 percent were supportive of using U.S. forces to turn the war around (as opposed to 32 percent who were opposed). A Harris poll released the same week found that 18 percent favored bombing North Vietnam while 20 percent backed withdrawal. Another Harris poll taken in the first week of January 1965 found that 25 percent of respondents wanted to "negotiate and get out" and another 45 percent were willing to do no more than "hold the line."[52] Taken together, these polls demonstrate that the pressure for escalation was minimal, at least at the grassroots level.

Granted, the public "rallied around the flag" once the United States began bombing North Vietnam. In early February 1965, after approving air strikes in retaliation for the Viet Cong attacks near Pleiku, Johnson quietly commissioned a set of polls to assess how the public was reacting to the bombing. The polls revealed overwhelming support for the air strikes, nearly 83 percent. All told, Johnson's approval rating on Vietnam jumped almost twenty points from before the February reprisal strikes (41 percent approval) to after (60 percent approval).[53] At the same time, large numbers of Americans continued to express interest in holding negotiations. For example, the same poll that registered 83 percent approval for the post-Pleiku air strikes found that 75 percent of respondents wanted the United States to ask for negotiations to settle the war. In March 1965, a Gallup poll revealed that whereas 42 percent of Americans wanted to send "more troops and airplanes" to Vietnam, 41 percent favored "negotiations now."[54] Louis Harris, a pollster, summed up the prevailing mood in a report for the Johnson administration, dated February 22, 1965: "The clear main-stream of American opinion is this: We should shore up the efforts of the South Vietnamese to resist further Communist advances, use retaliatory airstrikes only when extreme guerrilla activity warrants it, and when we have made enough show of power so that the Communists can see that we will not yield, then finally negotiate a settlement."[55] Public opinion, while hardly dovish, was not particularly hawkish either.

Johnson operated in a permissive context as he moved to expand the war in late 1964 and early 1965.[56] It would be going too far, however, to say that there was a public mandate for aggressive action. If anything, Johnson's landslide win over Goldwater, a renowned hawk, in the 1964 election suggests the opposite, that, when push came to shove, the public preferred disengagement over escalation.[57] This is a problem Johnson rec-ognized at the time. At one meeting in late July 1965, he wondered aloud whether "Congress and the people will go along with 600,000 people and billions of dollars 10,000 miles away?" In response to an aide's observa-tion that the polls showed popular support for the Vietnam commitment, Johnson mused, "But if you make a commitment to jump off a building, and you find out how high it is, you may withdraw the commitment."[58] Doubts such as these only reinforced Johnson's inclination to escalate the war by stealth, to preempt the kind of noisy debate that would polarize the public.

Shifting Blame to the Communists

Johnson recognized that Americanization was bound to be controver-sial. To avoid a divisive debate on the subject, he resorted to deception, exploiting a series of pretexts to justify the systematic bombing of North Vietnam and the insertion of large numbers of ground forces into South Vietnam. All the while, he denied that a major change in policy was in the offing. The effect was to shift blame for hostilities onto the communist side. Here I detail the deceptions that Johnson's strategy entailed—his per-sistent refusal to admit that the U.S. was heading toward war in Vietnam and the pretexts that he used to justify deepening U.S. involvement—and then assess whether there was a pattern of oversell in administration state-ments on the war.

Escalation by Stealth

In 1964, Johnson settled on what can only be called a policy of delay. The forthcoming election loomed large in his calculations, and Johnson was determined that Vietnam not be a front-burner issue during the fall campaign. His priority was to maintain the status quo and postpone controversial decisions about the U.S. commitment until after the election. "Politics became the enemy of strategy in 1964," as one observer has noted.[59] Especially troubling to some of Johnson's advisers was his lack of candor with the public as the campaign heated up. On several occasions, he came close to making hard promises that the United States would not take over the fighting. On September 25, 1964, while dedicating a dam in Eufaula, Oklahoma, Johnson declared, "We don't want our American boys to do the fighting for Asian boys." Referring to China, he continued, "We don't want to get involved in a nation with 700 million people and get tied down in a land war in Asia."[60] McGeorge Bundy, who feared that Johnson was foreclosing his options, asked the president not to make such categorical statements on the campaign trail. "I think you may wish to give a hint of firmness," he advised Johnson on October 1, 1964. "It is a better than even chance that we will be undertaking some air and land action in the Laotian corridor and even in North Vietnam within the next two months, and we do not want the record to suggest even remotely that we campaigned on peace in order to start a war in November."[61] Johnson disregarded Bundy's advice, telling an audience at the University of Akron on October 21, 1964, "Sometimes our folks get a little impatient. Sometimes they rattle their rockets some, and they bluff about their bombs. But we are not about to send American boys 9 or 10,000 miles away from home to do what Asian boys ought to be doing for themselves."[62]

Johnson made such pledges despite the fact that momentum had been building since spring 1964 for a program of "graduated pressure" against North Vietnam, culminating in air strikes, if the political and military situation in South Vietnam did not improve by the end of the year.[63] Johnson insisted that escalation be delayed at least that long because he did not want a war in Vietnam to interfere with his reelection prospects. He could be quite candid about the matter, even with the Joint Chiefs of Staff, who were pushing for stronger action at the time. Johnson explained his reasons for delay in a March 4, 1964, meeting with the chiefs, as recounted by Marine Commandant General Wallace Greene:

> He repeated again that the Congress and the country did not want war—that war at this time would have a tremendous effect on the approaching Presidential political campaign and might perhaps keep the Democrats from winning in November. He said that he thought it would be much better to keep out of any war until December; that would be after the election and whoever was going to be President could then go to Congress for a supporting and joint resolution, and the people of the United States to explain to them why we had to risk the chances of another war by expanding our operations in Southeast Asia. The political situation in December would be stabilized.[64]

True to his word, Johnson failed to act on a memorandum circulated by Bundy in mid-June 1964 recommending that the administration seek a congressional resolution that would provide a domestic foundation for expanded military action.[65] Bundy's fear was that the war would be lost before the election. His fears turned out to be overblown, and Johnson's strategy paid off handsomely at the polls. He was able to secure a landslide victory over his Republican opponent, Barry Goldwater, by successfully positioning himself as the candidate of peace, even as his administration laid the groundwork for new military measures. Logevall sums up the winning political formula:

> There can be no doubt that millions who cast their ballots for Johnson did so precisely because he was not Barry Goldwater. The Republican candidate scared them with his ideologically tinged speeches and his seeming proclivity for a direct confrontation with communist forces in Vietnam. In contrast, Johnson ran as the candidate of peace, as the man who would continue to support South Vietnam but also keep the United States out of a major war in Southeast Asia. Notwithstanding the attempt by White House speechwriters to leave slightly ajar the door to a larger American involvement in the conflict, the dominant impression left by LBJ in the final weeks of the campaign was that of a president telling voters that if they wanted to avoid a larger war in Vietnam, he was their man.[66]

In fact, final planning for a larger war in Vietnam was set in motion on November 2, 1964, the day before the election, when the NSC created a Working Group on South Vietnam/Southeast Asia.[67] The group was chaired by William Bundy, assistant secretary of state for East Asian affairs, and included other mid-echelon figures such as McNaughton; Vice Admiral Lloyd Mustin, the senior operations officer of the Joint Chiefs of Staff; and Harold Ford, the China-Asia officer at the Central Intelligence Agency (CIA). After considering three options—Option A (a continuation of existing policy), Option B (rapid escalation or the "fast/full squeeze"), and Option C (graduated escalation or the "slow squeeze")—the working group settled on a muscular version of Option C, specifically a two-phase plan of gradually intensifying air strikes against North Vietnam. The principal goals of the bombing were to stabilize the political situation in South Vietnam, cut down on infiltration from North Vietnam, and to coerce Hanoi into ending its support for the insurgency.[68] Less well known was that the final version of the planning also called for the introduction of ground forces to "handle any contingency," such as a North Vietnamese invasion.[69]

Johnson approved the working-group recommendations during the first week of December 1964 but asked that implementation wait pending a stable government in Saigon. The president did not want "to send a widow woman to slap Jack Dempsey," as he put it in a White House meeting on December 1.[70] He also made it abundantly clear that public disclosure was to be avoided, instructing his advisers in a covering memorandum, "I consider it a matter of the highest importance that the substance of this position should not become public except as I specifically direct."[71] Why all the secrecy? Johnson had agreed in principle to an expanded war, but he wanted to conceal the decision for as long as possible so as to head off a potentially divisive debate. Debate was to be avoided for several reasons. First, Johnson did not want to divert attention from his domestic agenda, the Great Society, which he intended to push through Congress before conservative opposition coalesced.[72] Second, he wanted to contain demands for an all-out war against North Vietnam or China.[73] Finally, and most important, Johnson knew that a full debate "would greatly complicate matters by revealing a wide difference of opinion about what the American posture should be," allowing the anti-escalation side, "with its formidable lineup of heavy hitters," to draw "a large proportion of the confused and undecided to its side." [74] Johnson, in other words, feared that he might lose a debate on its merits. This explains why, in Logevall's words,

"he set out to quash debate on the war" in the first half of 1965, "to manufacture consensus."[75]

Accordingly, when it came time to implement the December 1964 decisions, Johnson took several measures to ensure that the war would not
become a political issue. As already discussed, he put considerable pressure
on wavering lawmakers to get on the team or at least keep their reservations quiet.[76] He also misled members of Congress, reassuring a bipartisan
group of legislators on January 21, 1965, that "we have decided that more
U.S. forces are not needed in South Vietnam short of a decision to go to
full-scale war," adding, "The war must be fought by the South Vietnamese. We cannot control everything that they do and we have to count on
their fighting their war."[77] When confronted with evidence that the U.S.
role in the war was growing, Johnson deflected scrutiny by refusing to
acknowledge that there had been any change in policy. His stock claim
was that he was simply pursuing the policy of the two previous administrations, assisting the South Vietnamese against foreign aggression.[78] At
a press conference on March 13, 1965, less than two weeks after the initiation of Rolling Thunder, Johnson downplayed the significance of the air
campaign: "I would say that our policy there is the policy that was established by President Eisenhower, as I have stated, since I have been President, 46 different times, the policy carried on by President Kennedy, and
the policy that we are now carrying on. . . . Our policy is still the same,
and that is to any armed attack, our forces will reply."[79] Of course, by this
time, U.S. forces were doing much more than responding to communist
provocations.

To appease critics on the left, who were alarmed by the bombing, Johnson launched a half-hearted "peace offensive" in spring 1965. The campaign kicked off with an April 7 speech at Johns Hopkins University, in
which the president professed a willingness to enter into "unconditional
discussions" with the North Vietnamese, promising a billion-dollar development program for the Mekong River Valley region in the event Hanoi
set aside its ambitions to forcefully reunify the country.[80] Johnson's offer,
as he and his advisers had quipped at lunch the day before, was aimed
at placating "the sob sisters and peace societies" as much as at securing
an early settlement.[81] The Hopkins speech was followed by a five-day
bombing pause, code-named MAYFLOWER, which went into effect on
May 12, 1965.[82] These moves, although successful from a public relations

standpoint, were little more than invitations to surrender on the part of Hanoi and were promptly rebuffed. Johnson expected as much, remarking on one occasion, "If I were Ho Chi Minh, I would never negotiate."[83] MAYFLOWER can even be interpreted as an escalatory move in that it was intended, at least in part, to clear political space for more intensive bombing. The North Vietnamese saw through the ruse, denouncing the bombing pause as "a deceitful maneuver designed to pave the way for new U.S. acts of war."[84]

In hindsight, the "peace offensive" was destined to fail. From the Eisenhower administration onward, the U.S. position had been that "negotiations should be entered into only when there was nothing to negotiate," that is, when the insurgency in South Vietnam had been defeated.[85] In the meantime, the invocation of negotiations could be used as a propaganda tool "to pin the rose of aggression on the Communists," as McGeorge Bundy put it.[86] This strategy came with its own complications. By February 1965, United Nations Secretary-General U Thant had made several attempts to organize bilateral talks between the United States and North Vietnam. The Johnson administration not only stonewalled Thant but asked that he keep quiet about his diplomatic efforts. Thant finally lost patience with the two-faced approach of the administration, telling reporters on February 24, 1965, "I am sure that the great American people, if only they know the true facts and the background to the developments in South Vietnam, will agree with me that further bloodshed is unnecessary. And also that the political and diplomatic method of discussions and negotiations alone can create conditions which will enable the United States to withdraw gracefully from that part of the world. As you know, in times of war and of hostilities the first casualty is truth."[87] Thant's remarks elicited an angry phone call from Rusk, who dismissed Thant's proposals as "procedural" and rejected talks as "out of the question" because they were unlikely to be "fruitful"—that is, unlikely to lead to the communists' capitulation.[88]

The communists, every bit as skeptical of negotiations as their U.S. counterparts, kicked off a major offensive on May 11, 1965, centered in the highlands area of South Vietnam.[89] With the South Vietnamese suffering staggering losses, the Johnson administration moved to take over the ground war. McNamara played a central role in the process, mediating between Johnson and William Westmoreland, the senior officer at

Military Assistance Command, Vietnam, who had requested an additional 150,000 troops in early June 1965, to be used offensively.[90] McNamara, after conferring with Westmoreland, forwarded his final recommendations to the president on July 20, 1965. Rather than withdraw or muddle through, McNamara felt that the administration should "expand promptly and substantially the US military pressure against the Viet Cong in the South." This alternative, McNamara felt, "would stave off defeat in the short run and offer a good chance of producing a favorable settlement in the longer run."[91] In military terms, McNamara's program required that Johnson deploy 175,000 troops to South Vietnam by the end of 1965, with 100,000 more likely to follow in early 1966; call up 235,000 of the Reserves and National Guard; increase the size of the regular armed forces by 375,000 through heavier use of the draft and extended tours of duty; and approach Congress for a supplemental appropriation to fund the build-up. If all went well, friendly forces would eventually be able to take the offensive, "with the objects of putting the VC/DRV [Viet Cong/Democratic Republic of Vietnam] battalion forces out of operation and of destroying their morale." With larger formations out of the way, it would be up to the South Vietnamese government to mop up the insurgency. McNamara's overall evaluation was that his recommended course of action, if executed properly, stood "a good chance of achieving an acceptable outcome within a reasonable time in Vietnam."[92]

Between July 21 and July 27, 1965, Johnson chaired a series of meetings with his senior advisers, the Joint Chiefs of Staff, the NSC, and the congressional leadership, ostensibly to reach a decision on the Americanization of the ground war. That decision, in fact, had already been made, with Johnson approving Westmoreland's forty-four-battalion request on July 17.[93] With events already set in motion, the final round of meetings was meant to create the appearance of deliberation and to hash out how the troop decision would be presented to the public.[94] Fatefully, Johnson rebuffed McNamara's suggestion that he put the country on a war footing, contriving what Francis Bator has called the "Westmoreland Redux" option, which amounted to consenting to the field commander's troop request and rules of engagement while saying no to a declaration of national emergency, a reserve call-up, a tax increase, a new Senate resolution, a prime-time speech, or any other means of mobilizing the public.[95]

"The fewer theatrics the better," Johnson confided to Dirksen in the meeting with the congressional leadership on July 27.[96]

Johnson defended "Westmoreland Redux" in limited war terms, telling the NSC on July 27, "We have chosen to do what is necessary to meet the present situation, but not to be unnecessarily provocative to either the Russians or the Communist Chinese."[97] But, when pressed by the Joint Chiefs on July 24 about the decision not to call up the Reserves, McNamara admitted its political nature, acknowledging that "mobilization of the Reserves would . . . cause considerable debate, that a lot of minority votes would result, that there was certain to be a strong vote against a call-up, and that the Communists might get the wrong impression regarding division among our ranks."[98] Also revealing is an exchange that Johnson had with Cyrus Vance, McNamara's deputy, on July 16 about approaching Congress for a supplemental appropriation. Vance communicated the details of the conversation to McNamara the next day, summarizing Johnson's position: "(1) It is his current intention to proceed with 34 battalion plan. (2) It is impossible for him to submit supplementary budget request of more than $300–400 million to the Congress before next January. (3) If a larger request is made to the Congress, he believes this will kill domestic legislative program."[99] Johnson feared, in other words, that if Congress were forced to choose between guns and butter it would gladly pick the former over the latter.[100]

When it came time to announce the new deployments on July 28, Johnson chose a midday press conference rather than a prime-time speech. After reiterating why the United States was in Vietnam, the president broke the news matter-of-factly: "I have asked the Commanding General, General Westmoreland, what more he needs to meet this mounting aggression. He has told me. We will meet his needs." Johnson understated the magnitude of the troop increase, saying that fighting strength would be raised from 75,000 to 125,000 men, rather than the 175,000 that had been authorized.[101] He also finessed the matter of a budget request to Congress, indicating that a supplemental appropriation would be ready by January 1966 and that funds would be transferred within the Defense Department in the meantime. Finally, Johnson reminded those assembled of his readiness to negotiate, to "move from the battlefield to the conference table" and "begin unconditional discussions with any government, any place, at any time." With that, Johnson moved on to announce the appointment of John Chancellor as director of the Voice of America and the nomination of Abe Fortas to the Supreme Court. When asked later by a reporter whether the troop increase implied "any change in the existing policy of relying mainly on the South Vietnamese to carry out offensive operations and using American forces to guard American installations and to act as an emergency backup," Johnson replied, disingenuously, "It does not imply any change in policy whatsoever."[102]

To the end, Johnson was reluctant to admit that he was taking the country to war. When pressed by Bundy to be more candid with the public, Johnson retorted, colorfully, "You mean that if your mother-in-law—your very own mother-in-law—has only one eye, and it happens to be right in the middle of her forehead, then the best place for her is in the livin' room with all the company!"[103] Johnson's lack of transparency angered Bundy, who feared there would be disturbing consequences when the public "looked back and asked themselves if they had been led openly into this war or somehow bamboozled into it."[104] Bundy's fears turned out to be prescient. As Larry Berman has argued, Johnson's "greatest tactical error as a *political* leader came when he rejected the advice of civilian and military advisors on the question of mobilizing the nation's resources. In deciding *not* to mobilize the Reserves, *not* to seek a congressional resolution or declaration of national emergency, *not* to present the program in a prime-time address to Congress or the nation, and *not* to disclose publicly the full extent of the anticipated military call-up, the president's credibility soon came unraveled."[105] In the short term, however, Johnson's soft-pedaling allowed him to buy time and preempt debate, exactly the results he wanted.

Escalation by Pretext

If Johnson's public position was that he was not taking the country to war, how did he explain the escalatory steps that the United States was taking? At each juncture, the president was able to exploit an insult or provocation to justify progressively stronger military measures. First, in August 1964, he took advantage of a naval "incident" in the Gulf of Tonkin to order retaliatory air strikes and to secure congressional approval for an open-ended resolution that had been in the works for months. Six months

later, in February 1965, he set the escalation process in motion by calling
for a program of "sustained reprisals" against North Vietnam following a
series of Viet Cong attacks. These reprisals quickly morphed into Rolling
Thunder, the first systematic bombing campaign of the war. Finally, Rolling Thunder became the rationale for an expanded ground presence, with
American troops ostensibly deployed to protect air bases from retaliation.
It was not revealed that these troops were engaged in major combat operations until summer 1965.

In summer 1964, Johnson was looking for an opportunity to demonstrate his commitment to a faltering government in South Vietnam and
to rebut Republican charges that he was not doing enough to win the
war. The Tonkin Gulf incident was seemingly tailor-made for the occasion.[106] According to the official version of events, the incident ensued on
August 2, 1964, when three North Vietnamese patrol boats attacked the
U.S. destroyer *Maddox* without provocation in the Tonkin Gulf off the
central coast of North Vietnam.[107] The *Maddox*, with help from aircraft
from the USS *Ticonderoga*, successfully repulsed the attack. The president,
anxious to avoid war, elected not to retaliate, issuing a warning instead.
Two days later, however, the North Vietnamese launched a second attack,
this time on the *Maddox* and another destroyer, the *C. Turner Joy*. In the
face of "open aggression on the high seas," Johnson felt he had no choice
but to respond with air strikes against the bases housing the patrol boats
as well as a nearby oil storage facility. Congress rallied around the flag,
easily passing a resolution on August 7 authorizing the president to take
"all necessary measures to repel any armed attacks against the forces of
the United States and to prevent further aggression."[108] "The public," says
Edwin Moïse, "was left in no doubt that on August 2 and 4 there had been
totally unprovoked attacks on the U.S. Navy, and that the U.S. retaliation
had been both thoroughly justified and splendidly successful."[109]

The official version of events, as is well documented, was misleading
in a number of respects. First, the North Vietnamese attacks were hardly
unprovoked. At the time of the first attack, the *Maddox* was eavesdrop-
ping in close proximity to where U.S.-directed South Vietnamese guerillas
had shelled offshore islands a few nights before. The whole point of the
Desoto patrol that had brought the *Maddox* to the Tonkin Gulf was to
probe North Vietnamese coastal defenses in conjunction with such harass-
ing operations, which were part of a covert action program called OPLAN

34A.[110] Administration officials clearly understood that the North Vietnamese were lashing out in response to the OPLAN 34A raids.[111] Rusk, for example, cabled the embassy in South Vietnam after the first attack, "We believe that present OPLAN 34A activities are beginning to rattle Hanoi, and *Maddox* incident is directly related to their effort to resist these activities."[112] John McCone, the director of the CIA, made the same point to Johnson in an NSC meeting on August 4. "The North Vietnamese are reacting defensively to our attacks on their offshore islands," he explained.[113] Johnson clearly got the point. When briefed about the first attack on the *Maddox*, he likened it to being on a movie date in Texas: "You're sitting next to a pretty girl and you have your hand on her ankle and nothing happens. And you move it up to her knee and nothing happens. You move it up further and you're thinking about moving a bit more and all of a sudden you get slapped. I think we got slapped."[114] None of this stopped McNamara from testifying before Congress on August 6 that the *Maddox* had been "carrying out a routine patrol" and that the U.S. Navy "played absolutely no part in, was not associated with, and was not aware of any South Vietnamese actions, if there were any."[115] McNamara, in fact, knew full well that the North Vietnamese saw a connection between the OPLAN 34A raids and the Desoto patrol. After the first incident, when Johnson had wanted to head off pressures for retaliation, McNamara had advised him to inform Congress of the shelling of the offshore islands a few nights before, as a way of rationalizing the North Vietnamese actions in the Gulf.[116]

Second, the August 4 attack almost certainly did not occur.[117] More important for our purposes, administration officials had reason to believe that there had been no attack at the time. Within a few hours of the incident, Captain John Herrick, the commander of the task force in the Tonkin Gulf, reported, "Review of action makes many reported contacts and torpedoes fired appear doubtful. Freak weather effects on radar and over-eager sonarmen may have accounted for many reports. No actual visual sightings by *Maddox*. Suggest complete evaluation before any further action taken."[118] No evaluation was completed, however. The fact of the matter is that Johnson had decided early on August 4—when, according to some accounts, all he had were warnings that an attack was imminent—to use the incident as a means to get a congressional resolution passed.[119] From that point on, there was little doubt that a retaliation order would be given, and attention turned to picking out targets for the air strikes. When McNamara became aware, in the mid-afternoon of August 4, that Herrick, as well as Admiral Ulysses S. Grant Sharp, the commander-in-chief of U.S. forces in the Pacific, had doubts about the authenticity of the attack, it appears that he deliberately concealed the information from Johnson so as not to undermine the momentum for action.[120] To the extent that clarification was sought from the chain of command, it was to confirm that an attack had taken place, not to get to the bottom of what had actually happened in the Gulf on the night of August 4. The Joint Chiefs of Staff, on August 6, sent an urgent message to the commanders of all the units involved in the incident asking for "proof and evidence" of a second attack against the destroyers. After receiving this message, "the commanders in the Pacific provided far more support to the idea of a real attack than most of them had provided before."[121] Needless to say, none of this was divulged to the public, even after Johnson had become privately convinced that no second attack had occurred. By mid-September 1964, Johnson was remarking to Ball that "those dumb, stupid sailors were just shooting at flying fish."[122]

Third, a plausible case can be made that the administration tried to provoke the second incident, if not the first. After all, Johnson sent the *Maddox*, along with the *Turner Joy*, back into the Tonkin Gulf a few hours after the August 2 attack. He also approved another round of OPLAN 34A raids for the night of August 3, despite the fact that they had played a key role in inciting the first clash. Plans to retaliate in case of a North Vietnamese response were drawn up in advance and quickly implemented on August 4, well before all the facts were in. The evidence for a manufactured crisis is circumstantial at best, but it is surely relevant that the Johnson administration entered the month of August 1964 looking for an opportunity to demonstrate its strength and resolve.[123]

In the event, the Tonkin Gulf incident produced mixed results. Domestically, the crisis gave the administration an immediate boost: Johnson was able to secure bipartisan support for his policies, improve his standing in the polls, and defuse Vietnam as a campaign issue. Overnight, the public went from disapproving of Johnson's handling of the Vietnam issue by a margin of 58 to 42 percent to approving by a margin of 72 to 28 percent.[124] The Tonkin Gulf Resolution was particularly welcome, with Johnson quipping that "like grandma's nightshirt, it covered everything."[125] The resolution should not be seen as a blank check for war, however. The dominant tone among its Senate supporters "was one of apprehension, gloom, and resignation," according to one account, and few were willing to go on record supporting administration policy in vigorous terms.[126] Daniel Brewster (D-Maryland), who had served as a marine officer during World War II, recalled that he had "had the opportunity to see warfare not so very far from this area, and it was very mean," adding that he "would look with great dismay on a situation involving the landing of large land armies on the continent of Asia." Fulbright, who as chairman of the Foreign Relations Committee had shepherded the measure through the Senate, agreed, saying, "I personally feel it would be very unwise under any circumstances to put a large land army on the Asian continent. It has been a sort of article of faith ever since I have been in the Senate that we should never be bogged down."[127] Pressed by his colleagues, Fulbright admitted that the resolution could be used as advance authority for going to war, but he assured skeptics that this was not what the president had in mind and expressed confidence that Johnson would fully consult with Congress should more substantial escalation become necessary.[128] Ultimately, political expediency carried the day, with Democrats not wanting to create any trouble for Johnson in an election year, their reservations about the open-ended nature of the resolution notwithstanding. "Any apprehensions about Johnson's policies were dwarfed by fear of what Barry Goldwater might do in Vietnam or elsewhere if he became president," in Stone's words.[129]

Internationally, Johnson's belligerent response to an attack that the North Vietnamese had not launched convinced them that he was determined to maintain the U.S. presence in Vietnam, leading them to intensify the insurgency in South Vietnam in hopes of an early victory.[130] In September 1964, the first regiment from the North Vietnamese Army began to move down the Ho Chi Minh Trail, the Politburo having decided that the Viet Cong was not strong enough to destroy the South Vietnamese government on its own. China also stepped up its support for the Vietnamese cause, expanding the railroad network north of the Vietnamese border and beginning work on military airfields that would facilitate operations there. "The overall result," according to Moïse, "was that by the time the United States began major escalation of the American role in the war, in February and March of 1965, the Communist forces with which the Americans had to deal were stronger, better prepared, and better supplied than they would have been had the Tonkin Gulf incidents never occurred."[131] In South Vietnam, the Khanh government tried to take advantage of the crisis by declaring a state of emergency, which led only to mass unrest. Rather than bolstering the regime in Saigon, the incident nearly led to its disintegration.[132] Perhaps most important, the language of the congressional resolution dramatically raised the publicly articulated stakes in Vietnam, further foreclosing the possibility of a face-saving withdrawal. "Greater visible commitment was purchased at the price of reduced flexibility," as a chronicler of the *Pentagon Papers* has put it.[133] In this way, among others, the Tonkin Gulf incident contributed directly to Johnson's decision to expand the war in early 1965.

When it came time to implement that decision, Johnson faced the same dilemma he had in summer 1964: how to justify escalation in the absence of a declared state of war. At the time of the Tonkin Gulf incident, administration officials took note that "reprisal" strikes played well with the public, with the Joint Chiefs, among others, calling for deliberate attempts to provoke North Vietnam into taking actions that could be used to justify a sustained bombing campaign.[134] Although the idea was shelved at that time, it was revived in early January 1965, when serious discussions began about whether the United States should initiate Phase II bombing of North Vietnam. Maxwell Taylor, now ambassador in Saigon, was confident that a pretext could be found that would justify the bombing. At the end of a lengthy cable dated January 6, 1965, detailing the desperate political and military situation in South Vietnam, Taylor advised that the administration "look for an occasion to begin air operations" against Hanoi. "When decided to act," he suggested, "we can justify that decision on the basis of infiltration, of VC terrorism, of attacks on DeSoto patrols or any combination of the three."[135] The clear intent was to portray any bombing campaign as a response to North Vietnamese aggression, as opposed to a last-ditch attempt to save the South Vietnamese regime.

Despite Taylor's entreaties, Johnson would agree only to limited reprisals in early January 1965, not the systematic bombing of North Vietnam. By the end of the month, he had come around to the idea, however. A key forcing event was the "Fork in the Road" memorandum. On January 27, 1965, Bundy and McNamara informed Johnson that the time had come for hard choices. Both had become convinced that the current policy, of waiting and hoping for a stable government in South Vietnam, was leading only to "disastrous defeat." Two alternatives remained: the first was "to use our military power in the Far East and to force a change of Communist policy"; the second was "to deploy all our resources along a track of negotiation, aimed at salvaging what little can be preserved with no major addition to our present military risks."[136] Bundy and McNamara made it clear that they favored the first course. Confronted with this fait accompli, Johnson agreed that day to the initiation of Phase II bombing. "Stable government or no stable government," he said to his advisers, "we'll do what we have to do. . . . We will move strongly." To this end, Johnson authorized the resumption of destroyer patrols in the Tonkin Gulf, the first since September 1964, presumably to provoke a North Vietnamese attack, and dispatched Bundy to Saigon to confer with the embassy about bombing operations.[137]

The pretext for action arrived on February 7, 1965, on the last day of the Bundy mission. A company of Viet Cong guerrillas attacked a U.S. airfield and advisory compound near Pleiku in the central highlands, resulting in eight fatalities. Back in Washington, Johnson quickly approved a reprisal strike, code-named Flaming Dart, against military barracks in the southern portion of North Vietnam, telling members of the NSC that "he had kept the shotgun over the mantel and the bullets in the basement for a long time now," but "the enemy was killing his personnel and he could not expect them to continue their work if he did not authorize them to take steps to defend themselves."[138] Bundy felt that a one-off strike was insufficient, however. In a report drafted on the long return flight from Vietnam, Bundy summed up the desperate situation in South Vietnam and urged Johnson to adopt a policy of "sustained reprisal," in which continuing air and naval action against North Vietnam would be justified by the whole Viet Cong terror campaign in the South. In an annex to the report, Bundy acknowledged that this policy could fail—he estimated the odds of success as somewhere between 25 and 75 percent—but countered that, even if it did, sustained reprisal would have been worth it: "At a minimum it will damp down the charge that we did not do all that we could have done, and this charge will be important in many countries, including our own." If the opportunity to begin bombing was passed up, Bundy cautioned, "we face the grave danger that Pleiku, like the Gulf of Tonkin, may be a short-run stimulant and a long-term depressant."[139]

Bundy admitted to a reporter a few weeks later that his response to Pleiku was opportunistic. "Pleikus are like streetcars," he said, with incidents like it coming along regularly to be exploited when the time was right.[140] The next "streetcar" actually came just days later, on February 10, 1965, when an explosion in an enlisted man's barracks in the coastal city of Qui Nhon killed twenty-three more Americans. On February 13, 1965, Johnson formally approved the policy of sustained reprisal. The State Department cabled Taylor that day that the administration was ready to carry out "measured but effective actions against military targets in North Vietnam."[141] Johnson refused, however, to make any new statement of policy, disregarding Bundy's advice that he level with the public about the demands of the long war ahead.[142] In a meeting with congressional leaders the day after Pleiku, Johnson described sustained reprisal only in the most vague and general terms, as "an effort to defeat North Vietnamese aggression without escalating the war."[143] When Rolling Thunder finally got underway on March 2, 1965, Johnson made no announcement to mark its beginning, preferring to characterize the air strikes as retaliatory in nature and consistent with long-standing policy. "The administration," as Herring says, "was considerably less than candid in explaining to the American public the reasons for and significance of its decision to bomb North Vietnam."[144]

Rolling Thunder, in turn, provided a pretext for the introduction of ground forces. On February 23, 1965, before the first sorties of the air war, Westmoreland requested that a marine landing team be deployed to protect the air base at Da Nang from Viet Cong retaliation. Johnson consented to Westmoreland's request, despite warnings from Taylor that introducing combat units would set a dangerous precedent and tempt the South Vietnamese to shift the burden of the ground war onto the United States.[145] Not long after the first marines landed at Da Nang on March 8, 1965, the military began to pressure Johnson for more forces and for less restrictive rules of engagement, exactly as Taylor had predicted. Sent on a fact-finding mission to South Vietnam, General Harold K. Johnson, the army chief of staff, returned on March 15, 1965, with twenty-one recommendations for how to defeat the Viet Cong, including sending a division to occupy the central highlands and deploying an anti-infiltration force along the demilitarized zone (DMZ) to cut the Ho Chi Minh Trail. General Johnson's feeling was that it would take five years and 500,000 U.S. troops to win the war.[146] The Joint Chiefs of Staff followed on March 20, 1965, with a recommendation that sufficient combat forces be deployed to South Vietnam "not simply to withstand the Viet Cong, but to gain effective operational superiority and assume the offensive."[147] This would entail sending additional marines to Da Nang as well as deploying an army division to the Pleiku area; these troops would be authorized to engage in counterinsurgency combat operations.

Spurred along by the military, Johnson approved the deployment of two additional marine battalions on April 1, 1965, and, more important, expanded their mission from base security to counterinsurgency combat operations.[148] With the dispatch of logistics and engineering units, the groundwork was also laid for a larger, two-division deployment. Members of the administration went out of their way to conceal these decisions from the public. On April 2, Bundy instructed the NSC that, when interacting with the press, "under no circumstances should there be any reference to the movement of U.S. forces or other future courses of action."[149] In his instructions to the embassy in South Vietnam, Rusk struck a similar tone, emphasizing that troop deployments would be spaced out over a period of time with publicity regarding these deployments to be kept at the lowest key possible.[150] In case there was any remaining ambiguity on the need for discretion, NSAM 328, the document codifying the April 1 decisions, included the demand that "premature publicity be avoided by all possible precautions" when it came to the expanded U.S. role in the ground war. Johnson's desire was "that these movements and changes should be understood as being gradual and wholly consistent with existing policy," which clearly they were not.[151]

The expectation, in other words, was that the piecemeal introduction of forces would obscure the transition being made from advising and assisting the South Vietnamese to taking over the ground war. H. R. McMaster lays out the logic of this middle course: "Units smaller than division size already stationed overseas could be relocated to South Vietnam with less fanfare than the deployment of entire divisions from the United States. Offensive operations could be portrayed as active patrolling in support of what the administration would continue to describe as a primarily defensive operation."[152] In the meantime,

Congress would be kept in the dark. Testifying before an executive session of the Senate Foreign Relations Committee on April 7, 1965, McNamara blithely promised, "I am certain that it will be the President's desire and purpose to consult with the Congress, the leadership of the Congress, members of this Committee, before undertaking any combat moves of personnel that would potentially enlarge the war." Taylor had made similar statements before Congress on April 2, reassuring one member that in the event a large-scale troop deployment was being considered, "When that day comes, Senator, you are going to be consulted, I am perfectly sure."[153]

The Johnson administration's hush campaign was successful enough that it was not revealed that U.S. units were engaged in combat operations until June 8, 1965, when Robert McCloskey, a State Department spokesman, leaked the news under questioning from a *New York Times* reporter.[154] The revelation led the paper to editorialize, "The American people were told by a minor State Department official yesterday that, in effect, they were in a land war on the continent of Asia. This is only one of the extraordinary aspects of the first formal announcement that a decision has been made to commit American ground forces to open combat in South Vietnam: The nation is informed about it not by the President, nor by a Cabinet member, not even by a sub-Cabinet official, but by a public relations officer."[155] To mitigate the damage, White House Press Secretary George Reedy issued a brief statement to reporters on June 9: "There has been no change in the mission of U.S. ground combat units in Vietnam in recent days or weeks. The President has issued no order of any kind in this regard to General Westmoreland recently or any other time. The primary mission of these troops is to secure and safeguard important military installations like the air base at Danang. They have the associated mission of active patrolling and securing action in and near the areas thus safeguarded."[156] Needless to say, the White House attempt at a retraction was highly misleading. Not only had Johnson approved the change of mission from base security to counterinsurgency in early April, he had since committed thirteen battalions to the fight against the Viet Cong, with Westmoreland's request for forty-four battalions having arrived on June 7, 1965. It was that request that finally forced Johnson to acknowledge, however belatedly, that he was taking the country to war in South Vietnam.[157]

Did the Johnson Administration Oversell the Threat?

By now, it should be clear that the Johnson administration resorted to a considerable amount of blameshifting in the lead-up to the Vietnam War, failing to level with the public about the hard fight ahead and latching onto a series of pretexts to explain the escalatory steps it was taking. Is there comparable evidence that the administration was deliberately overselling the threat? Specifically, did its members peddle versions of the domino theory in public that they did not subscribe to in private?

One view is that leading officials were quite sincere in their assessments of the threat. Jerome Slater, who has written extensively on the domino theory, comes down on this side of the issue. "During the war," he says, "many assumed that the more extravagant public statements about the disastrous global consequences of the loss of South Vietnam were for public consumption, and were not taken seriously by policymakers. . . . This was not the case: the documentation makes it clear that there was little difference between the public statements and the private beliefs of the highest policymakers. Not only did the policymakers believe in the validity of the domino theory, but they accepted nearly without question very sweeping versions of it."[158] Gareth Porter, who devotes a chapter of his book *Perils of Dominance* to the domino theory, reaches the opposite conclusion. His position is that the domino theory had been largely discredited by the 1960s—in his words, it "had taken on the odd status among civilian national security officials of a relic of the distant past that was considered crude and unsophisticated"— but was deliberately manipulated for bureaucratic purposes by hawks in the Johnson administration such as Bundy, McNamara, and Rusk.[159] These officials, according to Porter, were concerned less about falling dominoes than the unraveling of a policy of isolation and pressure meant to topple the communist regime in China.[160]

When we parse the evidence, Porter's position receives some support but Slater's is ultimately more convincing. That is, official belief in the domino theory appears to have been sincere, if not unqualified. Take the so-called "Death of the Domino Theory Memo." In late May 1964, Johnson asked the intelligence community whether the loss of South Vietnam and Laos would precipitate a domino effect in the Far East. The Board of National Estimates (BNE), the most prestigious center for analysis in the intelligence community, returned with a mixed verdict. According to Sherman Kent, its chairman, the BNE did "not believe that the loss of South Vietnam and Laos would be followed by the rapid, successive communization of the other states of the Far East. . . . With the possible exception of Cambodia, it is likely that no nation in the area would quickly succumb to communism as a result of the fall of Laos and South Vietnam. Furthermore, a continuation of the spread of communism in the area would not be inexorable, and any spread which did occur would take time—time in which the total situation might change in any number of ways unfavorable to the Communist cause."[161] The BNE, in other words, put little stock in the territorial version of the domino theory and was unambiguous enough about the matter that the estimate quickly became known in the intelligence community as the "Death of the Domino Theory Memo."[162]

The moniker was misleading, however, insofar as the memo went on to warn about the psychological consequences of a communist victory in Vietnam. "The loss of South Vietnam and Laos to the Communists would be profoundly damaging to the US position in the Far East," the BNE concluded, "most especially because the US has committed itself persistently, emphatically, and publicly to preventing Communist takeover of the two countries. Failure here would be damaging to US prestige, and would seriously debase the credibility of US will and capability to contain the spread of communism elsewhere in the area. Our enemies would be encouraged and there would be an increased tendency among other states to move toward a greater degree of accommodation with the Communists."[163] In other words, whereas the territorial version of the domino theory could safely be dismissed, the psychological version could not.

What are the implications of the "Death of the Domino Theory Memo" for the oversell issue? On the one hand, the very fact that Johnson solicited the views of the intelligence community suggests that he harbored some doubts about the validity of the domino theory, which is Porter's point.[164] On the other hand, it does not appear that the memo had any impact. The BNE conclusions seem to have been simply ignored and left out of policy deliberations.[165] Aside from the fact that the Americanization of the war was still some way off, it must have mattered that the memo actually took down only one version of the domino theory, the territorial one.[166] If anything, it was the psychological version of the theory that preoccupied decision makers more, and it was this version that received some support in the BNE estimate, with its warnings about lost prestige and credibility.[167] Even Porter seems to concede the ultimate impact of the domino theory in two respects. First, Johnson himself must have put some stock in the theory; otherwise, Bundy, McNamara, and Rusk would have had little incentive to deploy it for bureaucratic purposes. Second, the threat of neutralism and accommodation with China that Porter cites as motivating administration hawks was quite consistent with the domino theory. South Vietnam, for hawks such as Bundy, was the "ultimate domino"; its fall would validate China's "wars of national liberation" strategy, potentially undermining the progress that had been made in containing the Soviet Union.[168]

In short, administration officials had access to intelligence casting doubt on the validity of the domino theory, especially its territorial version. Nevertheless, these estimates seem to have had little impact on the decision-making process. Rather than grapple with the BNE's conclusions, Johnson and his advisers simply ignored them, confident that a rationale for war remained.

Blowback

If the Johnson administration was as guilty of misleading the public as the evidence suggests, what were the consequences? As the reader will recall, deception is likely to backfire in the event that a war goes badly, especially if it degenerates into a costly stalemate. Under these conditions, public discontent will provide an opening for critics to revisit the origins of the war and the deceptive tactics that were used to sell it. Leaders will lose credibility as their dishonesty is exposed. In this case, the public will punish its leaders less for being misleading than for launching a failed war.

This is exactly what happened in the Vietnam case. Despite inflicting massive casualties on the enemy, U.S. forces could not break the will of the Vietnamese communists.[169] The main cause of U.S. defeat was an asymmetry in interests. Whereas for the United States the conflict in Vietnam was a limited war fought on behalf of abstract objectives such as maintaining credibility, for the communists it was a total war in which the main issue at stake was nothing less than national reunification. U.S. decision makers never fully grasped this fact, which led them to underestimate the enemy's tenacity and fighting power and to overestimate how long the U.S. public would tolerate a protracted, inconclusive war.[170] The United States also pursued a flawed military strategy in Vietnam, one predicated on search-and-destroy tactics and the use of overwhelming firepower to cause the attrition of the enemy forces.[171] A pacification effort rooted in classic principles of counterinsurgency warfare might have been more effective.[172] Even this approach faced long odds of success, however, given that the South Vietnamese government never developed the necessary level of political competence to enlist the loyalties of the population on its side, which was a necessary precondition for its surviving a U.S. withdrawal.[173]

The Tet Offensive proved to be a decisive turning point, coming as it did on the heels of a media campaign by White House, State Department, and military officials to promote the view that victory was just around the corner.[174] These pronouncements were based on dubious intelligence, as the "order of battle" controversy reveals.[175] In summer 1967, the CIA estimated that enemy strength in South Vietnam was perhaps twice that claimed by the military, when irregular elements were counted. The White House, fearful that the CIA dissent would undermine its claims that the "crossover point"[176] had been reached, pressured the intelligence agency to sign off on the lower number claimed by the military and then used the consensus estimate to convince the public that the war of attrition was being won. The White House manipulations backfired when the Tet Offensive discredited any notion that the communists were on the brink of defeat. The fact that the Viet Cong suffered crippling losses during the offensive mattered less than the fact that they had mounted it at all; Tet was widely seen as a political defeat for the United States. The Tet Offensive came to represent "a failure of U.S. intelligence, the puncture of U.S. optimism, the destruction of South Vietnam, the incapacity and illegitimacy of the regime in Saigon, the brutality and immorality of the war, as well as proof of the indefatigable will of the communist forces" to the public.[177] In its aftermath, Johnson reluctantly came to the conclusion that the Vietnam War, in its current form, had become domestically unsustainable.[178]

Johnson never recovered from widespread perceptions of a "credibility gap" surrounding his statements on the Vietnam War.[179] Helping to fuel these perceptions were ongoing revelations about the dubious circumstances surrounding the origins of the war. Most famously, the Senate Foreign Relations Committee, chaired by Fulbright, conducted an official inquiry into the Gulf of Tonkin incident in February 1968. Mc-Namara agreed to testify before the committee in executive session on February 20.[180] Over the course of seven and a half hours, Fulbright peppered him with questions about connections between the DeSoto patrols and the OPLAN 34A raids, as well as the ambiguous details of the second incident. McNamara stonewalled, insisting that "even with the advantage of hindsight I find the essential facts of the two attacks appear today as they did then, when they were fully explored with Congress."[181] The media were not deterred, interviewing in the weeks following dozens of sailors who had served aboard the *Maddox* and *Turner Joy*. The general consensus was that the destroyers had been on a secret mission in support of the South Vietnamese and that the second attack had never happened.[182]

The political implications for Johnson, as Randall Woods relates, were devastating: "The 1968 brouhaha struck a major and perhaps decisive blow at the president's credibility, and it did so at a crucial time. If Johnson had misled Congress and the American people concerning the North Vietnamese attack on the two American destroyers in 1964, then the Gulf of Tonkin Resolution, which the administration had so often invoked as justification for the presence of American troops in Vietnam, was invalid."[183] Shortly thereafter, on March 31, 1968, Johnson announced that he was putting a halt to the bombing of most of North Vietnam, that he was eager to open peace talks with Hanoi, and that he would not seek a second term as president.[184] In the end, he was undone by the very deceptions that had made the Vietnam War politically possible in the first place.

4

OVERSELLING THE IRAQ WAR

Unlike Roosevelt and Johnson, President George W. Bush faced a relatively permissive domestic political environment on the eve of war. With the public in a vengeful mood after the 9/11 attacks and Democrats in Congress not wanting to be seen as weak on national security, Bush had a relatively free hand in 2002–2003, although not so free as to allow for total candor. Accordingly, overselling played the leading role in his securing domestic support for the Iraq War. Bush and members of his administration misrepresented the available intelligence and suggested that Saddam Hussein was an undeterrable madman, in league with al Qaeda, and on the verge of acquiring nuclear weapons. The overall effect was to obscure the preventive nature of the war by depicting Iraq as a clear and present danger; in fact, it was a weak and isolated pariah. Bush was able to indulge in such blatant overselling, I argue, because of the widespread expectation that victory over Iraq would come cheaply and easily. This undermined the effective functioning of the marketplace of ideas by diluting whatever incentives Democrats might have had to expose even obvious instances of threat inflation. Bush was held to account for his misleading portrayal of the threat only when the deteriorating situation on the ground in Iraq renewed interest in the origins of the war and the arguments that were used to justify it.

In this chapter, I first discuss why Bush invaded Iraq. The key take-away is that, however much the public debate focused on Iraqi weapons of mass destruction (WMDs) and links to terrorism, the war was less about the threat posed by Iraq than the opportunity it presented to demonstrate U.S. power. I then focus on the domestic political environment, which was relatively pliable but still required that Bush obscure that he was advocating a preventive war. Next, I examine why Bush pursued the United Nations route and argue that the goal was to set a trap for Saddam Hussein, not to peacefully disarm him. I then describe how Bush oversold the threat, twisting the intelligence in the process, and address the failure of the marketplace of ideas, focusing in particular on the choice made by leading Democrats not to expose Bush's threat inflation. Finally, I assess whether the experience of the Iraq War has soured the U.S. public on future military adventures.

Why Invade Iraq? Threat versus Opportunity

Why did Bush invade Iraq? The first point to make is that Iraq's WMD programs and links to terrorism were not as crucial to the decision to invade as their prominence in the public debate would suggest they were. In other words, it is simply not the case that Iraq was an intelligence-driven crisis.[1] Rather, Bush had already decided on a confrontation with Saddam Hussein by the time the relevant intelligence was scrutinized in detail. The movement toward war began almost immediately in the wake of the 9/11 attacks, when hawks within the Bush administration, such as Secretary of Defense Donald Rumsfeld and his deputy Paul Wolfowitz, pressed for Iraq to be included in the initial phases of the war on terror.[2] Although the decision was made to deal with Afghanistan first, attention turned to Iraq as soon as Kabul fell, with military planning for what would become Operation Iraqi Freedom beginning in late November 2001.

It is difficult to pin down the exact timing, but it appears that by July 2002, at the latest, Bush was committed to regime change in Iraq, using force if necessary.[3] The key piece of evidence in this regard is the Downing Street memo. The memo, which records the minutes of a meeting of senior British officials held on July 23, 2002, is most notable for what Sir Richard Dearlove, chief of the British secret intelligence service, had to say about a recent set of talks in Washington. According to Dearlove, "There was a perceptible shift in attitude. Military action was now seen as inevitable. Bush wanted to remove Saddam, through military action, justified by the conjunction of terrorism and WMD. But the intelligence and facts were being fixed around the policy."[4] In Dearlove's telling, Bush had effectively decided on war with Iraq and was now shifting his attention to preparing the political ground for it. In this context, it is interesting to note that a National Intelligence Estimate (NIE) on Iraq's WMD programs was put together only in September 2002.[5] A NIE is meant to capture the collective judgment of the intelligence community (IC) on an important issue and is normally prepared over the course of several months as participating agencies hash out their differences. The NIE on Iraqi WMDs, in contrast, had to be completed in only three weeks after Democratic members of the Senate Intelligence Committee demanded to see one before voting on a resolution authorizing the use of force; they were stunned that Bush had not already made the request.

It appears that it was only in late December 2002 that Bush gave careful scrutiny to the intelligence underlying the case for war. On December 21, George Tenet, director of the CIA, and John McLaughlin, his deputy, went to the White House to brief Bush, Vice President Richard Cheney, National Security Advisor Condoleezza Rice, and Chief of Staff Andrew Card on intelligence that might be used to build a public case against Saddam Hussein. McLaughlin did the briefing, which was underwhelming. When he was finished, Bush was unhappy, commenting, "Nice try. I don't think this is quite—it's not something that Joe Public would understand or would gain a lot of confidence from." Turning to Tenet, Bush complained, "I've been told all this intelligence about having WMD and this is the best we've got?" Tenet reassured Bush, "Don't worry, it's a slam dunk."[6] Cheney, among others, has cited the "slam dunk" meeting as evidence that the Bush administration acted against Iraq on the basis of the best possible intelligence, but what it really reveals is that the decision to remove Saddam Hussein, which had been made months before, did not depend on a fine-grained picture of the WMD or terrorism threat.[7]

Since the Iraq War began, administration insiders have more or less conceded that intelligence on WMDs was not driving the decision-making process. On July 9, 2003, Rumsfeld testified before the Senate Armed Services Committee, "The coalition did not act in Iraq because we had discovered dramatic new evidence of Iraq's pursuit of weapons of mass murder. We acted because we saw the existing evidence in a new light through the prism of our experience on 9/11."[8] In the same vein, Douglas Feith, the undersecretary of defense for policy, has remarked in his memoirs, "It was a mistake for the Bush Administration to rely so heavily on intelligence community information to make the case for war in Iraq—and not just for the obvious reason that the information contained important errors. It was a mistake because *one did not need secret information* to understand or explain the threat from Saddam." That is, "the rationale for war did not actually stand or fall on the accuracy of . . . assessments of Iraq's WMD stockpiles."[9] If that is the case, why did the intelligence on WMDs play such a prominent role in the prewar debate? Wolfowitz provides an answer in an interview he gave to a *Vanity Fair* reporter in May 2003, acknowledging, "The truth is that, for reasons that have a lot to do with the U.S. government bureaucracy, we settled on the one issue that everyone could agree on, which was weapons of mass destruction, as the core reason" to go to war.[10] WMDs, in other words, served as a least common denominator, a consensus selling point, for hawks who had other reasons to confront Saddam Hussein.[11]

What, exactly, were those other reasons? Jeffrey Record has argued persuasively that "the case for war rested on what amounted to a loose coalition of arguments, motives, hopes, and expectations," with different elements of the pro-war camp embracing different rationales.[12] These included finishing what had been started in the first Gulf War, when the United States stopped short of marching on Baghdad; restoring U.S. credibility; legitimating preventive war; intimidating other rogue states such as Iran and North Korea; democratizing the Middle East; reducing the strategic dependence of the United States on Saudi Arabia; eliminating an enemy of Israel; vindicating Rumsfeld's "transformation" agenda at the Pentagon; and expanding the power of the presidency.[13] The Iraq War, in other words, was overdetermined, with multiple motives at play.

If there was an ideological thread tying these motives together, it was neoconservatism, with its unapologetic defense of democracy promotion, preventive war, unilateralism, and U.S. hegemony. As has been chronicled elsewhere, it was the neoconservatives who had been fixated on ousting Saddam Hussein throughout the 1990s; it was the neoconservatives who, from 9/11 on, pushed the hardest to make Iraq a central front in the war on terrorism; and, most important, it was the neoconservatives who provided the intellectual rationale for the Iraq War in the form of the Bush Doctrine.[14] In retrospect, the Iraq War makes little sense in anything but the Bush Doctrine's terms. As Robert Jervis has argued, "The war is hard to understand if the only objective was to disarm Saddam or even to remove him from power. Even had the inflated estimates of his WMD capability been accurate, the danger was simply too remote to justify the effort. But if changing the Iraqi regime was expected to bring democracy and stability to the Middle East, discourage tyrants and energize reformers throughout the world, and demonstrate the American willingness to provide a high degree of what it considers world order whether others like it or not, then as part of a larger project, the war makes sense."[15] The Iraq War, in other words, is best seen as a test case for neoconservatives' larger ideas about U.S. power and world leadership.[16]

What conclusions can be drawn about why the United States invaded Iraq? Two stand out. First, to the extent that the Bush administration was reacting to a threat, it was long term in nature. That is, the Iraq War was a preventive war.[17] This comes through clearly in the 2002 White House *National Security Strategy*, notwithstanding the misleading use of the term *preemption*: "The United States has long maintained the option of preemptive actions to counter a sufficient threat to our national security. The greater the threat, the greater is the risk of inaction—and the more compelling the case for taking anticipatory action to defend ourselves, even if uncertainty remains as to the time and place of the enemy's attack. To forestall or prevent such hostile acts by our adversaries, the United States will, if necessary, act preemptively."[18] Applied to Iraq, this meant that war was justified as long as there was a possibility that Saddam Hussein might develop a formidable unconventional arsenal and then use it for aggression, blackmail, or even direct attacks against the United States. If there was even a 1 percent chance of terrorists getting their hands on WMDs, according to Cheney, then the United States needed to act as if it were a certainty.[19] Second, the Iraq War was less about Iraq itself than about U.S. power and reputation. That is, "the invasion represented power exercised first and foremost for its own sake."[20] To the extent that WMDs mattered in this calculus, they were as a symbol of continued Iraqi defiance of the United States rather than as a near-term threat to regional stability, let alone U.S. security.

The Domestic Politics of the Iraq War: 2002–2003

What kind of domestic political environment did Bush face as he ramped up the selling of the Iraq War in 2002–2003? On the one hand, there was no equivalent to the anti-interventionism that Roosevelt had to contend with in 1940–1941. In other words, Bush had no reason to expect that an aggressive push for war would result in much mobilized opposition. On the other hand, the domestic political environment was not so pliable as to allow for total candor. Specifically, Bush could count on widespread support for the use of force only if he could make a compelling case that the threat was imminent and that diplomatic options had been exhausted. A preventive war, in other words, had to be dressed up as a preemptive war to appease elite and mass opinion.

Powell, the Military, and the Press

Among key elites, there was a preexisting consensus, dating from the passage of the Iraq Liberation Act in 1998, that regime change was desirable, but that consensus did not extend to war, or at least a preventive war initiated by the United States.[21] This was made manifest in summer 2002, when Brent Scowcroft and James Baker, Republican elder statesmen, publicly urged Bush to slow the rush to war, at least long enough to go to the United Nations and cultivate multilateral support for a hard line against Saddam.[22] The interventions by Scowcroft and Baker reinforced the efforts that Secretary of State Colin Powell had been making to get Bush to commit to the UN process. In a private session at the White House on August 5, 2002, Powell warned Bush that, in the event that he did successfully oust Saddam, he would become "the proud owner of 25 million people," which meant a major occupation that would "suck the oxygen out of everything" and dominate Bush's presidency. "It's nice to say we can do it unilaterally, except you can't," Powell said, pointing to the need for access

to bases in the region. There was simply no alternative to internationaliz-
ing the problem.[23] It is important to point out that Powell was never cat-
egorically opposed to military action; and once Bush sided with him and
agreed to work through the United Nations, Powell played the role of the
good soldier, lending his credibility to the case for war by going before the
UN Security Council on February 5, 2003, and laying out the assembled
evidence (as thin as it was) on Iraq's WMD programs and involvement in
terrorism.[24]

Within the national security bureaucracy, it was not hard to find dis-
comfort over how the decision-making process was unfolding. The military, especially, was leery of the role that Defense Department civilians
were playing in the war planning, with Rumsfeld pushing for a smaller
invasion force than the army thought was necessary to secure Iraq in the
wake of combat operations.[25] "The heart of the Army's argument," according to James Fallows, "was that with too few soldiers, the United States
would win the war only to be trapped in an untenable position during
the occupation."[26] Generally, however, concerns such as these bubbled
under the surface, and the few attempts made to bring them to the fore
were either ignored or rejected. The most famous case is that of General
Eric Shinseki, the army chief of staff, who, when pressed during Senate
testimony on February 25, 2003, estimated that "something on the order
of several hundred thousand soldiers" would be required to occupy Iraq.
Shinseki's statement invited a prompt rebuttal from Wolfowitz, who told
the House Budget Committee two days later that "some of the higher-end
predictions that we have been hearing recently, such as the notion that it
will take several hundred thousand U.S. troops to provide stability in post-
Saddam Iraq, are wildly off the mark."[27] As Fallows has observed, "this
was as direct a rebuke of a military leader by his civilian superior as the
United States had seen in fifty years."[28] It had the effect of ending serious
public discussion of the fundamentals of the war plan before it had even
begun.[29]

Outside the government, the mainstream media served to echo, and
even amplify, the White House talking points on Iraq.[30] Howard Kurtz, a
media critic, found that from August 2002 until the war was launched in
March 2003 there were about 140 front-page pieces in the *Washington Post*
making the administration's case for war but only a handful making the
opposite case or even raising questions.[31] Some of this can be attributed to

a desire to appear patriotic, but even more important was the fact that so few "authoritative" sources, especially members of Congress, were willing to go on record and challenge the administration's claims. As one Democratic veteran of Capitol Hill said to Thomas Ricks, a reporter, "The media didn't stand up because they had no one to quote."[32] With Congress more or less giving Bush a free pass, the mainstream media were relegated to reproducing the one-sided debate that was happening in the Beltway. This is consistent with the indexing hypothesis, which contends that "the perspectives expressed by Washington elites effectively determine the tone and content of the news that reaches the public."[33] For the most part, the media failed to pick up on alternative centers of opposition to the war, such as among realists in academe.[34]

Subdued Debate in Congress

Perhaps the most striking aspect of the prewar debate was the subdued role played by Congress. Jane Cramer presents compelling evidence that a large majority in Congress, including a fair number of Republicans, was not persuaded that attacking Iraq was necessary.[35] Notably, Senators Joseph Biden (D-Delaware), Richard Lugar (R-Indiana), and Chuck Hagel (R-Nebraska), all on the Foreign Relations Committee, spearheaded a bipartisan effort that nearly succeeded in drastically circumscribing Bush's authority. The Biden-Lugar-Hagel Resolution, which reportedly had the backing of at least sixty to seventy senators, including as many as twenty-five Republicans, was crafted to allow Bush to attack Iraq only for the purpose of destroying Iraqi WMDs and only after seeking authorization from the UN Security Council. In the event that UN approval was not forthcoming, the resolution required the president to return to Congress and demonstrate that the threat to the United States posed by Iraqi WMDs was so grave as to necessitate military action. As it happens, the Biden-Lugar-Hagel initiative fell apart when Richard Gephardt (D-Missouri), the House minority leader, agreed to grant broad war powers to Bush, even appearing with him in the Rose Garden on October 2, 2002, to announce that the text of the draft Iraq War Resolution had been finalized. The speculation among Democrats was that Gephardt, who was determined to run for president in 2004, did not want to repeat the mistake he had made in 1991 by voting against the first Persian Gulf

War, thereby creating an opening for Republicans to paint him as soft and hesitant to use force.[36]

Gephardt's defection precluded any possibility of a bipartisan alternative to the Iraq War Resolution because no Republican could afford to be seen as weaker on national security than the top Democratic leader in the House. Lacking bipartisan cover, Democrats who had been on the fence, especially those who were facing tough reelection fights and those who harbored presidential aspirations, shied away from directly challenging the administration. The way was now clear for Bush to secure a blank check from Congress. With the result foreordained, the debate in Congress over whether to go to war was anticlimactic. At their most intense points, the debates in the House and Senate attracted fewer than 10 percent of the members of each body.[37] Overall, the Senate devoted six days of debate to Iraq, which paled in comparison to the twenty-one days spent debating the Elementary and Secondary Education Act, the twenty-three days spent on the energy bill, the nineteen days spent on the trade bill, and the eighteen days spent on the farm bill.[38] This was despite the fact that the NIE on Iraqi WMDs had been delivered only on October 1, 2002, three days before debate began. Senate staff later calculated that no more than six members went to the secure room where the highly classified document was kept to read it for themselves.[39]

Bowing to the inevitable, leading Democrats in Congress authorized the president to use force even as they registered their doubts in floor speeches.[40] The final tallies were one-sided: 296 to 113 in the House and 77 to 23 in the Senate. In the Senate, twenty-nine of the fifty Democrats voted for the resolution. Biden, who was one of them, remained adamant that Iraqi WMDs did not pose an imminent threat to national security and that it was unlikely that Saddam would use them unless he was attacked. Nevertheless, he proceeded to authorize military action anyway, arguing, "The stronger the vote in favor of this resolution, the stronger the likelihood, in my view, that the Security Council will approve a tough UN Resolution. . . . The tougher a UN resolution, the less likely it is that we will have to use force in Iraq. That is because such a resolution would finally force Saddam to face the choice between inspectors and invaders, between giving up his weapons and giving up power, and there is at least a chance that he might make the right choice."[41] Senator Hillary Clinton (D-New York) provided a similar justification for her vote, arguing, "Because bipartisan support for this resolution makes success in the United Nations more likely and war less likely, and because a good faith effort by the United States, even if it fails, will bring more allies and legitimacy to our cause, I have concluded, after careful and serious consideration, that a vote for the resolution best serves the security of our Nation."[42] Biden and Clinton were among nine senators who explicitly rejected preventive war thinking in their testimony and then proceeded to vote *for* the Iraq War Resolution.[43]

Vocal opposition was confined to the fringes of the Democratic caucus, among liberal "lions" such as Senator Robert Byrd (D-West Virginia) who, in the midst of the debate in Congress, penned a fiery *New York Times* op-ed challenging Congress to resist the rush to war: "I have listened closely to the president. I have questioned the members of his war cabinet. I have searched for that single piece of evidence that would convince me that the president must have in his hands, before the month is out, open-ended Congressional authorization to deliver an unprovoked attack on Iraq. I remain unconvinced. The president's case for an unprovoked attack is circumstantial at best. Saddam Hussein is a threat, but the threat is not so great that we must be stampeded to provide such authority to this president just weeks before an election."[44] Byrd was representative of other early opponents of the war, such as Senator Edward Kennedy (D-Massachusetts). He held a secure seat and no longer harbored aspirations for national office, which freed him to speak his mind.[45]

The Public: Inclined toward War, but with Caveats

Rhetorically, the Bush administration framed the Iraq War as an extension of the war on terror, priming the public to think of the two together.[46] Its job was eased by the fact that Saddam Hussein had been demonized as Public Enemy #1 throughout the 1990s, leaving the public predisposed to believe the worst about him.[47] In fact, a surprising number of Americans were ready to blame Saddam Hussein for 9/11, or at least believe he was involved, in the days following the attacks. In a poll taken on September 13, 2001, 34 percent of respondents thought it "very likely" that Saddam Hussein was "personally involved in Tuesday's terrorist attacks," while another 44 percent thought it "somewhat likely."[48] This translated directly into support for folding Iraq into the war on terror. In a poll taken on September 22, 2001, 91 percent of respondents saw "destroying terrorist operations in Afghanistan" as a very important goal of military action;

68 percent nominated "removing Saddam Hussein from power in Iraq."[49] Clearly, the public was ready to draw a connection between Iraq and the war on terror well before the Bush administration explicitly cultivated it.

Support for military action against Iraq peaked in November 2001, at 74 percent. From there, it hovered at around 60 percent until the outbreak of war. Douglas Foyle infers from this that "if the administration successfully 'led' the public to war, it did so in large part because, after September 11, the public favored such a war."[50] Two qualifications should be noted, however. First, there were conditions attached to the public's support. Most important, large majorities preferred that congressional authorization be obtained, that diplomacy be given a chance, and that any invasion be done multilaterally. In nineteen surveys taken between February 2002 and March 2003, only 33 percent of respondents, on average, backed invading Iraq unilaterally, whereas a majority (averaging 55 percent) preferred doing so only with UN approval.[51] Public sentiment, like elite sentiment, pointed in the direction of the UN process.

Second, the public was not monolithic in its support for the war. From the beginning, Republicans and Democrats were divided about a potential invasion of Iraq. Partisan differences only grew over time, especially after September 2002, when the Bush administration ramped up its selling of the war. By March 2003, the partisan gap was nearly 40 percentage points, with close to 90 percent of Republicans and less than 50 percent of Democrats supporting military action. On March 16, 2003, just days before the start of hostilities, 64 percent of Democrats—compared to 30 percent of Republicans—said the United States should "wait and give the United Nations and weapons inspectors more time" rather than "take military action against Iraq fairly soon."[52] Partisan differences extended to assessments of the threat. In their analysis of polling data from summer 2003, Steven Kull, Clay Ramsay, and Evan Lewis found that the intention to vote for President Bush was the single most powerful predictor of various misperceptions that could have justified going to war with Iraq. These included beliefs that close links between Iraq and al Qaeda had been found, that WMDs had been found, and that world public opinion was favorable to the war.[53] The partisan gap on Iraq served as an early indicator that Bush would be vulnerable politically in the event that the Iraq War went badly.

When we survey the domestic political scene in 2002–2003, we find that Bush could count on widespread support for the use of force against

Saddam Hussein but only if he could make a compelling case that the threat was imminent and that all diplomatic options had been exhausted. War, in other words, had to be sold as a last resort, which Bush did by going to the United Nations and by inflating the threat.

The United Nations Process

Why did Bush go to the United Nations? Was it a sincere attempt to peacefully disarm Iraq or an instance of "counterfeit diplomacy" meant to shift blame for war onto Saddam Hussein?[54] The bulk of the evidence supports the latter interpretation. When, in spring and summer 2002, the British were attempting to sell the Americans on the merits of the UN process, the argument they made was that it could be leveraged to provide political cover for war. The Downing Street memo is indispensable evidence here. In the same July 23, 2002, meeting referenced earlier, Prime Minister Tony Blair "said that it would make a big difference politically and legally if Saddam refused to allow in the U.N. inspectors."[55] That is, if the United Nations could be made to agree on an ultimatum that Saddam accept inspectors, and if Saddam then refused to accept them, a legitimate justification for war would be supplied.[56] Cheney and Rumsfeld, the staunchest hawks in the Bush administration, were not convinced by Blair's logic. They had little confidence in the inspections and did not want to open the door to a peaceful resolution of the crisis.[57] They argued for bypassing the United Nations; otherwise, Bush would be inviting "a never-ending process of debate, compromise and delay."[58] Only joint pressure by Blair and Powell convinced Bush to go to the United Nations and pursue a Security Council resolution, with the caveat that the United States would disarm Iraq unilaterally if necessary.[59]

With the UN Security Council voting unanimously on November 8, 2002, to give Iraq a final chance to disarm, Saddam allowed intrusive inspections to resume on November 27. By late January and early February 2003, the inspectors had turned up little evidence that Iraq was producing or stockpiling WMDs, which led to calls by France, Germany, Russia, and others on the Security Council that the inspections be given more time. Vindicating Cheney's and Rumsfeld's misgivings, the UN process threatened to take the regime-change option off the table, leading many in Washington to view the work of the inspectors "not as a possible path to peace but as an obstacle to a fait accompli."[60] By this point, however, the approach to the United Nations had largely served its domestic political purpose, allowing leading Democrats to claim, however disingenuously, that their votes for the Iraq War Resolution had been votes in favor of multilateral inspections and UN diplomacy, not war.[61] And Bush was able to mitigate the damage from the inconclusive inspections by framing the issue in terms of Saddam's failure to fully come clean rather than the failure to find WMDs, effectively shifting the blame for war onto Saddam's shoulders.[62]

The fact of the matter is that Bush never intended for Saddam to be disarmed peacefully. Rather, he went to the United Nations to expose Saddam's duplicity, cementing the case for war. The inspections process was meant to be a trap.[63] Ari Fleischer, the White House press secretary, admitted as much to reporters on December 2, 2002, remarking, "If Saddam Hussein indicated that he has weapons of mass destruction and that he is violating United Nations resolutions, then we will know that Saddam Hussein again deceived the world. If he declared he has none, then we will know that Saddam Hussein is once again misleading the world."[64] Further suggestive evidence comes from a meeting that Bush had with Blair in the Oval Office on January 31, 2003. In the meeting, Bush acknowledged that no WMDs were likely to be found inside Iraq and talked about several ways to provoke a confrontation with Saddam in the event that the inspections process broke down, including a proposal to paint a U.S. surveillance plane in the colors of the United Nations in the hopes of drawing Iraqi fire.[65] By this point, there was almost nothing that the Iraqi leader could have done to avert war. Of course, this is not what was communicated to the public. Nor is it how Saddam read the situation. Incredibly, his attention was focused on internal and regional threats right up until the end. He had convinced himself that the United States, partly because of its troubles at the United Nations, would not attack and that if it did, it would stop short of marching on Baghdad.[66]

Overselling the Threat

What sets the Iraq War apart from the other cases featured in this book is the outsized role that overselling played in securing domestic support for it. Especially critical was the politicization of intelligence.[67] Starting in mid-2002, the Bush administration began to put pressure—more indirect than direct—on the IC to bring its threat assessments closer into line with policy statements. And in those areas in which the intelligence continued to lag behind what policymakers were saying in public, the administration misrepresented the IC findings. This included downplaying dissent among analysts, expressing unwarranted levels of certainty given the ambiguity of the underlying evidence, and cherry-picking favorable bits of intelligence for release.

Most egregious was the insinuation of an alliance between Saddam Hussein's regime and al Qaeda, one that could result in the handoff of WMDs to terrorists for attacks on the United States. In the 2003 State of the Union, Bush warned,

> Evidence from intelligence sources, secret communications, and statements by people now in custody reveal that Saddam Hussein aids and protects terrorists, including members of Al Qaeda. Secretly, and without fingerprints, he could provide one of his hidden weapons to terrorists, or help them develop their own. Before September the 11th, many in the world believed that Saddam Hussein could be contained. But chemical agents, lethal viruses and shadowy terrorist networks are not easily contained. Imagine those 19 hijackers with other weapons and other plans—this time armed by Saddam Hussein. It would take one vial, one canister, one crate slipped into this country to bring a day of horror like none we have ever known.[68]

As is now well documented, administration claims to this effect contradicted the available intelligence.[69] Multiple reports dismissed the allegation that Iraq and al Qaeda were cooperating partners; and the 2002 NIE went out of its way to say that Saddam would consider aiding al Qaeda in attacks on the homeland only if the prospect of regime change made him sufficiently desperate.[70] It was exactly because the IC was unwilling to validate accusations about operational links between Iraq and al Qaeda that the Policy Counter Terrorism Evaluation Group (PCTEG) was stood up in the Pentagon after 9/11. Directed by Feith, the cell combed through raw intelligence reports looking for evidence that the relationship between the Iraqi regime and al Qaeda was more extensive than the IC had acknowledged and might have involved a facilitating role in the 9/11 attacks. The most important PCTEG "discovery" in this regard was a supposed meeting between Mohammed Atta, the lead 9/11 hijacker, and an Iraqi intelligence agent in Prague in April 2001. Both the CIA and the Federal Bureau of Investigation (FBI) quickly concluded that the meeting had probably never taken place, which did not stop Cheney from referring to it when asked whether Saddam was connected to 9/11. "It's been pretty well confirmed that [Atta] did go to Prague and he did meet with a senior official of the Iraq intelligence service," Cheney insisted during a December 9, 2001 appearance on *Meet the Press*, a charge he repeated on September 8, 2002, during another appearance on the show.[71]

Nearly as problematic were claims that Iraq was close to having a nuclear weapon.[72] In remarks to a gathering of the Veterans of Foreign Wars on August 26, 2002, Cheney declared, "[W]e now know that Saddam has resumed his efforts to acquire nuclear weapons. . . . Many of us are convinced that Saddam will acquire nuclear weapons fairly soon."[73] In an address in Cincinnati, Ohio, on October 7, 2002, Bush elaborated on the charge: "The evidence indicates that Iraq is reconstituting its nuclear weapons program. . . . Iraq has attempted to purchase high-strength aluminum tubes and other equipment needed for gas centrifuges, which are used to enrich uranium for nuclear weapons. If the Iraqi regime is able to produce, buy, or steal an amount of highly-enriched uranium a little larger than a single softball, it could have a nuclear weapon in less than a year."[74] The 2003 State of the Union brought the additional revelation, "The British Government has learned that Saddam Hussein recently sought significant quantities of uranium from Africa."[75]

What administration officials failed to acknowledge was the extent of the disagreement within the IC over each of these claims.[76] On the issue of whether Iraq had reconstituted its nuclear weapons program, the 2002 NIE expressed the majority view that the program was being reconstituted but included a dissent by the State Department Bureau of Intelligence and Research (INR). The INR view was that "The activities we have detected do not add up to a compelling case that Iraq is currently pursuing what INR would consider to be an integrated and comprehensive approach to acquire nuclear weapons. Iraq may be doing so, but INR considers the available evidence inadequate to support such a judgment."[77] The authors of the NIE were also careful to state that the Iraqis would not be able to make a nuclear weapon for five to seven years unless they acquired the needed fissile material from abroad.[78] On the issue of the aluminum tubes, the CIA had determined in April 2001 that the tubes were intended for use in gas centrifuges that would enrich uranium for a nuclear weapon, but engineers at the Department of Energy (DOE) had immediately disputed the CIA findings. They noted that the specifications of the tubes were not consistent with known centrifuge designs and that they were unlikely to withstand the stress of the enrichment process, in which tubes were spun continuously at extremely high speeds. When DOE analysts got their hands on a sample of the tubes, they found that they matched those Iraq had previously used as casings for artillery rockets. "Rocket production," not nuclear weapons, "is the more likely end-use for these tubes," read a classified DOE report dated August 17, 2001.[79] The NIE incorporated the DOE assessment that the aluminum tubes were probably not part of Iraq's reconstituted nuclear weapons program in its "Key Judgments."[80]

Finally, on the uranium issue, the phrasing used in the 2003 State of the Union—"The British Government has learned that Saddam Hussein recently sought significant quantities of uranium from Africa"—was deliberate. It was meant to get around the fact that the *U.S.* IC had repeatedly advised the White House not to use the claim in its public statements because of its doubtful credibility. The specific charge—that Iraq had arranged to buy 500 tons of yellowcake uranium from Niger—first surfaced in October 2001, when the Servizio per le Informazioni e la Sicurezza Militare (SISMI; the Italian military intelligence agency) alerted the CIA to the sale, sending along documentary "proof" in February 2002.[81] Over time, intelligence analysts developed stronger and stronger doubts about the Iraq-Niger connection. First, Iraq already had a sizable stockpile of uranium ore in its inventory. Second, a French consortium tightly controlled the two uranium mines in Niger and its director had assured the U.S. ambassador to Niger that there was "no possibility" that any of the 3,000 tons of yellowcake uranium produced there could have been diverted.[82] Finally, the logistical difficulties involved in transporting large amounts of uranium made it highly unlikely that any deal could have taken place covertly.[83] As one Foreign Service officer who had served in Niger stated, "Twice a year 25 semi tractor trailer loads of yellowcake would have to be driven down roads where one seldom sees even a bush taxi. In other words, it would be very hard to hide such a shipment."[84]

Because of these and related doubts, the CIA had repeatedly warned the White House not to use the yellowcake uranium story in its public statements, successfully getting a reference to it struck from Bush's Cincinnati speech. Yet, when it came time to draft the State of the Union address, the allegation resurfaced; Bush's speechwriters could not resist the temptation to show, in the most concrete terms possible, that Saddam was seeking nuclear weapons. This time the White House was able to get Alan Foley, a proliferation expert at the CIA, to sign off on it as long as the information was attributed to the British, who had included the yellowcake uranium story in a white paper on Iraq. Foley says that he was explicit with Robert Joseph, his contact at the NSC, that the CIA could not support the charge; Joseph eventually asked Foley to confirm only that the British had reported the information.[85] For his part, Tenet received a draft of the speech before Bush delivered it but did not read it, inadvertently allowing the bogus intelligence into the State of the Union address.[86] Shortly thereafter, the Niger charge disintegrated completely, with Mohamed ElBaradei, the director of the International Atomic Energy Agency (IAEA), reporting to the UN Security Council on March 7, 2003, that the documents purporting to show a uranium transaction between Iraq and Niger were "not authentic."[87]

Methodically, the Bush administration had developed a portrait of Saddam Hussein as an undeterrable madman, in league with al Qaeda, and on the verge of acquiring nuclear weapons.[88] The situation was intolerable, as Bush explained in an address to the nation on March 17, 2003, as Operation Iraqi Freedom kicked off, "Intelligence gathered by this and other governments leaves no doubt that the Iraq regime continues to possess and conceal some of the most lethal weapons ever devised. . . . The regime has a history of reckless aggression in the Middle East. It has a deep hatred of America and our friends. And it has aided, trained, and harbored terrorists, including operatives of Al Qaeda. The danger is clear: Using chemical, biological or, one day, nuclear weapons obtained with the help of Iraq, the terrorists could fulfill their stated ambitions and kill thousands or hundreds of thousands of innocent people in our country or any other."[89] The problem with such rhetoric is that it grossly exaggerated the gravity and imminence of the threat that Iraq posed. Wracked by a decade of sanctions and misrule, Iraq was a weak and isolated pariah at the time of the invasion and hardly posed a danger to the Gulf region, let alone the United States. What was actually a war of choice was sold as a war of necessity.[90] And while top officials in the Bush administration may have been sincere in their description of Iraq as an intolerable threat, their manipulation of intelligence to artificially beef up the case for war crossed the line into oversell.[91]

Explaining the Failure of the Marketplace of Ideas

The remaining question is why the marketplace of ideas did not expose the distortions in the Iraq debate, as it is supposed to do in a mature democracy.[92] Chaim Kaufmann, notably, has emphasized executive powers in this failure. Five factors appear to have been critical.[93] First, the Bush administration was able to shift the terms of debate from regional aggression to terrorist attack, splitting whatever consensus there had been against forcible regime change. Second, the administration used its control of the intelligence apparatus to present a selective, and menacing, view of the threat. Third, the White House enjoys a privileged position in foreign policy debates, which allowed the administration to concentrate attention on its claims while marginalizing those of critics. Fourth, countervailing institutions such as the political opposition and the press failed to perform their policing function; leading Democrats, for example, criticized the administration from the right lest they appear weak on national security. Finally, the shock surrounding the 9/11 attacks meant that the public was more receptive to threat inflation than it might otherwise have been.

The executive powers argument, in turn, has not gone unchallenged. The president's ability to set the terms of debate and to lead public opinion is limited in important respects, some argue.[94] In the specific case of Iraq, sufficient information was publicly available to discredit the administration's more alarming threat claims. The real puzzle, then, is why Bush encountered so little resistance in the marketplace of ideas, especially from Democrats, when his threat inflation was so transparent. Ronald Krebs and Jennifer Lobasz emphasize the framing of the Iraq War as part of the war on terror. This framing served to silence Democratic opponents by depriving them of socially sustainable arguments against the war. By fall 2002, there was general agreement that a war on terror should be fought and that Saddam Hussein was a terrorist. By connecting the dots between the two, Bush narrowed the scope for debate, ensuring that Democrats could contest his claims only at the margins. The Democrats, in effect, were victims of "rhetorical coercion."[95] Alternatively, Jane Cramer has argued that norms of "militarized patriotism," left over from the Cold War, silenced the Democrats. Despite the fact that a majority of the Senate harbored misgivings about the war, bipartisan opposition collapsed because of the political risks entailed in appearing soft on national security and challenging the executive branch in a time of crisis.[96]

Each of the explanations for the failure of the marketplace of ideas in the Iraq case has merit. The executive branch certainly occupies a privileged position in foreign policy debates, a position that Bush leveraged to frame the Iraq War as part of the war on terror. And this framing, along with norms of militarized patriotism, certainly made leading Democrats think twice about rising up in opposition. At the same time, each explanation suffers from shortcomings. Arguments that emphasize executive powers and pressures to be patriotic underestimate the political opposition. However institutionally disadvantaged, opposition parties have historically not shied away from registering their dissent when they felt it was in their self-interest. A partial list includes Republican opposition to the 1799 quasi-war with France, Federalist opposition to the War of 1812, Whig opposition to the Mexican-American War, Democratic opposition to the first Persian Gulf War, and Republican opposition to the Kosovo War.[97] Arguments that emphasize rhetorical coercion suffer from the opposite problem. Insofar as they highlight the transformative effects of 9/11, they are overly contingent. It is not clear what kinds of external shocks might facilitate rhetorical coercion in the future. Perhaps a simpler explanation is in order for the Democrats' timidity: like Bush, they expected the war to result in a quick and decisive victory and so had few incentives to register their dissent. If they had anticipated the protracted war to follow, the Democrats would have been more likely to expose the worst instances of threat inflation. Political incentives, in short, provide a neat explanation for the failure of the marketplace of ideas in the Iraq case.

What evidence is there that this was the dynamic at play? First, there was the widespread expectation that the United States would depose Saddam Hussein in short order. As planning for what would become Operation Iraqi Freedom began in late November 2001, the United States was coming off an unexpectedly easy victory in Afghanistan, in which the combination of Special Forces, air power, and indigenous allies had led to the rapid collapse of the Taliban.[98] One of the lessons taken away from that conflict was that the United States could substitute firepower for manpower, exploiting the "revolution in military affairs" to dispatch foes at minimal cost.[99] These expectations were incorporated into the war planning, with the result that the final invasion force, which numbered about

160,000 troops, was less than half the size of the one originally envisioned by military planners. Even with this reduced force, military commanders were confident that they could wrap up combat in about a month.[100]

Nor was there much concern about what would happen once the fighting stopped. As is now well established, planning for postwar Iraq was slow to come together, with more of a focus on humanitarian relief than reconstruction.[101] The operating assumption was that the invading army would decapitate the regime, install friendly Iraqis in positions of power, and then withdraw quickly as local forces assumed responsibility for providing law and order. The intention was to shrink the U.S. military presence down to two divisions—between 30,000 and 40,000 troops—by fall 2003. Reconstruction would be financed by Iraqi oil revenues and international assistance. George Packer sums up the official thinking about the postwar situation: "If there was never a coherent postwar plan, it was because the people in Washington who mattered never intended to stay in Iraq."[102]

Granted, there were warnings that the Iraq venture would be more difficult than had been forecast. James Fallows, writing in the January 2004 issue of the *Atlantic Monthly*, was one of the first to focus attention on this issue, citing prewar planning efforts by the CIA, the State Department, the U.S. Army and Marine Corps, and the U.S. Agency for International Development, among others:

> Almost everything, good and bad, that has happened in Iraq since the fall of Saddam Hussein's regime was the subject of extensive prewar discussion and analysis. This is particularly true of what have proved to be the harshest realities for the United States since the fall of Baghdad: that occupying the country is much more difficult than conquering it; that a breakdown in public order can jeopardize every other goal; that the ambition of patiently nurturing a new democracy is at odds with the desire to turn control over to the Iraqis quickly and get U.S. troops out; that the Sunni center of the country is the main security problem; that with each passing day Americans risk being seen less as liberators and more as occupiers, and targets. All this, and much more, was laid out in detail and in writing long before the U.S. government made the final decision to attack.[103]

To take one example, in January 2003 the National Intelligence Council (NIC) prepared a classified report for Bush describing the building of democracy in Iraq as a long, difficult, and potentially turbulent process;

predicting that domestic groups would engage in violent internal conflict with one another unless an occupying force prevented them from doing so; and warning of a possible insurgency against the new Iraqi government or U.S.-led forces.[104] But warnings such as this were disregarded at the highest levels. If the administration had been forced to reckon with the costs and risks of a prolonged occupation, the momentum for war would have been slowed and the public would have become less supportive of an invasion. Exactly because it could be construed as an "antiwar" undertaking, leading officials discouraged the kind of thorough planning that would have prepared them for the worst case. "The desire to sell a war of choice trumped prudent planning and public candor about the difficulties ahead," as Michael Isikoff and David Corn argue.[105]

The situation was not much better in Congress, which largely abdicated its oversight role. As the vote on the Iraq War Resolution approached, Democrats worried about how the issue would play in the upcoming midterm elections.[106] They suspected that Republicans had timed the vote on the resolution to distract the public from the economic situation and other bread-and-butter issues that might advantage Democrats in the campaign.[107] When it became clear that the vote would not be postponed until after the election, the Democratic caucus decided on September 19, 2002, to get it out of the way so that they could shift the conversation to more favorable terrain.[108] Peter Zimmerman, the scientific adviser to the Senate Foreign Relations Committee, sums up the party's thinking this way: "The whole notion was, 'Let's get the war out of the way as fast as possible and turn back to the domestic agenda.'"[109] Presumably, Democrats would not have been so anxious to move on to other issues had they anticipated that the Iraq War would provide them with a political opening in coming election cycles.

During the debate itself, there was minimal discussion of potential costs and risks. Congress requested a NIE on Iraq's WMD programs but not one on the likely postwar situation. Analyses such as that produced by the NIC warning of a lengthy occupation were not completed until after the vote had been taken. The result was that supporters of the war tended to do so unconditionally, while among opponents the potential costs and risks competed with other considerations, most prominently the preventive nature of the war, as reasons to withhold support.[110] In the House of Representatives, for example, 70 percent of all opponents, or 23 percent of all debate participants, rejected preventive war on normative grounds, while only 31 percent of opponents, or 11 percent of all debate participants, cited the practical costs of war to justify their stance.[111]

A useful contrast can be drawn with the debate preceding the first Gulf War. Despite the fact that Saddam Hussein clearly had triggered the 1990–1991 crisis by invading Kuwait, President George H. W. Bush had a much tougher time securing congressional authorization for the use of force than George W. Bush did. Indeed, it was the closest vote on going to war in U.S. history: 250 to 183 in the House and 52 to 47 in the Senate.[112] In the House, 86 Democrats voted for the Persian Gulf War Resolution while 179 Democrats voted against it. In the Senate, only ten Democrats supported the resolution while forty-five opposed it. What accounts for the Democrats' stronger stand in 1991 than in 2002? Partly it was the legacy of the Vietnam War and the sense that Congress had been manipulated into granting Lyndon Johnson the authority to wage it.[113] More important, however, were widespread expectations that the ground war in Kuwait would last months and cost thousands of U.S. lives.[114] Expecting a tough fight, influential Democrats did not shy away from voicing their disagreement with the Bush administration, with notables such as Senator Sam Nunn (D-Georgia), chairman of the Armed Services Committee, demanding that the president allow additional time for diplomacy and economic sanctions to work.[115] By all accounts, the prewar congressional debate hinged on casualty expectations.[116]

The Iraq Syndrome

When the Gulf War came in January–February 1991, the United States and its coalition allies routed the Iraqis, winning with an unprecedentedly low loss rate.[117] The damage done to the Democrats' reputation on national security issues was considerable, leading them to adopt a more accommodating stance in 2002–2003.[118] This time, however, a quick and decisive victory was not in the cards. By summer 2003, the march on Baghdad had given way to a violent occupation. Simultaneously, the stated rationale for the war evaporated when it was confirmed that there were no WMDs in Iraq and that the ties between Saddam Hussein's regime and al Qaeda had been insignificant. With public support eroding at a rapid clip, Bush shifted his rhetorical emphasis away from the threat that Iraq had posed and toward the importance of spreading democracy and "staying the course."[119] The downward slide in support could be only partially arrested, however. Demands for withdrawal were slow to materialize, but the Republican Party suffered a heavy political price for its identification with a failed war, being repudiated in the 2006 and 2008 elections.[120]

As far as how the war was sold, official inquiries have generally exonerated Bush, finding that he inflated the threat, to the extent that he did, because he relied on faulty intelligence. This is the conclusion reached, for example, by the Commission on the Intelligence Capabilities of the United States Regarding Weapons of Mass Destruction—also known as the Silberman-Robb Commission—which was created by Bush in February 2004. In a letter accompanying its final report, the commission found "that the Intelligence Community was dead wrong in almost all of its pre-war judgments about Iraq's weapons of mass destruction."[121] The Iraq War, if the commission is to be believed, was the product of an intelligence failure, not top-down manipulation.

The marketplace of ideas, no longer dormant, has not been as kind to Bush. There is a near-consensus among expert commentators that members of his administration manipulated intelligence and misled the public in their sales campaign for the war. In fall 2006, Jane Cramer and Trevor Thrall conducted an online survey of scholars and other foreign policy experts asking them why they thought the United States had invaded Iraq. The results demonstrated broad agreement that the stated justifications for war were not in fact the most important ones. Most strikingly, "the vast majority of respondents did not believe that the administration truly believed that Iraq represented an urgent WMD threat."[122] Mirroring the expert consensus, a CNN/ORC poll conducted in March 2013 found that 54 percent of respondents thought the Bush administration had deliberately misled the American public about whether Iraq had WMDs.[123]

A compelling argument can also be made that an Iraq Syndrome has set in, comparable to the one that constrained U.S. interventionism after the Vietnam War. As John Mueller predicted in 2005, "the impact of deteriorating support will not end when the war does. In the wake of the wars in Korea and Vietnam, the American public developed a strong aversion to embarking on such ventures again. A similar sentiment—an 'Iraq Syndrome'—seems to be developing now, and it will have important consequences for U.S. foreign policy for years after the last American battalion leaves Iraqi soil."[124] Bearing this prediction out, Robert Gates, then the secretary of defense, told an audience of West Point cadets in February 2011, "In my opinion, any future defense secretary who advises the president to again send a big American land army into Asia or the Middle East or Africa should 'have his head examined,' as General MacArthur so delicately put it."[125] The Iraq Syndrome can be seen concretely in the cautious way that the administration of President Barack Obama has approached the use of force. His heavy reliance on drone strikes and other covert actions that leave a "light footprint" suggests that one of Obama's top priorities has been to limit liability in terms of costs and risks, partly out of deference to a wary public.[126] This is an ironic legacy of a war that was meant to restore U.S. swagger.

CONCLUSION

Deception and Democracy in International Relations

Liberal institutionalists argue that democracy should serve as a deterrent to deception. This book makes the opposite case—that deception is a natural outgrowth of the democratic process. Elected leaders have powerful incentives to maximize domestic support for war and retain considerable ability to manipulate domestic audiences without being fully exposed. Most important, they can exploit information and propaganda advantages to frame issues in misleading ways, cherry-pick supporting evidence, suppress damaging revelations, and otherwise skew the public debate in advantageous directions. These tactics are particularly effective in the prewar period when the information gap between leaders and the public is greatest and the public's perception of reality is most elastic.

In practice, leaders resort to varying degrees and types of deception to sell wars. As a general rule, however, the more contentious the domestic politics surrounding a war, the more leaders engage in blameshifting. When the expected costs are high or success is uncertain, leaders can encounter serious resistance to going to war. They will not be inclined to welcome domestic debate under these conditions; rather, they will do their best to conceal the fact that they are actively considering war while seeking out provocations that shift blame for hostilities onto the adversary. If the public becomes convinced that the other side has forced the issue, it will be more tolerant of the high costs and initial setbacks that can attend war against a capable opponent.

In contrast, the more permissive the domestic political environment, the more deception takes the form of overselling. In the event that expected costs are low or an easy victory seems assured, public discontent will be latent and will center on the fact that war seems unnecessary. In this case, leaders will oversell the threat to convince the public that the stakes are high enough to justify the use of force. Any threat inflation will go uncontested because the expectations of a one-sided victory dilute whatever incentives the political opposition might have to force a contentious debate.

When resorting to deception, leaders take a calculated risk that the outcome of war will be favorable, with the public adopting a forgiving attitude after victory is secured. In the event that the outcome is unfavorable, leaders will suffer a political cost, less for misleading the public than for launching a failed war.

The three case studies featured in the book test these claims in an intensive fashion. Each is marked by a different level of domestic opposition to war, with more opposition associated with blameshifting and less opposition with overselling.

The World War II case is the most striking of the three in that it is characterized by the highest levels of prewar opposition as well as the use of the most sophisticated forms of deception. Franklin Roosevelt wanted to bring a unified country into the European war but faced an energized anti-interventionist movement, an obstructionist Congress, and a public that supported aiding the Allies but opposed declaring war. Mindful of domestic opinion, Roosevelt engaged in blameshifting. He maneuvered the country in the direction of war, seeking out pretexts in the Atlantic and Pacific while allowing the public to believe that the United States was being pushed into the conflict. He was finally able to ask for a declaration of war when matters came to a head with Japan in December 1941. With domestic opinion galvanized by the attack on Pearl Harbor and the Allies winning a decisive victory over the Axis in 1945, Roosevelt was spared much in the way of damaging scrutiny.

In 1964–1965, Lyndon Johnson faced a milder version of the domestic political predicament that had confronted Roosevelt prior to World War II. He felt he had no choice but to expand the U.S. presence in Vietnam to contain communism. At the same time, he understood that whatever domestic support he enjoyed was brittle and could quickly evaporate in the event the costs and risks of war were highlighted. Following Roosevelt's lead, Johnson engaged in a creeping form of blameshifting, exploiting a series of pretexts to justify the bombing of North Vietnam and the insertion of ground forces into South Vietnam. All the while, he denied that a major change in policy was in the offing, subverting debate. In the end Johnson's deceptions backfired when the war degenerated into a quagmire.

George W. Bush, unlike his predecessors, faced a relatively permissive domestic political environment on the eve of war, although not so permissive as to allow for total candor. Accordingly, overselling played the leading role in his securing domestic support for the Iraq War. Misrepresenting the available intelligence, Bush suggested that Iraq was a clear and present danger when it was, in fact, a weak and isolated pariah. The effect was to obscure the preventive nature of the war. As we have seen, Bush was able to indulge in such blatant overselling because of the widespread expectation that a victory over Iraq would come cheaply and easily. This undermined the effective functioning of the marketplace of ideas by diluting whatever incentives Democrats might have had to expose obvious instances of threat inflation. Bush was held to account for his misleading portrayal of the threat only when the deteriorating situation on the ground in Iraq renewed interest in the origins of the war and the arguments that had been used to justify it.

Democracy, Deception, and Entry into War: Surveying the International Relations Literature

Dan Reiter has noted elsewhere that the existing body of empirical knowledge on the relationship between democracy, deception, and entry into war is narrow.[1] One of the goals of this book has been to provide extensive case evidence that deception is a recurrent feature of democratic politics when war is on the horizon. Still, it is a fair question to ask how well the argument travels outside the cases studied here. What broader evidence is there that democracy, deception, and entry into war go together? A brief survey of the international relations literature turns up the following cases.

- Germany and World War I.

"World War I looms large in international relations theory," as Keir Lieber has argued.[2] It has inspired some of the core concepts in the field of international relations—such as the security dilemma, the spiral model, and the offense-defense balance—and has provided a fertile testing ground for theories of the causes and conduct of war.[3] It is also a paradigmatic case of blameshifting, with Germany exploiting the provocations and responses of the July Crisis to pin the blame for starting the war on Russia.[4] For example, German leaders went out of their way to soften their warnings to Russia late in the crisis so that the Russians would not capitulate and rob Germany of the opportunity to fight a general war.[5] And although Germany was hardly a mature democracy in 1914, it was arguably as democratic as France and Britain when it came to the conduct of foreign policy.[6] Most relevant to the issue at hand is that German leaders were intent on avoiding blame for the outbreak of war because they feared that the German public would be against any war seen as too aggressive.[7]

- Israel and the Suez and Lebanon wars.

Israel has played a prominent role in the ongoing debate over why democracies tend to win their wars. As Michael Desch has noted, "Very few democracies have fought in so many wars in such a short period of time and amassed such an impressive record of victories."[8] One problem with making Israel the "poster child" for democratic triumphalism, however, is that its leaders have been anything but candid with the public about the circumstances surrounding the wars it has started. The 1956 Suez and 1982 Lebanon wars stand out in this regard, with Israeli leaders such as David Ben-Gurion and Ariel Sharon "able to use secrecy and outright deception to mislead the public about the costs, benefits, risks, and even outcome of these wars."[9] In the 1956 case, Ben-Gurion colluded with the British and French to seize the Suez Canal and topple Gamal Abdel

Nasser, the Egyptian nationalist leader. He sought cabinet approval for the operation only the night before it was launched, too late to stop it. To the public, the war was portrayed as a preemptive war of self-defense rather than a war of conquest and regime change.[10] The 1982 case is even more egregious, with Sharon taking advantage of his position as defense minister to create a series of "facts on the ground" that incrementally led to the implementation of an ambitious plan to remake Lebanon and the larger Middle East, a plan that the cabinet had rejected just months earlier. Whatever support the Lebanon War enjoyed early on rested on the false notion that it was limited in scope to pushing Palestine Liberation Organization forces back from the border so that they could no longer shell Israeli settlements.[11]

- The United States and politicizing intelligence.

Joshua Rovner, near the end of his study on intelligence-policy relations, concludes that democracy actually increases the likelihood that intelligence will be politicized because elected leaders "have strong incentives to use intelligence as a promotional vehicle for their policy decisions."[12] In his words, "Politicization is inexorably rooted in domestic politics. Leaders try to fix the facts when they need intelligence to overcome skeptical domestic audiences."[13] The Iraq War bears out Rovner's model of policy oversell, as do the other cases featured in his book: the "order of battle" controversy during the Vietnam War; clashes between the Richard Nixon administration and the CIA over the feasibility of a Soviet first-strike; and the Team B affair under the Gerald Ford administration.

- The United States and counterfeit diplomacy.

Building on some of the arguments in this book, Evan Braden Montgomery has shown that, when democratic leaders need to mobilize support for hardline measures without appearing overly aggressive, they can use "counterfeit diplomacy" to shift responsibility for any deterioration of relations onto the adversary. Montgomery highlights two cases of counterfeit diplomacy in practice: the decision by the Harry Truman administration to invite the Soviet Union and its Eastern European satellites to participate in the Marshall Plan in 1947, and the efforts by the George H. W. Bush administration to mobilize support for the Persian Gulf War in 1990–1991. In both cases, "American policymakers adopted diplomatic measures that they hoped would fail in an effort to placate domestic and international audiences that were reluctant to support more aggressive measures."[14] In the Persian Gulf case, Bush arranged a last-minute meeting between Secretary of State James Baker and Iraqi Foreign Minister Tariq Aziz to show members of Congress that he was "going the extra mile for peace" even though he had privately concluded that war was the preferred outcome.[15]

- The United States and the Korean War: Deception in the cause of peace.

The focus of this book has been on the relationship between democracy, deception, and entry into war; however, there is intriguing evidence that deception has been used in the cause of great power peace as well. Specifically, Austin Carson documents how U.S. leaders minimized the role of the Soviet Union in the Korean War to lower the risks of further escalation.[16] From the beginning, U.S. leaders went out of their way to avoid accusing the Soviet Union of having ordered or directed the North Korean invasion of South Korea, even though they privately suspected as much. One reason for their restraint was to tamp down on any war hysteria that might crop up in domestic opinion.[17] More remarkably, U.S. leaders tacitly colluded with their Soviet counterparts to conceal the de facto air war that the two sides waged against each other from November 1950 until the end of the conflict in 1953. Despite the fact that Soviet pilots shot down hundreds of U.S. aircraft during this period, the United States played along with the fiction of Soviet noninvolvement to head off pressures for escalation.[18] As a State Department official recounted in an interview with Jon Halliday, "the argument [for a cover-up] was that if we publicized the facts, the public would expect us to do something about it and the last thing we wanted was for the war to spread to more serious conflict with the Soviets."[19] The potential implication is that democratic leaders will resort to deception not only when they face an overly dovish public but also an overly hawkish one.[20]

Implications

The evidence presented in this book and in the larger international relations literature suggests that deception is a feature, and not a bug, of democratic politics when it comes to issues of war and peace. Three implications follow.

The first implication has to do with the constraining effect of democratic institutions. On the one hand, it would be incorrect to argue that the domestic political constraints that democratic leaders face are inoperative or weak.[21] The institutional logic is right to emphasize that domestic support for war cannot be taken for granted and that the process of mobilizing it can be complex and difficult. On the other hand, proponents of the logic have underestimated the ability of democratic leaders to overcome the constraints that they face, even when those constraints are fairly formidable. It is difficult to dispute empirically that democracies have formed a separate peace with each other or that they have won an impressive percentage of their wars, but it remains open to question whether these outcomes are due to the constraining effect of democratic institutions.

The second implication has to do with how effectively the marketplace of ideas functions in the run-up to war. In theory, mature democracies are supposed to be characterized by free and open debates in which leaders are called to account for making false or misleading claims, ensuring that the decision to go to war is publicly vetted and underpinned by the best available information. On the one hand, it would be going too far to say that the marketplace of ideas poses no constraint on the ability of leaders to manufacture consent for war. Democratic leaders have to contend with the prospect of public scrutiny, which forces them to be creative and subtle in their tactics, eschewing the crudest forms of deception used by their autocratic counterparts.[22] Indeed, if the marketplace of ideas were not effective at all at fomenting debate, leaders would have little reason to deceive in the first place. On the other hand, the marketplace of ideas rarely lives up to its full potential as a deterrent to deception. This is partly because opposition parties have political incentives to jump on the pro-war bandwagon when a war is expected to be popular or successful, depriving the marketplace of ideas of dissenting viewpoints. As important is that leaders benefit from considerable information and propaganda advantages when engaging in debate with their critics, advantages that tilt the rhetorical playing field in their direction. Of course, leaders cannot say whatever they please, but they retain the ability to set the terms of the debate, which is often enough to open up the political space needed for war.[23]

The third implication concerns the impact of deception on foreign policy. Public opinion, from a liberal perspective, is rational and exerts a moderating influence on leaders. Deception is to be frowned on because it erodes the constraints that keep leaders honest, increasing the risk of policy failure. Realists, in contrast, have traditionally distrusted the public, seeing it as hostile to balance-of-power thinking. Democracy, from a realist perspective, is less a moderating influence than a distorting one, so that deception is justified when public opinion deviates from what is in the national interest. Which of these two perspectives is borne out by the evidence? The safest conclusion is that the effects of deception on foreign policy are conditional; they depend on whether war is justified in a particular case. A distinction should be drawn, for example, between World War II, in which vital interests were threatened, and Vietnam and Iraq, in which they were not.[24] The lesson to be learned from the U.S. experience is *not* that dishonesty should be avoided at all costs but that we must learn to discriminate between deception that advances the national interest and deception that harms the national interest.[25] Of course, this is easier to do in hindsight and necessarily involves value judgments about the conditions under which war is justified. But, at the very least, deception cannot be ruled out a priori as contrary to the national interest.

For help in making distinctions of this kind, there is no substitute for sound strategy. Since the end of the Cold War, if not before, the United States has pursued a grand strategy of global dominance animated by two broad objectives: maintaining U.S. primacy and spreading democracy.[26] This has led ineluctably to a series of wars against minor powers, both to demonstrate U.S. credibility and to forcibly export liberal values. In these cases, leaders have been compelled to overstate the dangers to U.S. interests to mobilize domestic support for the use of force. As John Mearsheimer has argued, "The United States spends more on its military than the rest of the world put together; it has a robust nuclear deterrent and is insulated from most dangers by two enormous oceans. Given how secure America really is, the only way its leaders can justify ambitious global crusades is to convince the American people that relatively minor problems are in fact dire and growing dangers."[27] The surest way to minimize this kind of overselling and the blowback that can come with it is to adopt a more restrained grand strategy.[28]

Three Final Questions

I conclude with a reflection on three questions that this book raises but ultimately does not answer.

First, when does deception blur into self-deception?[29] Roosevelt and Johnson were no doubt sincere, at least up to a point, when they assured the public that they did not want war. The same could be said of Bush when he described the Iraq threat in the starkest terms. Nevertheless, they could make these claims in the strong forms they did only by discounting or ignoring information that was available to them and that clearly contradicted their preferred narratives. To successfully deceive others, in other words, these leaders needed to first deceive themselves, at least in some measure. In the absence of "smoking gun" evidence, it is difficult to pin down exactly what the balance was between deception and self-deception in each instance.

Second, elites should not be as vulnerable to deception as the public, given that they are better informed. So what strategies do leaders use to coopt them and keep them from blowing the whistle? The success of the deception campaigns featured in the book depended vitally on key elites—powerful legislators, high-ranking bureaucrats, and senior military officers—keeping their reservations to themselves rather than going public with them. To some extent, this was because those elites were themselves misled, but just as important were efforts by leaders to coopt them and convince them that the benefits of going along outweighed the costs. What mixture of carrots and sticks did leaders use to accomplish this? What compromises resulted? Ongoing work by Elizabeth Saunders, who has developed an elite-centric theory of democratic foreign policymaking, promises to shed more light on this topic.[30]

Third, to what extent is deception a bottom-up phenomenon? Deception is usually portrayed as a top-down phenomenon, something that is foisted on an unsuspecting public by scheming leaders. To a large extent, this is the tact that has been taken in this book. In contrast, Warren Kimball has observed something about the World War II case that may apply more broadly: in a sense, the public wanted to be lied to when it came to entry into the war.[31] In cases in which the opponent is formidable, the public wants to be told that the other side has forced the issue and that the country has no choice but to take up arms. And in cases in which the opponent is weak, the public wants to be told that the most vital of interests are nonetheless threatened. The public, in other words, does not reward politicians who are forthcoming about the trade-offs inherent in major decisions about war and peace; it rewards those who pretend that no such trade-offs exist. Until the public demonstrates that it values candor, it only seems fair to treat deception as a bottom-up phenomenon as much as a top-down one.

NOTES

Introduction

1. Bruce Russett, *Grasping the Democratic Peace: Principles for a Post-Cold War World* (Princeton: Princeton University Press, 1993), 38.

2. Dan Reiter and Allan Stam, *Democracies at War* (Princeton: Princeton University Press, 2002).

3. Chaim Kaufmann, "Threat Inflation and the Failure of the Marketplace of Ideas: The Selling of the Iraq War," *International Security* 29, no. 1 (2004): 5–48.

4. For contemporary reporting to this effect, see Daniel Pearl and Robert Block, "Despite Tales, the War in Kosovo Was Savage, but Wasn't Genocide," *Wall Street Journal*, December 31, 1999.

5. On the politicized origins of the 10,000 dead figure, see Kelly M. Greenhill, "Counting the Cost: The Politics of Numbers in Armed Conflict," in *Sex, Drugs, and Body Counts: The Politics of Numbers in Global Crime and Conflict*, ed. Peter Andreas and Kelly M. Greenhill (Ithaca: Cornell University Press, 2010), 148–55. On the critical role of the KLA in provoking violence, see Alan J. Kuperman, "Suicidal Rebellions and the Moral Hazard of Humanitarian Intervention," in *Gambling on Humanitarian Intervention: Moral Hazard, Rebellion and Civil War*, ed. Timothy W. Crawford and Alan J. Kuperman (London, UK: Routledge, 2006), 11–12; Kelly M. Greenhill, *Weapons of Mass Migration: Forced Displacement, Coercion, and Foreign Policy* (Ithaca: Cornell University Press, 2010), 163–66.

6. Greenhill, *Weapons of Mass Migration*, 153–57.

7. Arman Grigorian, "Third-Party Intervention and Escalation in Kosovo: Does Moral Hazard Explain It?" in *Gambling on Humanitarian Intervention: Moral Hazard, Rebellion and Civil War,* ed. Timothy W. Crawford and Alan J. Kuperman (London, UK: Routledge, 2006), 58–59; Greenhill, *Weapons of Mass Migration*, 149–51

8. Dag Henriksen, *NATO's Gamble: Combining Diplomacy and Airpower in the Kosovo Crisis, 1998–1999* (Annapolis, MD: Naval Institute Press, 2007), 194–96; Greenhill, *Weapons of Mass Migration*, 158–60. Although we can draw only tentative conclusions, a similar dynamic appears to have unfolded in the case of the 2011 NATO intervention in Libya. In mid-March 2011, Libyan rebels warned of an impending bloodbath if forces loyal to the regime of Muammar al-Qaddafi were allowed to enter Benghazi, their stronghold. They pointed to instances of Qaddafi targeting peaceful protestors with indiscriminate violence. In fact, the available evidence indicates that "the Qaddafi regime committed no bloodbaths during the war, and had no intention of doing so." If anything, outside intervention escalated and prolonged the violence. Backed by NATO airpower, a rebellion that was on the verge of defeat was able to topple Qaddafi, ushering in a period of prolonged instability that has had spillover effects throughout the region. Alan J. Kuperman, "A Model Humanitarian Intervention? Reassessing NATO's Libya Campaign," *International Security* 38, no. 1 (2013): 105–36, quotation on 134.

9. Alexander B. Downes, "The Myth of Choosy Democracies: Examining the Selection Effects Theory of Democratic Victory in War," in *Democracy and Victory*, H-Diplo/ISSF Roundtable 2, no. 12 (2011): 79–100.

10. Marc Trachtenberg, *The Craft of International History: A Guide to Method* (Princeton: Princeton University Press, 2006), chap. 4.

11. Quotation from Reiter and Stam, *Democracies at War*, 144.

12. See also John J. Mearsheimer, *Why Leaders Lie: The Truth about Lying in International Politics* (Oxford: Oxford University Press, 2011), 59–60.

13. See, especially, Dan Reiter, "Democracy, Deception, and Entry into War," *Security Studies*. 21, no. 4 (2012): 594–623.

14. Benjamin I. Page and Robert Y. Shapiro, *The Rational Public: Fifty Years of Trends in Americans' Policy Preferences* (Chicago: University of Chicago Press, 1992), chap. 9; Kaufmann, "Threat Inflation"; Jon Western, *Selling Intervention and War: The Presidency, the Media, and the American Public* (Baltimore: Johns Hopkins University Press, 2005), esp. 16–20, 224–29.

15. On the "elasticity of reality," see Matthew A. Baum and Philip B.K. Potter, "The Relationships between Mass Media, Public Opinion, and Foreign Policy: Toward a Theoretical Synthesis," *Annual Review of Political Science* 11 (2008): 56–57; Matthew A. Baum and Tim J. Groeling, *War Stories: The Causes and Consequences of Public Views of War* (Princeton: Princeton University Press, 2010), 10–11, 32–44, chap. 7.

16. The UN process can be construed as a form of blameshifting, as I elaborate on in chapter 4.

17. Making the argument that democracies benefit from a competitive marketplace of ideas are Jack Snyder, *Myths of Empire: Domestic Politics and International Ambition* (Ithaca: Cornell University Press, 1991), 39; Jack Snyder, *From Voting to Violence: Democratization and Nationalist Conflict* (New York: Norton, 2000), 54–55; Reiter and Stam, *Democracies at War*, 23; Reiter, "Democracy, Deception, and Entry into War," 602.

18. Opposition parties, as Kenneth Schultz argues, publicly oppose the use of force to present voters with an alternative. There is no benefit in presenting an alternative to a policy that is popular or widely regarded as successful. See Kenneth A. Schultz, *Democracy and Coercive Diplomacy* (Cambridge, UK: Cambridge University Press, 2001), 79–81.

19. Kaufmann, "Threat Inflation"; Western, *Selling Intervention and War*.

20. Miroslav Nincic, *Democracy and Foreign Policy: The Fallacy of Political Realism* (New York: Columbia University Press, 1992).

21. Reiter and Stam, *Democracies at War*, 159–62.

22. In the post–World War II period, a consensus reigned among researchers that public opinion was volatile, incoherent, but thankfully irrelevant to policy. This consensus formed the backdrop for the classical realist position, best articulated by George Kennan and Hans Morgenthau, that democracy was a potential obstacle to an effective foreign policy. On the post–World War II consensus on public opinion, see Ole R. Holsti, *Public Opinion and American Foreign Policy* (Ann Arbor: University of Michigan Press, 1996), chap. 2. On the (mistaken) assumption among realists that public opinion is hostile to them, see Daniel W. Drezner, "The Realist Tradition in American Public Opinion," *Perspectives on Politics* 6, no. 1 (2008), 51–70.

1. Explaining Democratic Deception

1. Sissela Bok, *Lying: Moral Choice in Public and Private Life* (New York: Vintage Books, 1999), 13. For an additional definitional discussion of deception and related concepts, see Thomas L. Carson, *Lying and Deception: Theory and Practice* (Oxford: Oxford University Press, 2010), chap. 2.

2. John J. Mearsheimer, *Why Leaders Lie: The Truth about Lying in International Politics* (Oxford: Oxford University Press, 2011), 15.

3. Carson, *Lying and Deception*, 47.

4. Jack Snyder, *Myths of Empire: Domestic Politics and International Ambition* (Ithaca: Cornell University Press, 1991), 2–6. The myths of empire include beliefs in the domino theory, offensive advantage, and bandwagoning.

5. Bok, *Lying*, 6.

6. Mearsheimer ascribes this to the fact that "it is usually difficult to bamboozle another country's leaders." *Why Leaders Lie*, 28.

7. Ibid., 31, 34.

8. On strategic versus selfish lies, see ibid., 11, 23–24. On lies for the public good, see Bok, *Lying*, chap. 12.

9. Dan Reiter, "Democracy, Deception, and Entry into War," *Security Studies* 21, no. 4 (2012): 594–623.

10. On lying, spinning, and concealment, see Mearsheimer, *Why Leaders Lie*, 9–10, 16–20. Mearsheimer argues that "lying will be the option of last resort for leaders seeking to deceive" (20).

11. On the need to ensure broad popular support for war in democracies, see Bruce Russett, *Grasping the Democratic Peace: Principles for a Post-Cold War World* (Princeton: Princeton University Press, 1993), 38.

12. See also Mearsheimer, *Why Leaders Lie*, 59–60.

13. Dan Reiter and Allan Stam, *Democracies at War* (Princeton: Princeton University Press, 2002), 144.

14. As is well established in the American politics literature, the public is relatively uninformed about politics in general and foreign policy in particular. See Michael X. Delli Carpini and Scott Keeter, *What Americans Know about Politics and Why It Matters* (New Haven: Yale University Press, 1996); Ole R. Holsti, *Public Opinion and American Foreign Policy* (Ann Arbor: University of Michigan Press, 1996), 45.

15. Thomas J. Christensen, *Useful Adversaries: Grand Strategy, Domestic Mobilization, and Sino-American Conflict, 1947–1958* (Princeton: Princeton University Press, 1996), 27. Important findings in the public opinion literature support Christensen's claim. To take one example, Herrmann, Tetlock, and Visser embedded five experiments within a nationally representative survey to explore the conditions under which the public supports the use of force. They found that participants were more willing to intervene (1) when national interests were at stake, (2) when the aggressor was powerful rather than weak, (3) when the adversary was nuclear-armed rather

than not, and (4) when the aggressor had revisionist rather than ambiguous or potentially defensive motives; Richard K. Herrmann, Philip E. Tetlock, and Penny S. Visser, "Mass Public Decisions to Go to War: A Cognitive-Interactionist Framework," *American Political Science Review* 93, no. 3 (1999): 553–73. Jentleson's argument, that the public is most likely to support the use of force for the restraint of an aggressive adversary, is also relevant here; Bruce W. Jentleson, "The Pretty Prudent Public: Post Post-Vietnam American Opinion on the Use of Military Force," *International Studies Quarterly* 36 (1992): 49–74; Bruce W. Jentleson and Rebecca L. Britton, "Still Pretty Prudent: Post-Cold War American Public Opinion on the Use of Military Force," *Journal of Conflict Resolution* 42, no. 4 (1998): 395–417; Richard C. Eichenberg, "Victory Has Many Friends: U.S. Public Opinion and the Use of Military Force, 1981–2005," *International Security* 30, no. 1 (2005): 140–77.

16. Martha Finnemore, *The Purpose of Intervention: Changing Beliefs about the Use of Force* (Ithaca: Cornell University Press, 2003), 19.

17. See Michael W. Doyle, "Kant, Liberal Legacies, and Foreign Affairs," in *Debating the Democratic Peace,* ed. Michael E. Brown, Sean M. Lynn-Jones, and Steven E. Miller (Cambridge, MA: MIT Press, 1996), 24–25; Reiter and Stam, *Democracies at War,* 167. As Rosato argues, this assumption is not entirely unproblematic because the costs of war typically fall on a small subset of the population; Sebastian Rosato, "The Flawed Logic of Democratic Peace Theory," *American Political Science Review* 97, no. 4 (2003), 594–95.

18. John Mueller, *War, Presidents, and Public Opinion* (New York: John Wiley and Sons, 1973); Scott Sigmund Gartner and Gary M. Segura, "War, Casualties, and Public Opinion," *Journal of Conflict Resolution* 42, no. 3 (1998): 278–300; Scott Sigmund Gartner, "The Multiple Effects of Casualties on Public Support for War: An Experimental Approach," *American Political Science Review* 102, no. 1 (2008): 95–106. A cost-sensitive public would explain an intriguing finding by Horowitz and Levendusky, who assess how a military's recruitment policy influences mass support for war. Using an original survey experiment, they find strong support for the argument that conscription decreases mass support for war by spreading its costs more evenly throughout society; Michael C. Horowitz and Matthew S. Levendusky, "Drafting Support for War: Conscription and Mass Support for Warfare," *Journal of Politics* 73, no. 2 (2011): 524–34. Also relevant is the finding that highly democratic states suffer fewer military and civilian casualties in their wars than do other states; Benjamin A. Valentino, Paul K. Huth, and Sarah E. Croco, "Bear Any Burden? How Democracies Minimize the Costs of War," *Journal of Politics* 72, no. 2 (2010): 528–44.

19. Christopher Gelpi, Peter D. Feaver, and Jason Reifler, *Paying the Human Costs of War: American Public Opinion and Casualties in Military Conflicts* (Princeton: Princeton University Press, 2009). See also Peter D. Feaver and Christopher Gelpi, *Choosing Your Battles: American Civil-Military Relations and the Use of Force* (Princeton: Princeton University Press, 2004); Christopher Gelpi, Peter D. Feaver, and Jason Reifler, "Success Matters: Casualty Sensitivity and the War in Iraq," *International Security* 30, no. 3 (2005/2006): 7–46.

20. Kenneth A. Schultz, *Democracy and Coercive Diplomacy* (Cambridge, UK: Cambridge University Press, 2001), 79.

21. Ibid., 80–81. Opposition parties can register their dissent through legislative enactments or, more commonly, public appeals. See, for example, William G. Howell and Jon C. Pevehouse, *While Dangers Gather: Congressional Checks on Presidential War Powers* (Princeton: Princeton University Press, 2007), 10–27.

22. On the polarization effect, see John R. Zaller, *The Nature and Origins of Mass Opinion* (Cambridge, UK: Cambridge University Press, 1992), 100–113. For an application of Zaller's model to the foreign policy realm, see Adam J. Berinsky, *In Time of War: Understanding American Public Opinion from World War II to Iraq* (Chicago: University of Chicago Press, 2009).

23. On the indexing hypothesis, see Howell and Pevehouse, *While Dangers Gather,* 156–66; Matthew A. Baum and Philip B. K. Potter, "The Relationships between Mass Media,

Public Opinion, and Foreign Policy: Toward a Theoretical Synthesis," *Annual Review of Political Science* 11 (2008), 50.

24. On strategic bias in the media, see Matthew A. Baum and Tim J. Groeling, *War Stories: The Causes and Consequences of Public Views of War* (Princeton: Princeton University Press, 2010).

25. For an elite-centric theory of democratic foreign policymaking, one in which leaders attempt to coopt elites lest they trigger public attention, see Elizabeth N. Saunders, "War and the Inner Circle: Democratic Elites and the Politics of Using Force," *Security Studies* (forthcoming).

26. Jon Western, *Selling Intervention and War: The Presidency, the Media, and the American Public* (Baltimore: Johns Hopkins University Press, 2005), 20–22.

27. Jack S. Levy, "Declining Power and the Preventive Motivation for War," *World Politics* 40, no. 1 (1987), 87. Copeland, consistent with this logic, has found that major wars are typically initiated by dominant military powers that fear significant decline; Dale C. Copeland, *The Origins of Major War* (Ithaca: Cornell University Press, 2000).

28. Randall L. Schweller, "Domestic Structure and Preventive War: Are Democracies More Pacific?" *World Politics* 44, no. 2 (January 1992), 248.

29. Jack S. Levy and Joseph R. Gochal, "Democracy and Preventive War: Israel and the 1956 Sinai Campaign," *Security Studies* 11, no. 2 (2001/2002): 1–49; Marc Trachtenberg, "Preventive War and U.S. Foreign Policy," *Security Studies* 16, no. 1 (2007): 1–31; Scott A. Silverstone, *Preventive War and American Democracy* (New York: Routledge, 2007); Jack S. Levy, "Preventive War and Democratic Politics," *International Studies Quarterly* 52, no. 1 (2008): 1–24.

30. Walt argues that states balance against threats, which are a function of aggregate power, geographical proximity, offensive power, and aggressive intentions; Stephen M. Walt, *The Origins of Alliances* (Ithaca: Cornell University Press, 1987). See also Jack S. Levy and William R. Thompson, "Hegemonic Threats and Great-Power Balancing in Europe, 1495–1999," *Security Studies* 14, no. 1 (2005): 1–33.

31. For an argument that democracies will be particularly slow to balance against threats, see Randall L. Schweller, *Unanswered Threats: Political Constraints on the Balance of Power* (Princeton: Princeton University Press, 2006), 48–49.

32. John J. Mearsheimer, *The Tragedy of Great Power Politics* (New York: Norton, 2001), 141.

33. Ibid., chap. 7.

34. Jeffrey W. Taliaferro, *Balancing Risks: Great Power Intervention in the Periphery* (Ithaca: Cornell University Press, 2004).

35. Robert Jervis and Jack Snyder, eds., *Dominoes and Bandwagons: Strategic Beliefs and Great Power Competition in the Eurasian Rimland* (Oxford: Oxford University Press, 1991). It is important to note in this context that the more extreme domino predictions have rarely been fulfilled; Jerome Slater, "Dominos in Central America: Will They Fall? Does it Matter?" *International Security* 12, no. 2 (1987): 105–34; Jerome Slater, "The Domino Theory and International Politics: The Case of Vietnam," *Security Studies* 3, no. 2 (1993/1994): 186–224.

36. Robert J. McMahon, "Credibility and World Power: Exploring the Psychological Dimension in Postwar American Diplomacy," *Diplomatic History* 15, no. 4 (1991): 455–71. Press argues convincingly that great powers should not fight wars for the sake of preserving their credibility; Daryl G. Press, *Calculating Credibility: How Leaders Assess Military Threats* (Ithaca: Cornell University Press, 2005).

37. Andrew Mack, "Why Big Nations Lose Small Wars: The Politics of Asymmetric Conflict," *World Politics* 27, no. 2 (1975): 175–200; Ivan Arreguín-Toft, "How the Weak Win Wars: A Theory of Asymmetric Conflict," *International Security* 26, no. 1 (2001): 93–128.

38. Making the liberal institutionalist case is Reiter, "Democracy, Deception, and Entry into War."

39. See, for example, Benjamin I. Page and Robert Y. Shapiro, *The Rational Public: Fifty Years of Trends in Americans' Policy Preferences* (Chicago: University of Chicago Press, 1992), chap. 9;

Chaim Kaufmann, "Threat Inflation and the Failure of the Marketplace of Ideas: The Selling of the Iraq War," *International Security* 29, no. 1 (2004): 5–48; Western, *Selling Intervention and War*, esp. 16–20, 224–29.

40. On the elasticity of reality, see Baum and Potter, "Relationships," 56–57; Baum and Groeling, *War Stories*, 10–11, 32–44, chap. 7.

41. The term *blameshifting* comes from Stephen Van Evera, *Causes of War: Power and the Roots of Conflict* (Ithaca: Cornell University Press, 1999), 230–31. Of course, nondemocracies engage in blameshifting, too; see, for example, Reiter, "Democracy, Deception, and Entry into War," 604.

42. The term *oversell* comes from Theodore J. Lowi, *The End of Liberalism: The Second Republic of the United States* (New York: W. W. Norton, 1979), 139–45. On the related concept of threat inflation, see A. Trevor Thrall and Jane K. Cramer, *American Foreign Policy and the Politics of Fear: Threat Inflation since 9/11* (London: Routledge, 2009).

43. Controversial policies, according to Mearsheimer, are more likely to be hidden from the public in democracies than nondemocracies; Mearsheimer, *Why Leaders Lie*, 69.

44. Evan Braden Montgomery, "Counterfeit Diplomacy and Mobilization in Democracies," *Security Studies* 22, no. 1 (2013), 35, 41. Montgomery correctly points out that counterfeit diplomacy can backfire when the adversary takes advantage of the opening to string out talks and defuse momentum for hardline measures (46–51).

45. Richard Ned Lebow, *Between Peace and War: The Nature of International Crisis* (Baltimore: Johns Hopkins University Press, 1981), 25.

46. Ibid., 29.

47. Ibid.

48. Ibid., 37–40. On the political costs of striking first, see Dan Reiter, "Exploding the Power Keg Myth: Preemptive Wars Almost Never Happen," *International Security* 20, no. 2 (1995): 25–28.

49. "Experience suggests that skillfully managed justification of hostility crises usually succeed in garnering at least the internal support leaders seek." Ned Lebow, *Between Peace and War*, 40. For a review of the literature on the rally-round-the-flag phenomenon, see Baum and Potter, "Relationships," 45–46.

50. Samuel Kernell, *Going Public: New Strategies of Presidential Leadership* (Washington, DC: CQ Press, 1997).

51. Schultz, *Democracy and Coercive Diplomacy*.

52. Kaufmann, "Threat Inflation"; Jon Western, "The War over Iraq: Selling War to the American Public," *Security Studies* 14, no. 1 (2005): 106–39; Ronald R. Krebs and Jennifer K. Lobasz, "Fixing the Meaning of 9/11: Hegemony, Coercion, and the Road to War in Iraq," *Security Studies* 16, no. 3 (2007): 409–51; Jane Kellett Cramer, "Militarized Patriotism: Why the U.S. Marketplace of Ideas Failed before the Iraq War," *Security Studies* 16, no. 3 (2007): 489–524.

53. Eric Alterman, *When Presidents Lie: A History of Official Deception and Its Consequences* (New York: Viking, 2004), 20.

54. Ibid., 22.

55. Mearsheimer, *Why Leaders Lie*, 10; see also 92.

56. Michael W. Doyle, "Liberalism and World Politics," *American Political Science Review* 80, no. 4 (1986): 1151–69.

57. James Lee Ray, "Does Democracy Cause Peace?" *Annual Review of Political Science* 1 (1998): 27–46.

58. See, for example, Russett, *Grasping the Democratic Peace*, chap. 2.

59. John M. Owen IV, *Liberal Peace, Liberal War: American Politics and International Security* (Ithaca: Cornell University Press, 1997).

60. In other words, democratic institutions both constrain and inform; Kenneth A. Schultz, "Do Democratic Institutions Constrain or Inform? Contrasting Two Perspectives on Democracy and War," *International Organization* 53, no. 2 (1999): 233–66.

61. Immanuel Kant, *Perpetual Peace and Other Essays on Politics, History, and Morals* (Indianapolis: Hackett, 1983), 113.

62. Doyle, "Kant, Liberal Legacies, and Foreign Affairs," 25.

63. Russett, *Grasping the Democratic Peace*, 38–39.

64. See Reiter and Stam, *Democracies at War,* table 1 (29). Lake also finds that democracies win their wars; David Lake, "Powerful Pacifists: Democratic States and War," *American Political Science Review* 86, no. 1 (1992): 24–37.

65. Reiter and Stam, *Democracies at War,* 30. Downes cautions that the statistical significance of Reiter and Stam's results depends on two choices: their decision to equate war targets and joiners and their decision to exclude draws; Alexander B. Downes, "How Smart and Tough are Democracies? Reassessing Theories of Democratic Victory in War," *International Security* 33, no. 4 (2009): 9–51.

66. See Reiter and Stam, *Democracies at War*, chaps. 2 and 3. Reiter and Stam's warfighting argument is that democratic armies outperform nondemocratic armies on the battlefield because their soldiers, products of a political culture that emphasizes individualism, fight with greater initiative and exhibit better leadership than soldiers from nondemocracies. An important critique of this argument is Risa A. Brooks, "Making Military Might: Why Do States Fail and Succeed? A Review Essay," *International Security* 28, no. 2 (2003): 149–91. For a comprehensive critique of the democratic victory thesis, see Michael C. Desch, *Power and Military Effectiveness: The Fallacy of Democratic Triumphalism* (Baltimore: Johns Hopkins University Press, 2008).

67. See also Bruce Bueno De Mesquita, James D. Morrow, Randolph M. Siverson, and Alastair Smith, "An Institutional Explanation of the Democratic Peace," *American Political Science Review* 93, no. 4 (December 1999): 791–807.

68. Reiter and Stam, *Democracies at War*, 23.

69. Reiter, "Democracy, Deception, and Entry into War," esp. 600–603.

70. Reiter and Stam, *Democracies at War*, 146.

71. On collective deliberation, see Page and Shapiro, *Rational Public*, 362–66.

72. Snyder, *Myths of Empire*, 39. See also Jack Snyder, *From Voting to Violence: Democratization and Nationalist Conflict* (New York: Norton, 2000), 54–55. For a conceptual critique of the marketplace of ideas, see A. Trevor Thrall, "A Bear in the Woods? Threat Framing and the Marketplace of Values," *Security Studies* 16, no. 3 (2007): 454–62.

73. Reiter, "Democracy, Deception, and Entry into War," 602–3.

74. Kaufmann, "Threat Inflation," 32–46.

75. Ronald R. Krebs, "Selling the Market Short? The Marketplace of Ideas and the Iraq War," *International Security* 29, no. 4 (2005), 198–99.

76. Krebs and Lobasz, "Fixing the Meaning of 9/11."

77. Cramer, "Militarized Patriotism."

78. Krebs, "Selling the Market Short?" 201.

79. Reiter and Stam, *Democracies at War*, 160.

80. Miroslav Nincic, *Democracy and Foreign Policy: The Fallacy of Political Realism* (New York: Columbia University Press, 1992), 128.

81. Ibid., 149.

82. On blowback, see Snyder, *Myths of Empire*, 41–42; Alterman, *When Presidents Lie*, 20–22.

83. Nincic, *Democracy and Foreign Policy*, 150.

84. Alterman, *When Presidents Lie*, 22.

85. This was most true of the classical realists. They were influenced by scholars such as Gabriel Almond and Walter Lippmann, who saw public opinion as volatile and incoherent. On the rise and fall of the Almond-Lippmann consensus, see Holsti, *Public Opinion and American Foreign Policy*, chaps. 2–3. On the (mistaken) assumption among realists that public opinion is hostile

to them, see Daniel W. Drezner, "The Realist Tradition in American Public Opinion," *Perspectives on Politics* 6, no. 1 2008): 51–70.

86. Hans J. Morgenthau, *Politics among Nations: The Struggle for Power and Peace*, brief ed. (New York: McGraw-Hill, 1993), 161.

87. Ibid.

88. There are important exceptions. Jack Snyder, for example, argues in *Myths of Empire* that democracies are less prone to overexpansion than nondemocracies.

89. Rosato, "Flawed Logic," 599; Desch, *Power and Military Effectiveness*, 173.

90. On realist concerns about disruptions from below, see Nincic, *Democracy and Foreign Policy*, 6–11. Recent examples of realist work in this vein include Christensen, *Useful Adversaries*; Schweller, *Unanswered Threats*; John J. Mearsheimer and Stephen M. Walt, *The Israel Lobby and U.S. Foreign Policy* (New York: Farrar, Straus and Giroux, 2007).

91. Hans J. Morgenthau, *In Defense of the National Interest: A Critical Examination of American Foreign Policy* (New York: Alfred A. Knopf, 1951), 224.

92. Mearsheimer, *Why Leaders Lie*, 99. Mearsheimer is sensitive to the fact that lying can have significant downsides; *Why Leaders Lie*, chap. 8.

93. Gerring defines the *case study approach* as "the intensive study of a single unit or a small number of units (the cases), for the purpose of understanding a larger class of similar units (a population of cases)." John Gerring, *Case Study Research: Principles and Practices* (Cambridge, UK: Cambridge University Press, 2007), 37.

94. Marc Trachtenberg, "Dan Reiter and America's Road to War in 1941," in *Democracy, Deception, and Entry into War*, H-Diplo/ISSF Roundtable 5, no. 4 (2013), 35.

95. Thick analysis, which is typical of qualitative research, is more useful for gathering such evidence than is thin analysis, which is typical of quantitative research. See David Collier, Henry E. Brady, and Jason Seawright, "Sources of Leverage in Causal Inference: Toward an Alternative View of Methodology," in *Rethinking Social Inquiry: Diverse Tools, Shared Standards*. ed. Henry E. Brady and David Collier (Lanham, MD: Rowman and Littlefield, 2004), 248–49.

96. On self-deception, see Robert Jervis, "Understanding Beliefs and Threat Inflation," in Thrall and Cramer, *American Foreign Policy*, 16–39.

97. Alexander L. George and Andrew Bennett, *Case Studies and Theory Development in the Social Sciences* (Cambridge, MA: MIT Press, 2005), 21.

98. John Gerring, "What Is a Case Study and What Is It Good for?" *American Political Science Review* 98, no. 2 (2004), 348.

99. On process-tracing, see George and Bennett, *Case Studies and Theory Development*, chap. 10.

100. Marc Trachtenberg, *The Craft of International History: A Guide to Method* (Princeton: Princeton University Press, 2006). For useful discussions of historical method, see also Ian S. Lustick, "History, Historiography, and Political Science: Multiple Historical Records and the Problem of Selection Bias," *American Political Science Review* 90, no. 3 (1996): 605–18; Colin Elman and Miriam Fendius Elman, eds., *Bridges and Boundaries: Historians, Political Scientists, and the Study of International Relations* (Cambridge, MA: MIT Press, 2001); Cameron G. Thies, "A Pragmatic Guide to Qualitative Historical Analysis in the Study of International Relations," *International Studies Perspectives* 3, no. 4 (2002): 351–72; Jonathan B. Isacoff, "Writing the Arab-Israeli Conflict: Historical Bias and the Use of History in Political Science," *Perspectives on Politics* 3, no. 1 (2005): 71–88.

101. Trachtenberg, *Craft of International History*, 45.

102. On the method of structured, focused comparison, see George and Bennett, *Case Studies and Theory Development*, chap. 3.

103. The full universe included the Spanish-American War (1898), World War I (1914–1918), World War II (1939–1945), the Korean War (1950–1953), the Vietnam War (1965–1975),

the Gulf War (1990–1991), the Kosovo War (1999), the invasion of Afghanistan (2001–present), and the invasion of Iraq (2003–2011).

104. Auerswald characterizes the United States as a weak presidential system; David P. Auerswald, "Inward Bound: Domestic Institutions and Military Conflicts," *International Organization* 53, no. 3 (1999), 478–79. Auerswald is among a group of scholars who emphasize that democracies vary in how much autonomy their leaders enjoy when it comes to war and peace decisions. See also Miriam Fendius Elman, "Presidentialism, Parliamentarism, and Theories of Democratic Peace," *Security Studies* 9, no. 4 (2000): 91–126; Norrin M. Ripsman, *Peacemaking by Democracies: The Effect of State Autonomy on the Post-World War Settlements* (University Park: Pennsylvania State University Press, 2002).

105. Colin Dueck, *Reluctant Crusaders: Power, Culture, and Change in American Grand Strategy* (Princeton: Princeton University Press, 2006), 29.

106. In coding cases for domestic opposition, I considered political trends at both the mass and elite levels. Public opinion polling is obviously relevant, but so are grassroots activism, media commentary, legislative activity, and bureaucratic politics. In other words, it is important to capture the myriad indicators that contemporary leaders might have used to gauge domestic sentiment because it is their perceptions that ultimately matter most.

107. An additional rationale for including the Vietnam War as a case study is that the historiographical evidence on it is fairly settled, which means that it provides firmer support for the argument than the World War II and Iraq War cases can, given the limits of the evidentiary record in each one. The Vietnam War narrative is a familiar one and not much new historiographical ground can be broken, but these costs are outweighed by the benefits the case provides as a strong confirmation of the argument.

2. Shifting Blame to the Axis

1. David M. Kennedy, *The American People in World War II: Freedom from Fear, Part Two* (Oxford: Oxford University Press, 1999), 431.

2. Robert Dallek makes this point in his classic account of Roosevelt's foreign policy, *Franklin D. Roosevelt and American Foreign Policy, 1932–1945* (Oxford: Oxford University Press, 1979), 267.

3. Roosevelt's deceptions were a prominent theme in the first wave of revisionist scholarship on U.S. entry into World War II. See, for example, Charles A. Beard, *President Roosevelt and the Coming of War, 1941: Appearances and Realities* (New Haven: Yale University Press, 1948).

4. On offshore balancing, see John J. Mearsheimer, *The Tragedy of Great Power Politics* (New York: Norton, 2001), 141, 234–66.

5. For the impact of the Munich Crisis on Roosevelt's thinking, see Barbara Rearden Farnham, *Roosevelt and the Munich Crisis: A Study of Political Decision-Making* (Princeton: Princeton University Press, 1997), esp. chap. 5.

6. This warning, from a fireside chat on national security in December 1940, is fairly typical: "Some of us like to believe that even if Great Britain falls, we are still safe, because of the broad expanse of the Atlantic and of the Pacific. But the width of those oceans is not what it was in the days of clipper ships. At one point between Africa and Brazil the distance is less than from Washington to Denver, Colorado—five hours for the latest type of bomber. . . . Even today we have planes that could fly from the British Isles to New England and back again without refueling. And remember that the range of the modern bomber is ever being increased." Franklin D. Roosevelt, *The Public Papers and Addresses of Franklin D. Roosevelt, vol. 9: War—and Aid to Democracies* [for 1940], comp. Samuel Rosenman (New York: Russell and Russell, 1941), 636.

7. On the perceived Nazi threat to the Western Hemisphere, see Michael C. Desch, *When the Third World Matters: Latin America and United States Grand Strategy* (Baltimore: Johns Hopkins

University Press, 1993), chap. 3; Farnham, *Roosevelt and the Munich Crisis*, pp. 158–162; Justus D. Doenecke, *Storm on the Horizon: The Challenge to American Intervention, 1939–1941* (Lanham, Md.: Rowman and Littlefield, 2000), chap. 8; David Reynolds, *From Munich to Pearl Harbor: Roosevelt's America and the Origins of the Second World War* (Chicago: Ivan R. Dee, 2001), 43–44, 178–79; John A. Thompson, "Conceptions of National Security and American Entry into World War II," *Diplomacy and Statecraft* 16 (2005), 674.

8. David Reynolds, *The Creation of the Anglo-American Alliance, 1937–41: A Study in Competitive Cooperation* (Chapel Hill: University of North Carolina Press, 1981), 41.

9. On September 17, 1938, Roosevelt disclosed to Harold Ickes how he envisaged a European war unfolding. According to Ickes, Roosevelt "would make the war principally one of the air. He believes that with England, France, and Russia all pounding away at Germany from the air, Germany would find it difficult to protect itself even with its present preponderance in the air. It is his opinion that the morale of the German people would crack under aerial attacks much sooner than that of the French or the English. He says that this kind of war would cost less money, would mean comparatively few casualties, and would be more likely to succeed than a traditional war by land and sea." Quoted in Farnham, *Roosevelt and the Munich Crisis*, 103. See also Reynolds, *Creation of the Anglo-American Alliance*, 41–42.

10   Roosevelt, *Public Papers*, *vol. 9*, 635.

11. Initially, military planners recommended a posture of hemispheric defense in response to Hitler's victories in Europe, but that consensus was short-lived. Mark A. Stoler, *Allies and Adversaries: The Joint Chiefs of Staff, the Grand Alliance, and U.S. Strategy in World War II* (Chapel Hill: University of North Carolina Press, 2000), 24–29.

12. The Plan Dog memorandum is reprinted in Steven T. Ross, ed., *American War Plans, 1919–1941, vol. 3: Plans to Meet the Axis Threat, 1939–1940* (New York: Garland Publishing, 1992), 225–50; direct quotations from 228–29, 241, 247. For more on Plan Dog, see Stoler, *Allies and Adversaries*, 29–34.

13. On Plan Dog's reception, see James R. Leutze, *Bargaining for Supremacy: Anglo-American Naval Collaboration, 1937–1941* (Chapel Hill: University of North Carolina Press, 1977), 202–5, 219; Stoler, *Allies and Adversaries*, 34–37; Marc Trachtenberg, "Dan Reiter and America's Road to War in 1941," in *Democracy, Deception, and Entry into War*, H-Diplo/ISSF Roundtable 5, no. 4 (2013), 12–13.

14. The Victory Program's official title was Joint Board Estimate of the United States Over-All Production Requirements. Interestingly, it was leaked to the *Chicago Tribune* on December 4, 1941, just three days before Pearl Harbor. "Publication of the report," as David Kennedy notes, "made liars out of those administration spokesmen who had been denying the possibility of sending American troops overseas." *American People in World War II*, 62. Fleming has gone so far as to argue that Roosevelt himself orchestrated the leak of the Victory Program to goad Hitler into a declaration of war. The evidence for this claim is thin; Thomas Fleming, "The Big Leak," *American Heritage* 38, no. 8 (1987), http://www.americanheritage.com/content/big-leak.

15. The Victory Program, along with appendices, is reprinted in Steven T. Ross, ed., *American War Plans, 1919–1941, vol. 5: Plans for Global War: Rainbow-5 and the Victory Program, 1941* (New York: Garland Publishing, 1992), 158–298, direct quotations from 163, 169. Substantial portions of the Victory Program can also be found in Robert E. Sherwood, *Roosevelt and Hopkins: An Intimate History*, rev. ed. (New York: Harper and Brothers, 1950), 410–18.

16. Stoler, *Allies and Adversaries*, 49. In an estimate attached to the Victory Program, the Army War Plans Division concluded that German defeat would require the creation of a ground force of 215 divisions and nearly 9 million men; Ross, *American War Plans*, *vol. 5*, 201–4.

17. Ross, *American War Plans*, *vol. 5*, 193. See also Joseph Maiolo, *Cry Havoc: How the Arms Race Drove the World to War, 1931–1941* (New York: Basic Books, 2010), 383–84.

18. Justus D. Doenecke, "Historiography: U.S. Policy and the European War, 1939–1941," *Diplomatic History* 19, no. 4 (1995), 696.

19. Reynolds, *Creation of the Anglo-American Alliance*, 288.

20. Ibid., 218–19. See also Reynolds, *From Munich to Pearl Harbor*, 157. It is interesting to note in this context that Winston Churchill, the British prime minister, did not subscribe to Reynolds's logic that a declaration of war would be counterproductive. As he told Roosevelt at the Atlantic Conference, "I would rather have an American declaration of war now and no supplies for six months than double the supplies and no declaration." Quoted in Reynolds, *Creation of the Anglo-American Alliance*, 218.

21. Stoler, *Allies and Adversaries*, 56–57.

22. Reynolds, *Creation of the Anglo-American Alliance*, 212. See also Kennedy, *American People in World War II*, 3; Reynolds, *From Munich to Pearl Harbor*, 185–86. According to Joseph Maiolo, what really worried Roosevelt was the threat that militarization posed to the American way of life. Relying on air power, rather than a mass army, promised a way around this problem; *Cry Havoc*, 310–11.

23. In Ross, *American War Plans, vol. 5*, 194.

24. Dallek, *Franklin D. Roosevelt*, 285. Kershaw reads the evidence as suggesting that Roosevelt "had gradually and reluctantly come to the conclusion that American involvement was both inevitable and necessary if Hitler were to be defeated," even if he wanted to defer the moment of entry for as long as possible. Ian Kershaw, *Fateful Choices: Ten Decisions that Changed the World, 1940–1941* (New York: Penguin Press, 2007), 328.

25. Stoler, *Allies and Adversaries*, 50–58. Roosevelt was among the optimists, by the way. On June 26, 1941, he wrote to William Leahy, ambassador to Vichy France, "Now comes this Russian diversion. If it is more than just that it will mean the liberation of Europe from Nazi domination." Quoted in Waldo Heinrichs, *Threshold of War: Franklin D. Roosevelt and American Entry into World War II* (Oxford: Oxford University Press, 1988), 102. According to Heinrichs, maintaining a Russian front against Hitler had become the centerpiece of Roosevelt's world strategy by the time of the Atlantic Conference (159).

26. Steven Casey, *Cautious Crusade: Franklin D. Roosevelt, American Public Opinion, and the War against Nazi Germany* (Oxford: Oxford University Press, 2001), 42.

27. Ibid., 43–45.

28. Heinrichs, *Threshold of War*, 159.

29. Jonathan G. Utley, *Going to War with Japan, 1937–1941* (Knoxville: The University of Tennessee Press, 1985), 157.

30. Casey, *Cautious Crusade*, 13.

31. Stoler, *Allies and Adversaries*, 39.

32. In Ross, *American War Plans, vol. 3*, 249.

33. Quoted in Jeffrey Record, *A War It Was Always Going to Lose: Why Japan Attacked America in 1941* (Washington, DC: Potomac Books, 2011), 40.

34. Heinrichs, *Threshold of War*, 145. Heinrichs represents the dominant view among historians when he describes U.S. policy in the Pacific in terms of containment. See also Gerhard L. Weinberg, *A World at Arms: A Global History of World War II* (Cambridge, UK: Cambridge University Press, 2005), 245.

35. Scott D. Sagan, "From Deterrence to Coercion to War: The Road to Pearl Harbor," in *The Limits of Coercive Diplomacy,* ed. Alexander L. George and William E. Simons (Boulder: Westview, 1994), 61.

36. Doenecke, *Storm on the Horizon*, 8.

37. Ibid., 165–66. On the "great debate" between interventionists and anti-interventionists, see also Casey, *Cautious Crusade*, 24–26; Reynolds, *From Munich to Pearl Harbor*, 92–95, 110–112;

Michaela Hoenicke Moore, *Know Your Enemy: The American Debate on Nazism, 1933–1945* (Cambridge, UK: Cambridge University Press, 2010), 96–101.

38. Hoenicke Moore, *Know Your Enemy*, 95–96.

39. These are taken verbatim from Reynolds, *From Munich to Pearl Harbor*, 94. Interestingly, many in the army shared the AFC continentalist perspective; Stoler, *Allies and Adversaries*, 9–15.

40. Roosevelt, outraged, shot back that he regarded this "as the most dastardly, unpatriotic thing . . . that has been said in public life in my generation." The exchange is quoted in Reynolds, *From Munich to Pearl Harbor*, 111–12.

41. Doenecke expands on all these themes in *Storm on the Horizon*.

42. As Desch summarizes their thinking, "many isolationists believed that interventionist arguments about a Nazi threat from Latin America were little more than a cynical attempt to play on public insecurities in order to build support for greater U.S. involvement in the European war, and that the real threat to the American way of life lay in the irreconcilable tension between military preparations and civil liberties." *When the Third World Matters*, 57.

43. Lindbergh's testimony is quoted in Thompson, "Conceptions of National Security," 683. "If anti-interventionists had a favorite weapon, it lay in aviation," according to Doenecke. *Storm on the Horizon*, 108.

44. Quoted in Thompson, "Conceptions of National Security," 683. In April 1941, Baldwin published *United We Stand!*, in which he assessed U.S. defenses and found that the country could not be invaded; Doenecke, *Storm on the Horizon*, 246–47.

45. Casey, *Cautious Crusade*, 26.

46. Ibid., 44.

47. Dallek, *Franklin D. Roosevelt*, 109.

48. Reynolds, *Creation of the Anglo-American Alliance*, 54.

49. Dallek, *Franklin D. Roosevelt*, 199–204.

50. The Senate vote was 50 to 37, the smallest majority on any foreign policy issue since the European war had started. This was after the House had voted to extend the draft by only one vote in August 1941.

51. Dallek, *Franklin D. Roosevelt*, 292. After the votes on the draft and neutrality revision, Roosevelt "feared that a request for war would not merely meet a damaging filibuster but would actually be defeated, possibly by as much as two or even three to one." Reynolds, *Creation of the Anglo-American Alliance*, 217.

52. Casey, *Cautious Crusade*, 20.

53. Ibid., 24–26. In summer 1940, there was a sharp increase in the number of Americans who believed they would be personally affected by the war.

54. Adam J. Berinsky, *In Time of War: Understanding American Public Opinion from World War II to Iraq* (Chicago: University of Chicago Press, 2009), 49–50.

55. Bear F. Braumoeller, "The Myth of American Isolationism," *Foreign Policy Analysis* 6, no. 4 (2010), 364.

56. Casey, *Cautious Crusade*, 30.

57. Berinsky, *In Time of War*, 46.

58. Quoted in Casey, *Cautious Crusade*, 30.

59. Schroeder argues that over the course of the 1930s the American people had built up a profound hatred and distrust of Japan, largely on moral grounds. This made any relaxation of pressure on Japan politically difficult; Paul W. Schroeder, *The Axis Alliance and Japanese-American Relations* (Ithaca: Cornell University Press, 1958), 182–99.

60. Utley, *Going to War with Japan*, 55.

61. Casey, *Cautious Crusade*, 30

62. Steven M. Gillon, *Pearl Harbor: FDR Leads the Nation into War* (New York: Basic Books, 2011), 85.

63. Quoted in Casey, *Cautious Crusade*, 29–30.

64. Gillon, *Pearl Harbor,* 85–86.

65. In a critique of the argument advanced in this chapter, Dan Reiter makes much of the fact that the hard line that Roosevelt adopted toward Japan in late summer 1941 was popular. The public, with the help of the media, understood how severe the oil sanctions were and the risk of war that was attached to them and approved of them anyway. It is not clear how this is inconsistent with the deception thesis, however. It just means that Roosevelt took advantage of the public's belligerence toward Japan to bring matters to a head in the Pacific, which in turn provided a back door into the European war. It is important that there were limits to the public's bellicosity toward Japan. Just because Americans approved of stiff measures to contain the Japanese does not mean they wanted to be responsible for bringing on a war in the Pacific. In this sense, public attitudes toward Imperial Japan were roughly symmetrical to those toward Nazi Germany. Majorities detested both aggressors and wanted to see them stopped but hoped that this could be accomplished well short of a U.S. declaration of war. It was this dichotomy in opinion that Roosevelt exploited through blameshifting. For the Reiter critique, see "Democracy, Deception, and Entry into War," *Security Studies* 21, no. 4 (2012), 619–21.

66. Dallek, *Franklin D. Roosevelt*, 39, 227. Roosevelt regularly consulted a variety of sources to stay abreast of popular attitudes. These included newspapers, media surveys, mail, and, increasingly, opinion polls; Casey, *Cautious Crusade*, 16–19, 215. On Roosevelt's governing style, see Heinrichs, *Threshold of War*, 17–20; Kershaw, *Fateful Choices*, 200–203.

67. Kershaw, *Fateful Choices*, 480.

68. Roosevelt came around to a policy of aiding the European democracies as early as fall 1938, after the Munich Crisis. His priority was to sell them bombers to deter Hitler. In public, Roosevelt stressed the need for rearmament to mask his intention to help France and Great Britain. He did so even after a Douglas bomber crashed in California with an official of the French Air Ministry aboard, claiming that selling planes to France would put unused factories to work and build up U.S. productive capacity; Farnham, *Roosevelt and the Munich Crisis*, 192–97.

69. On the cash-and-carry debate, see Dallek, *Franklin D. Roosevelt*, 199–205; Reynolds, *Creation of the Anglo-American Alliance*, 65–67; Reynolds, *From Munich to Pearl Harbor*, 63–68.

70. Robert A. Divine, *The Illusion of Neutrality* (Chicago: University of Chicago Press, 1962), 297.

71. Franklin D. Roosevelt, *The Public Papers and Addresses of Franklin D. Roosevelt, vol. 8: War–and Neutrality* [for 1939], comp. Samuel Rosenman (New York: Macmillan, 1941), 520.

72. Quoted in Reynolds, *From Munich to Pearl Harbor*, 66. Privately Vandenberg wrote in his diary, "My quarrel is with this notion that America can be half in and half out of this war." Ibid., 66.

73. Dallek, *Franklin D. Roosevelt*, 246. In addition to securing the base sites, Roosevelt got Churchill to issue an assurance that the fleet would not be surrendered to Germany in the event of a British collapse.

74. The Lend-Lease law was given the symbolic number House Resolution 1776, the date of the American Revolution. On lend lease, see Dallek, *Franklin D. Roosevelt*, 251–60; Reynolds, *Creation of the Anglo-American Alliance*, 155–61; Reynolds, *From Munich to Pearl Harbor*, 110–16; Kershaw, *Fateful Choices*, 220–32.

75. On the Western Hemisphere Defense Plans, see Heinrichs, *Threshold of War*, 47–48, 56, 66–67, 113–15. On the stretching of the concept of the Western Hemisphere, see Reynolds, *From Munich to Pearl Harbor*, 127–129, 179.

76. Heinrichs, *Threshold of War*, 82. John Thompson is more skeptical, arguing that hemispheric security was used as a rationale for pursuing a policy of seeking the defeat of the Axis

that had more to do with a growing awareness of the power of the United States to determine the outcome of the war than with self-defense, narrowly defined; "Conceptions of National Security."

77. On the common-law alliance between the United States and Great Britain, see Reynolds, *Creation of the Anglo-American Alliance*, part 3. In Heinrichs's words, Roosevelt "sought the most intimate cooperation, in fact coordination, with Churchill. But he resisted formal combination and commitment." *Threshold of War*, 154.

78. Quoted in Casey, *Cautious Crusade*, 27.

79. Quoted in Dallek, *Franklin D. Roosevelt*, 250. Roosevelt was unhappy that he had to make such pledges, but by late October 1940, Willkie had surged to within 4 percentage points in the polls and Democratic party leaders were pressuring the president to emphasize his peaceful intentions. As Susan Dunn sums up the situation, "In October 1940, as Election Day approached, both Roosevelt and Willkie were fighting for their political lives. Like all politicians, their number one priority was winning the election. If the two internationalists needed to talk peace, peace, peace to win, then so be it. If they had to shade or disguise the truth . . . then so be it. Their concessions to isolationists and their promises of peace were equally dismal and unrealistic. They were playing their assigned parts in the customary campaign script, wrangling for votes, vying for a knockout punch, hiding their true thoughts and positions—and concealing their fundamental agreement on many crucial issues." Susan Dunn, *1940: FDR, Willkie, Lindbergh, Hitler—the Election amid the Storm* (New Haven: Yale University Press, 2013), 217–18.

80. When a speechwriter asked about the omission, Roosevelt replied, "Of course we'll fight if we're attacked. If somebody attacks us, then it isn't a foreign war, is it?" Quoted in Reynolds, *From Munich to Pearl Harbor*, 101.

81. Roosevelt, *Public Papers, vol. 9*, 640.

82. It was only when British records were opened in 1972 that it could be determined that Roosevelt had authorized the staff talks; Leutze, *Bargaining for Supremacy*, 202–5.

83. Reynolds, *Creation of the Anglo-American Alliance*, 184.

84. "Rainbow-5, 1941" is reprinted in Ross, *American War Plans, vol. 5*, 3–60.

85. Sherwood, *Roosevelt and Hopkins*, 273.

86. Leutze, *Bargaining for Supremacy*, 217–18.

87. Ibid., 223. On November 29, 1940, when the British ambassador to the United States reported home that the staff talks were going forward, he emphasized, "It is of the utmost importance that no knowledge of this should be allowed to obtain any kind of publicity. The officers should come over here attached in some way to British Purchasing Commission as if they were here for the purpose of export advice or inspection" (205).

88. Ibid., 223.

89. Sherwood, *Roosevelt and Hopkins*, 274.

90. Heinrichs, *Threshold of War*, 27.

91. Ibid., 30.

92. Reynolds, *From Munich to Pearl Harbor*, 129.

93. Dallek, *Franklin D. Roosevelt*, 267.

94. Heinrichs, *Threshold of War*, 109; Kershaw, *Fateful Choices*, 400–401.

95. Roosevelt likened the patrols to the band of scouts sent out far ahead of a wagon train to find Indians and prevent an ambush; Heinrichs, *Threshold of War*, 48; Dallek, *Franklin D. Roosevelt*, 261.

96. Quoted in Kershaw, *Fateful Choices*, 322. See also Heinrichs, *Threshold of War*, 167.

97. Franklin D. Roosevelt, *The Public Papers and Addresses of Franklin D. Roosevelt, vol. 10: The Call to Battle Stations* [for 1941], comp. Samuel Rosenman, (New York: Russell and Russell, 1950), 181, 189–90.

98. This is how Churchill summarized his talks with Roosevelt to the War Cabinet once he returned home from Argentia; Dallek, *Franklin D. Roosevelt*, 285–86; Reynolds, *Creation of the Anglo-American Alliance*, 214–15.

99. Dallek, *Franklin D. Roosevelt*, 265. See also Reynolds, *Creation of the Anglo-American Alliance*, 347n. 38. The fact that Roosevelt regularly used such language with advisors cuts against the notion that Churchill's account of the Atlantic Conference is embellished or that Roosevelt's belligerent rhetoric should not be taken at face value. For the latter critique, see Reiter, "Democracy, Deception, and Entry into War," 612–13.

100. Trachtenberg, "Dan Reiter," 16–17.

101. Dallek, *Franklin D. Roosevelt*, 287.

102. Roosevelt, *Public Papers, vol. 10*, 384–92, direct quotations from 384–86, 390–91.

103. Heinrichs, *Threshold of War*, 168. Interestingly, Roosevelt authorized Stark to give a more complete account of the *Greer* incident to Congress, which Stark did on September 20, 1941, just nine days after Roosevelt's fireside chat. Trachtenberg argues that this is an example of Roosevelt wanting to have it both ways, emphasizing the defensive nature of U.S. policy initially and then subtly correcting the record later. If that was Roosevelt's intent, the approach worked. The *New York Times*, for example, dutifully updated its reporting on the incident but did not derive the obvious implication that Roosevelt had misled the public. On Stark's testimony, see Reiter, "Democracy, Deception, and Entry into War," p. 611; Trachtenberg, "Dan Reiter," 24–25. For an example of the *New York Times* coverage, see Robert F. Whitney, "U-Boat It Hunted Attacked Greer," *New York Times*, October 15, 1941.

104. Also relevant is that the Atlantic fleet was able to exploit deciphered German naval messages to steer convoys around U-boat concentrations, which is not to say that the United States was trying to *avoid* confrontations with German warships. On the latter issue, see Weinberg, *World at Arms,* 240–41. See also the rebuttal in Marc Trachtenberg, *The Craft of International History* (Princeton: Princeton University Press, 2006), 84–87. For dueling takes on the degree of deliberate provocation underlying Roosevelt's policies in the Atlantic, see Reiter, "Democracy, Deception, and Entry into War," 610–15; Trachtenberg, "Dan Reiter," 19–22.

105. Quoted in Dallek, *Franklin D. Roosevelt*, 292. See also Reynolds, *Creation of the Anglo-American Alliance*, 217–18.

106. Kershaw, *Fateful Choices*, 329.

107. Kennedy, *American People in World War II*, 90.

108. Record, *War*, 12.

109. Reynolds, *From Munich to Pearl Harbor*, 163. Wohlstetter's account of the Pearl Harbor attack remains definitive; Roberta Wohlstetter, *Pearl Harbor: Warning and Decision* (Stanford: Stanford University Press, 1962).

110. Trachtenberg, *Craft of International History*, chap. 4. The back door argument is made most famously in Charles Callan Tansill, *Back Door to War: The Roosevelt Foreign Policy, 1933–1941* (Chicago: Regnery, 1952).

111. At the Imperial Conference that granted official approval to the Southern Advance on July 2, 1941, the foreign minister assured the emperor that "a war against Great Britain and the United States is unlikely to occur if we proceed with great caution." Quoted in Nobutaka Ike, ed. and trans., *Japan's Decision for War: Records of the 1941 Policy Conference* (Palo Alto, CA: Stanford University Press, 1967), 87.

112. The most detailed account of the freeze decision is in Edward S. Miller, *Bankrupting the Enemy: The U.S. Financial Siege of Japan before Pearl Harbor* (Annapolis, MD: Naval Institute Press, 2007), 173–78.

113. Ibid., 190. According to Miller, "Japanese buying did not at any time pinch American oil users, but the facts were complex. There was both a predicted shortage on the Atlantic Coast and

a glut of oil on the Pacific Coast. Roosevelt linked the two circumstances in his policy even though neither coast could solve the other's imbalance" (181, also app. 1).

114. Heinrichs, *Threshold of War*, 177.

115. Miller, *Bankrupting the Enemy*, 162.

116. As early as summer 1939, Joseph Grew, the U.S. ambassador to Japan, warned Roosevelt that "if we once start sanctions against Japan we must see them through to the end, and the end may conceivably be war." Quoted in Utley, *Going to War with Japan*, 66. For additional evidence that Roosevelt understood that an oil embargo could lead to war, see Dallek, *Franklin D. Roosevelt*, 274–75; Reynolds, *Creation of the Anglo-American Alliance*, 234; Utley, *Going to War with Japan*, 66–67, 153; Heinrichs, *Threshold of War*, 153–54; Sagan, "From Deterrence to Coercion to War," 64, 67–68; Trachtenberg, *Craft of International History*, 95–96; Record, *War*, 51–52.

117. Memorandum by the Acting Secretary of State, July 24, 1941, *Foreign Relations of the United States* (hereafter *FRUS*), Japan 1931–1941, Vol. 2: 527 [emphasis added].

118. Excerpt from Radio Bulletin No. 176, July 25, 1941, *FRUS*, Japan 1931–1941, Vol. 2: 265.

119. See, especially, Utley, *Going to War with Japan*, 153–56; Miller, *Bankrupting the Enemy*, chap. 16.

120. These recollections come from Ickes; in Sagan, "From Deterrence to Coercion to War," 69.

121. Utley, *Going to War with Japan*, 154.

122. Sagan, "From Deterrence to Coercion to War," 69–70. Anti-Japanese hardliners like Acheson, Secretary of the Interior Harold Ickes, and Secretary of the Treasury Henry Morgenthau had been pushing for an oil embargo against Japan for some time. Until late July 1941, Roosevelt had sided against them, citing the provocative effects of strong economic sanctions. Among the hardliners, there was a view that an oil embargo would deter rather than provoke Japan, mainly because the United States was so much more powerful than Japan that it would be suicidal for the latter to attack. For Ickes, however, an oil embargo was worth imposing even if it did provoke Japan because war in the Pacific would provide a back door into the war in Europe. The key piece of back door evidence linked to Ickes is "Ickes to Roosevelt," June 23, 1941, President's Secretary Files, Interior, Box 55, FDR Library.

123. Heinrichs, *Threshold of War*, 141–42, 246–47n. 68; Trachtenberg, *Craft of International History*, 99. Heinrichs argues that "Roosevelt and Welles were loath to permit any shipments of oil which might encourage or permit a Japanese attack on the Soviet Union." *Threshold of War*, 141. What is puzzling from this perspective is why the embargo remained in effect even after it was clear that a Japanese attack on the Soviet Union was unlikely and why the United States insisted on a Japanese withdrawal from China as a condition of its removal.

124. Trachtenberg, *Craft of International History*, 100.

125. Bolstering the case that Roosevelt must have been aware of the complete nature of the oil embargo is the fact that the media reported it accurately as a full cut-off of trade from the time it was imposed; Reiter, "Democracy, Deception, and Entry into War," 619.

126. Trachtenberg, *Craft of International History*, 98.

127. Ibid., 100. At the Atlantic Conference, Roosevelt and Welles did express an interest in *postponing* war with Japan for a month or two, but this does not mean they were ready to make a serious effort to *avoid* war with Japan. On this issue, see Reiter, "Democracy, Deception, and Entry into War," 617; Trachtenberg, "Dan Reiter," 29–30.

128. On September 6, 1941, the Japanese government formally decided that it would commence hostilities if diplomacy failed to yield fruit by mid-October. At the Imperial Conference ratifying the decision, General Suzuki Teiichi, the National Planning Board director, warned, "At this stage our national power with respect to physical resources has come to depend entirely upon the productive capacity of the Empire itself, upon that of Manchuria, China, Indochina . . .

and upon vital materials stockpiled so far. Therefore, as a result of the present overall economic blockade imposed by Great Britain and the United States, our Empire's national power is declining day by day. Our liquid fuel stockpile, which is the most important, will reach bottom by June or July of next year, even if we impose strict wartime controls on civilian demand. Accordingly, I believe it is vitally important for the survival of our Empire that we make up our minds to establish and stabilize a firm economic base." Quoted in Ike, *Japan's Decision for War*, 147–48. On the reaction in Tokyo to the oil embargo, see Sagan, "From Deterrence to Coercion to War," 71–73.

129. Robert J. C. Butow, *Tojo and the Coming of War* (Princeton: Princeton University Press, 1961), 245.

130. Quoted in Noriko Kawamura, "Emperor Hirohito and Japan's Decision to Go to War with the United States: Reexamined," *Diplomatic History* 31, no. 1 (2007), 65. According to Kawamura, "There was no doubt in anyone's mind at the conference that the emperor wanted the supreme command to pursue diplomatic means, not war preparations" (65).

131. This is how Kawamura summarizes his findings: "The emperor was personally against war with the United States and exerted his influence to delay the decision for war for one and a half months; but his influence was circumscribed within the nebulous triangular relations among the court, the government, and the military. He eventually succumbed to the persistent pressure of the military bureaucracy and accepted its argument that war with the United States was inevitable and possibly winnable." Ibid., 79.

132. Schroeder, *Axis Alliance and Japanese-American Relations*, 54.

133. Jonathan Utley believes that Hull demanded a Japanese withdrawal from China because he wanted to "break the power of the army in Tokyo." Only after the military had been humiliated and displaced by moderates would coexistence with Japan become possible; *Going to War with Japan*, 146.

134. Tojo went on to say, "But when I think about all the lives that will be further lost if there is a war between Japan and the United States, we must even think about withdrawing troops. That will be hard to decide." Quoted in James W. Morley, ed., *The Final Confrontation: Japan's Negotiations with the United States, 1941* (New York: Columbia University Press, 1994), 217; see also 250 for a similar statement by Tojo on October 23, 1941.

135. Trachtenberg, *Craft of International History*, 91.

136. Schroeder, *Axis Alliance and Japanese-American Relations*, 177, also 203.

137. Record, *War*, 115.

138. Stoler, *Allies and Adversaries*, 58. It is true that, in late summer and early fall 1941, Roosevelt received some support from the army for his hard line against Japan. The army's fear was that a relaxation of pressure would lead to a Japanese attack on Russia. By November 1941, however, when the likelihood of such an attack had diminished considerably, the army had reverted to its previous caution regarding the Far East. The navy favored a more conciliatory approach throughout (58–60).

139. Trachtenberg, *Craft of International History*, 121.

140. On November 5, 1941, the Joint Board of the Army and Navy recommended that the United States take no action that might precipitate war unless Japan attacked U.S., British, or Dutch possessions; William L. Langer and S. Everett Gleason, *The Undeclared War, 1940–1941* (New York: Harper and Brothers, 1953), 844–46; Heinrichs, *Threshold of War*, 204; Stoler, *Allies and Adversaries*, 60–61.

141. On October 21, 1941, Stimson wrote to Roosevelt, "A strategic opportunity of the utmost importance has suddenly arisen in the southwestern Pacific. Our whole strategic possibilities of the past twenty years have been revolutionized by the events in the world in the past six months. From being impotent to influence events in that area, we suddenly find ourselves vested with the possibility of great effective power. . . . We are rushing planes and other preparations to the

Philippines from a base in the United States which has not yet in existence the number of planes necessary for our immediate minimum requirements in that southwestern Pacific Theater. . . . Yet even this imperfect threat, if not promptly called by the Japanese, bids fair to stop Japan's march to the south and secure the safety of Singapore, with all the revolutionary consequences of such actions." Quoted in Sagan, "From Deterrence to Coercion to War," 79–80. On the "B-17 fever" that swept through the army in fall 1941, see also Utley, *Going to War with Japan*, 163.

142. Record, *War*, 109. See also Schroeder, *Axis Alliance and Japanese-American Relations*, 179–80.

143. Heinrichs, *Threshold of War*, 186. Considerable doubt remains about whether such a fait accompli would have worked. The key point is that a narrow window for diplomacy opened in fall 1941, which the Roosevelt administration failed to exploit. On Konoe's willingness to make concessions at a meeting with Roosevelt, see Morley, *Final Confrontation*, 189–94.

144. Quoted in Schroeder, *Axis Alliance and Japanese-American Relations*, 57.

145. Utley, *Going to War with Japan*, 162. See also Kershaw, *Fateful Choices*, 366. This wording is taken from a diary entry by Grew, who used similar language in a report to Washington.

146. On the "clean slate," see Butow, *Tojo and the Coming of War*, 301–2; Kawamura, "Emperor Hirohito," 71. Kawamura speculates that the emperor pushed for Tojo to become prime minister, despite the fact that he was the leading advocate for war in the Cabinet, because of his unswerving loyalty and his ability to keep the armed forces in check in the event of a settlement.

147. Plan B is reproduced in Ike, *Japan's Decision for War*, 210–11. On the merits of the proposal, see Schroeder, *Axis Alliance and Japanese-American Relations*, 76–81.

148. Roosevelt's *modus vivendi* proposal can be found in Langer and Gleason, *Undeclared War*, 872.

149. Dallek, *Franklin D. Roosevelt*, 307–8. "Chiang Kai-shek," according to Heinrichs, "was determined to defeat any possibility of a temporary arrangement with Japan." *Threshold of War*, 210.

150. Hull told Stimson on November 27, 1941, "I have washed my hands of it and it is now in the hands of you and Knox—the Army and the Navy." Quoted in Utley, *Going to War with Japan*, 173.

151. Dallek, *Franklin D. Roosevelt*, 309; Heinrichs, *Threshold of War*, 216–17.

152. Record, *War*, 104.

153. Schroeder, *Axis Alliance and Japanese-American Relations*, 100–101.

154. Hara made the statement as part of an Imperial Conference held on December 1, 1941; Ike, *Japan's Decision for War*, 282.

155. On the assumption that the United States and Great Britain were strategically inseparable, see Record, *War*, 66. On the objectives for the Pearl Harbor attack, see 92.

156. On Japan's "iron wall" strategy, see ibid., 70–74. Many Japanese felt that "as a creature-comforted society, America was simply too soft to sustain the blood and treasure burdens of a long, harsh war, especially in a region where the strength of U.S. interests was weak relative to the strength of Japanese interests" (75).

157. Sherwood, *Roosevelt and Hopkins*, 428.

158. Ibid., 431. On the sense of relief surrounding Pearl Harbor, see also Dallek, *Franklin D. Roosevelt*, 311; Casey, *Cautious Crusade*, 47; Gillon, *Pearl Harbor*, 53, 61–62, 148.

159. Evidence of this can be found in the back and forth of the ABC talks; Leutze, *Bargaining for Supremacy*, 225, 242.

160. See, for example, F. H. Hinsley, *British Intelligence in the Second World War: Its Influence on Strategy and Operations*, Vol. 2 (New York: Cambridge University Press, 1981), 75; Trachtenberg, *Craft of International History*, 124–25.

161. Richard F. Hill, *Hitler Attacks Pearl Harbor: Why the United States Declared War on Germany* (Boulder: Lynne Rienner, 2003), 18, 28, 195.

162. Ibid., 18, 195, 209n. 37.

163. Kershaw, *Fateful Choices*, 427.

164. Roosevelt, *Public Papers, vol. 10,* 529–30.

165. Casey, *Cautious Crusade.*

166. On the "secret map," see Desch, *When the Third World Matters,* 51–53. In the same speech, Roosevelt claimed he had evidence that Hitler planned to abolish all existing religions and establish an International Nazi Church; Roosevelt, *Public Papers, vol. 10,* 439–40.

167. In this Roosevelt has hardly been alone. John A. Thompson, "The Exaggeration of American Vulnerability: The Anatomy of a Tradition," *Diplomatic History* 16, no. 1 (1992): 23–43.

168. On the latter point, see ibid., 28–30; Desch, *When the Third World Matters,* 58–62, 64; Thompson, "Conceptions of National Security," 674–75. Russett has made the provocative argument that World War II was an unnecessary war in that the United States was no more secure at the end than it could have been had it stayed out; Bruce M. Russett, *No Clear and Present Danger: A Skeptical View of the United States Entry into World War II* (New York: Harper and Row, 1972).

169. There was only one dissenting vote (Representative Jeanette Rankin [R-Montana]) when Congress voted for war against Japan.

170. Gillon, *Pearl Harbor,* 182. On the night of the Pearl Harbor attack, Gerard Nye, an antiinterventionist senator, told a crowd in Pittsburgh, "We have been maneuvered into this by the President, but the only thing now is to declare war and to jump into it with everything we have and bring it to a victorious conclusion." Quoted in Gillon, *Pearl Harbor,* 120. See also Casey, *Cautious Crusade,* 47; Doenecke, *Storm on the Horizon,* 321.

171. Dallek, *Franklin D. Roosevelt,* 530–31.

172. Ibid., 289.

173. Warren F. Kimball, "Franklin D. Roosevelt and World War II," *Presidential Studies Quarterly* 34, no. 1 (2004), 98.

174. Marc Trachtenberg, "Preventive War and U.S. Foreign Policy," *Security Studies* 16, no. 1 (2007), 28.

175. On Asia-first sentiment and Roosevelt's efforts to combat it, see Casey, *Cautious Crusade,* chaps. 2–3.

176. Quoted in Dallek, *Franklin D. Roosevelt,* 289. See also Reynolds, *From Munich to Pearl Harbor,* 185.

3. Shifting Blame to the Communists

1. For a comprehensive overview of the orthodox-revisionist debate, see Gary R. Hess, *Vietnam: Explaining America's Lost War* (Oxford: Blackwell Publishing, 2009).

2. The expression is from Stanley Karnow, *Vietnam: A History* (New York: Viking, 1983), 430.

3. George C. Herring, *America's Longest War: The United States and Vietnam, 1950–1975,* 2nd ed. (New York: Alfred A. Knopf, 1986), 133.

4. David Kaiser, *American Tragedy: Kennedy, Johnson, and the Origins of the Vietnam War* (Cambridge, MA: Harvard University Press, 2000), 5.

5. Fredrik Logevall, *Choosing War: The Lost Chance for Peace and the Escalation of War in Vietnam* (Berkeley: University of California Press, 1999), 305.

6. On the Truman and Eisenhower years, see Herring, *America's Longest War,* chaps. 1–2.

7. For a more bullish assessment of the military progress made under Diem, see Mark Moyar, *Triumph Forsaken: The Vietnam War, 1954–1965* (Cambridge, UK: Cambridge University Press, 2006).

8. Notes on the National Security Council Meeting, Washington, November 15, 1961, *Foreign Relations of the United States* (hereafter *FRUS*), 1961–1963, Vol. 1: 254.

9. The deliberations in fall 1961 revolved around a report by General Maxwell Taylor, Kennedy's military assistant, and Walt Rostow, his deputy special assistant for national security affairs, who had traveled to South Vietnam in October to survey the military requirements. The Taylor-Rostow report recommended, among other things, that Kennedy deploy an 8,000-man task force to South Vietnam, disguised as a flood-relief team. This is compelling evidence that, from an early point, U.S. officials understood that some pretext would have to be found to justify a major intervention.

10. Mark Moyar argues that from the beginning of the enhanced advisory effort in December 1961 Kennedy was determined to hide the extent of U.S. involvement in Vietnam, largely for domestic political reasons. At a press conference on January 15, 1962, Kennedy lied about whether U.S. troops were involved in combat; Moyar, *Triumph Forsaken*, 144–48.

11. Logevall, *Choosing War*, 395–400; Gordon M. Goldstein, *Lessons in Disaster: McGeorge Bundy and the Path to War in Vietnam* (New York: Henry Holt, 2008), chap. 6. A common argument is that Kennedy would have been better positioned than Johnson to weather the domestic political storm that was likely to follow any liquidation of the commitment to South Vietnam. For an overview of the debate surrounding the Kennedy exceptionalism thesis that Kennedy would have avoided Americanization of the war, see Hess, *Vietnam*, 57–64.

12. Selverstone argues that the withdrawal schedule approved by Kennedy was more a bureaucratic planning exercise than a firm shift in policy and could easily have been reversed; Marc J. Selverstone, "It's a Date: Kennedy and the Timetable for a Vietnam Troop Withdrawal," *Diplomatic History* 34, no. 3 (2010): 485–95.

13. Quoted in Andrew L. Johns, *Vietnam's Second Front: Domestic Politics, the Republican Party, and the War* (Lexington: University Press of Kentucky, 2010), 28.

14. Logevall, *Choosing War*, chap. 1. Porter claims that Kennedy was quite open to a negotiated withdrawal from Vietnam but concealed this not only from the public but also from most of his own advisers; Gareth Porter, *Perils of Dominance: Imbalance of Power and the Road to War in Vietnam* (Berkeley: University of California Press, 2005), chap. 5.

15. The Kennedy administration was deeply divided over whether Diem should be ousted. The key point is that, once momentum started building toward a coup in late summer and early fall 1963, momentum generated to a considerable degree by members of his administration, Kennedy did little to stop it.

16. Mueller argues that the attrition strategy was not unreasonable. The Vietnamese communists were willing to accept virtually unprecedented losses in pursuit of a political goal, reunification, that was far from central to their survival as an organization; John E. Mueller, "The Search for the 'Breaking Point' in Vietnam: The Statistics of a Deadly Quarrel," *International Studies Quarterly* 24, no. 2 (1980): 497–519.

17. Downes goes so far as to argue that Johnson "chose stalemate" in Vietnam; Alexander B. Downes, "How Smart and Tough are Democracies? Reassessing Theories of Democratic Victory in War," *International Security* 33, no. 4 (2009): 31–46.

18. Jerome Slater, "The Domino Theory and International Politics: The Case of Vietnam," *Security Studies* 3, no. 2 (1993/1994), 188.

19. Goldstein, *Lessons in Disaster*, 139. Slater has argued along similar lines that "not only did policymakers believe in the validity of the domino theory, but they accepted nearly without question very sweeping versions of it." "Domino Theory and International Politics," 189. Porter dissents, arguing that the domino theory had been largely discredited by the 1960s but was deliberately manipulated for bureaucratic purposes by hawks in the administration; *Perils of Dominance*, chap. 8. I address Porter's point more fully in a later section.

20. On the two versions of the domino theory, see Joshua Rovner, *Fixing the Facts: National Security and the Politics of Intelligence* (Ithaca: Cornell University Press, 2011), 50–51.

21. On the different mechanisms by which communism was expected to expand, see Slater, "Domino Theory and International Politics," 193–95.

22. Rovner, *Fixing the Facts*, 53.

23. Memorandum from the Secretary of Defense (McNamara) to the President, March 16, 1964, *FRUS*, 1964–1968, Vol. 1: 84.

24. On the U.S. preoccupation with credibility, see Robert J. McMahon, "Credibility and World Power: Exploring the Psychological Dimension in Postwar American Diplomacy," *Diplomatic History* 15, no. 4 (1991): 455–71. Logevall concludes that for Johnson *American* credibility was less important in driving the decision to go to war than *personal* credibility. Johnson, simply put, "saw the war as a test of his own manliness." Logevall, *Choosing War*, 393.

25. Paper by Secretary of State Rusk, July 1, 1965, *FRUS*, 1964–1968, Vol. 3: 39. Slater is skeptical that the Asian dominoes would have fallen; even if they had, he asks, would the consequences have been that severe for U.S. national interests? Slater, "Domino Theory and International Politics."

26. For a dissent, see Moyar, *Triumph Forsaken*, 289–90, 375–76.

27. Paper Prepared by the Assistant Secretary of Defense for International Security Affairs (McNaughton), March 10, 1965, *FRUS*, 1964–1968, Vol. 2: 193.

28. McNaughton, as quoted in Logevall, *Choosing War*, 272. Diary evidence suggests that McNaughton was actually a dove; Benjamin T. Harrison and Christopher L. Mosher, "The Secret Diary of McNamara's Dove: The Long-Lost Story of John T. McNaughton's Opposition to the Vietnam War," *Diplomatic History* 35, no. 3 (2011): 505–34.

29. The quotation is taken from private notes that Bundy composed on March 21, 1965. In the same notes, Bundy asks, "In terms of U.S. politics which is better: to 'lose' now or to 'lose' after committing 100,000 men? Tentative answer: the latter." Quoted in William Conrad Gibbons, *The U.S. Government and the Vietnam War: Executive and Legislative Roles and Relationships, Part 3: January–July 1965* (Princeton: Princeton University Press, 1989), 179–80 [emphasis in original]. See also Goldstein, *Lessons in Disaster*, 166–67.

30. Johnson had personally experienced the divisive debate over "who lost China" that had wrecked Harry Truman's presidency, and he understandably feared that withdrawal from Vietnam would trigger a heated round of accusations by Republicans and conservative Democrats that he was guilty of "appeasement." The accompanying backlash had the potential to kill his domestic program, the Great Society, in its infancy. On this issue, see Francis M. Bator, "No Good Choices: LBJ and the Vietnam/Great Society Connection," *Diplomatic History* 32, no. 3 (2008): 309–40.

31. Logevall, *Choosing War*, xvii–xviii.

32. Johns, *Vietnam's Second Front*, 8–9.

33. Ibid., 335.

34. Logevall, *Choosing War*, 359.

35. Ibid., 141.

36. See Gary Stone, *Elites for Peace: The Senate and the Vietnam War, 1964–1968* (Knoxville: University of Tennessee Press, 2007), 51; Logevall, *Choosing War*, 349.

37. Stone, *Elites for Peace*, 51. On the Vietnam Debate, see also Gibbons, *U.S. Government and the Vietnam War, pt. 3*, 131–41.

38. Paper by the Under Secretary of State (Ball), n.d., *FRUS*, 1964–1968, Vol. 3: 26.

39. On Ball's famous October 1964 memo, see Brian VanDeMark, *Into the Quagmire: Lyndon Johnson and the Escalation of the Vietnam War* (Oxford: Oxford University Press, 1995), 85–90; Logevall, *Choosing War*, 243–46; Kaiser, *American Tragedy*, 349–51.

40. Logevall, *Choosing War*, 248–50.

41. Ibid., 402.

42. Stone, *Elites for Peace*, 45. See also Robert David Johnson, *Congress and the Cold War* (Cambridge, UK: Cambridge University Press, 2006), 108.

43. It must be pointed out that the prospects for neutralization were grim by 1964. In December 1963, the Communist Party in Hanoi—led by "South-firster" Le Duan—adopted the General Offensive and General Uprising strategy, which aimed to combine a military offensive with a political uprising to topple the already fragile Saigon regime. Le Duan was essentially "going for broke" in 1964, hoping to achieve a total victory before the United States could intervene; Lien-Hang T. Nguyen, *Hanoi's War: An International History of the War for Peace in Vietnam* (Chapel Hill: University of North Carolina Press, 2012), 63–65.

44. This exchange occurred during a telephone conversation on May 27, 1964; Logevall, *Choosing War*, 138.

45. Stone, *Elites for Peace*, 46. An Associated Press survey of eighty-three senators, released on January 6, 1965, found that only three senators fully supported expanding the war into North Vietnam; just five others thought that U.S. troops could be sent to South Vietnam at some future date if the situation warranted it. Ten advocated an immediate move to negotiations, and three wanted a unilateral U.S. withdrawal; Logevall, *Choosing War*, 306; Kaiser, *American Tragedy*, 391.

46. Logevall, *Choosing War*, 307.

47. Johnson, *Congress and the Cold War*, 120. According to his biographer, "As of the spring of 1965 Fulbright still believed that Lyndon Johnson was the main advocate of restraint in an administration of hard-liners." Randall Bennett Woods, *Fulbright: A Biography* (Cambridge, UK: Cambridge University Press, 1995), 370.

48. Logevall, *Choosing War*, 381. See also Stone, *Elites for Peace*, 59–63.

49. Logevall, *Choosing War*, 358.

50. In this section, I draw heavily on the analysis in Alexander B. Downes, "The Myth of Choosy Democracies: Examining the Selection Effects Theory of Democratic Victory in War," in *Democracy and Victory,* H-Diplo/ISSF Roundtable 2, no. 12 (2011), 93–99.

51. Logevall, *Choosing War*, 288.

52. Ibid., 282.

53. On the post-Pleiku polling, see VanDeMark, *Into the Quagmire*, 76.

54. Ibid., 120.

55. Gibbons, *U.S. Government and the Vietnam War, pt. 3,* 75.

56. Logevall, *Choosing War*, 403.

57. Ibid., 253.

58. Notes of Meeting, July 22, 1965, *FRUS*, 1964–1968, Vol. 3: 76.

59. Goldstein, *Lessons in Disaster*, 132.

60. *Public Papers of the Presidents of the United States* (hereafter *PPPUS*), Lyndon B. Johnson, 1936–64, Book 2 (Washington, D.C.: United States Government Printing Office, 1965), 597.

61. In Andrew Preston, *The War Council: McGeorge Bundy, the NSC, and Vietnam* (Cambridge, MA: Harvard University Press, 2006), 157; Goldstein, *Lessons in Disaster*, 129–30.

62. *PPPUS*, Lyndon B. Johnson, 1963–64, Book 2, 693.

63. On the spring 1964 deliberations, see Logevall, *Choosing War*, chap. 4; Kaiser, *American Tragedy*, chap. 10; Preston, *War Council*, chap. 6. For a critical take on the strategy of graduated pressure then being formulated by McNamara, see H. R. McMaster, *Dereliction of Duty: Lyndon Johnson, Robert McNamara, the Joint Chiefs of Staff, and the Lies that Led to Vietnam* (New York: HarperCollins, 1997), chap. 4.

64. Quoted in Kaiser, *American Tragedy*, 304.

65. Draft Memorandum by the President's Special Assistant for National Security Affairs (Bundy), June 10, 1964, *FRUS*, 1964–1968, Vol. 1: 211. Bundy's support for a congressional resolution was qualified. He recognized that pursuing one prematurely could ignite a noisy debate. He

thus recommended waiting until rapid passage was assured. The memo is referenced in Preston, *War Council*, 149–50; Goldstein, *Lessons in Disaster*, 116.

66. Logevall, *Choosing War*, 253.

67. On the working group, see VanDeMark, *Into the Quagmire*, chap. 2; McMaster, *Dereliction of Duty*, chap. 9; Logevall, *Choosing War*, 255–73; Kaiser, *American Tragedy*, 355–81.

68. Robert A. Pape, *Bombing to Win: Air Power and Coercion in War* (Ithaca: Cornell University Press, 1996), 177.

69. Kaiser, *American Tragedy*, 376–78.

70. Notes on a Meeting, White House, December 1, 1964, *FRUS*, 1964–1968, Vol. I: 432. Actually, Johnson was prepared to take the war to North Vietnam whether or not the political situation in South Vietnam stabilized. At this point, he wanted Maxwell Taylor, his ambassador to South Vietnam, to make one more attempt to unite the various factions in Saigon around the war effort.

71. Memorandum from the President to the Secretary of State, the Secretary of Defense (McNamara), and the Director of Central Intelligence (McCone), December 7, 1964, *FRUS*, 1964–1968, Vol. 1: 440.

72. VanDeMark puts overriding emphasis on Great Society considerations; *Into the Quagmire*, xv, 54, 71, 217.

73. Melvin Small, *At the Water's Edge: American Politics and the Vietnam War* (Chicago: Ivan R. Dee, 2005), 38–39.

74. Logevall, *Choosing War*, 306.

75. Ibid., 304. On Johnson's aversion to debate, see also Herring, *America's Longest War*, 132–33.

76. Logevall, *Choosing War*, 305.

77. Quoted in Gibbons, *U.S. Government and the Vietnam War*, pt. 3, 40. On the January 21 meeting, see McMaster, *Dereliction of Duty*, 210–11; Logevall, *Choosing War*, 314–15.

78. Kaiser, *American Tragedy*, 443.

79. *PPPUS*, Lyndon B. Johnson, 1965, Book 1, 106.

80. On the Hopkins speech, see VanDeMark, *Into the Quagmire*, 120–24; McMaster, *Dereliction of Duty*, 258–61; Logevall, *Choosing War*, 371–72; Kaiser, *American* Tragedy, 423–26.

81. McMaster, *Dereliction of Duty*, 260.

82. On MAYFLOWER, see VanDeMark, *Into the Quagmire*, 135–43; McMaster, *Dereliction of Duty*, 283–85; Kaiser, *American Tragedy*, 434–35.

83. Quoted in VanDeMark, *Into the Quagmire*, 123.

84. Moyar, *Triumph Forsaken*, 370.

85. Logevall, *Choosing War*, 22. A theme of Logevall's book is that "American policymakers from mid 1963 onward were not merely skeptical of the possibility of finding an early political solution to the war but acutely fearful of such a prospect and strongly determined to prevent one" (295).

86. Quoted in Preston, *War Council*, 202.

87. Quoted in Bernard J. Firestone, "Failed Mediation: U Thant, the Johnson Administration, and the Vietnam War," *Diplomatic History* 37, no. 5 (2013), 1076.

88. Ibid., 1077. See also VanDeMark, *Into the Quagmire*, 117; Logevall, *Choosing War*, 353.

89. In an article exploring the diplomatic strategy of Hanoi from 1965 to 1968, Asselin argues that Hanoi had come to reject negotiations with Washington by spring 1965 for fear of showing weakness. Diplomacy, for Hanoi, was a weapon of war, useful for securing political and material support from the Soviet Union and China as well as for mobilizing world opinion behind the cause of resistance but not for reaching a settlement with Washington and Saigon, which needed to be decisively defeated. "In retrospect," Asselin concludes, "there seems to have been no 'lost chance' chance for peace in Vietnam during the period covered in this study.

Confident that proletarian internationalism and its own determination would propel it to victory, Hanoi showed no inclination to engage in serious negotiations with its adversaries and even less desire to end the war by means of a compromise agreement." Pierre Asselin, "'We Don't Want a Munich': Hanoi's Diplomatic Strategy, 1965–1968," *Diplomatic History* 36, no. 3 (2012), 550.

90. For Westmoreland's request, see Telegram from the Commander, Military Assistance Command, Vietnam (Westmoreland) to the Joint Chiefs of Staff, Saigon, June 7, 1965, *FRUS*, 1964–1968, Vol. 2: 337.

91. Memorandum from Secretary of Defense McNamara to President Johnson, July 20, 1965, *FRUS*, 1964–1968, Vol. 3: 67.

92. Ibid.

93. See Larry Berman, *Planning a Tragedy: The Americanization of the War in Vietnam* (New York: Norton, 1982), 99; McMaster, *Dereliction of Duty*, 308; Kaiser, *American Tragedy*, 467–68.

94. On the July 21–27 deliberations, see Berman, *Planning a Tragedy*, 105–29; VanDeMark, *Into the Quagmire*, chap. 9; McMaster, *Dereliction of Duty*, 313–20; Kaiser, *American Tragedy*, 473–82.

95. Bator, "No Good Choices," 317.

96. VanDeMark, *Into the Quagmire*, 210.

97. Summary Notes of the 553rd Meeting of the National Security Council, July 27, 1965, *FRUS*, 1964–1968, Vol. 3: 93.

98. Quoted in Kaiser, *American Tragedy*, 478–79.

99. Telegram from Acting Secretary of Defense Vance to Secretary of Defense McNamara, in Vietnam, July 17, 1965, *FRUS*, 1964–1968, Vol. 3: 61.

100. In a July 19 memorandum to Johnson, Bundy listed "the reasons for avoiding a billion dollar appropriation in Vietnam." The third reason was that "it would create the false impression that we have to have guns, not butter—and would help the enemies of the President's domestic legislative program." Johnson put a line through the entire memorandum, crossed out the third point, and wrote at the bottom, "Rewrite eliminating 3." See Memorandum from the President's Special Assistant for National Security Affairs (Bundy) to President Johnson, July 19, 1965, *FRUS*, 1964–1968, Vol. 3: 63.

101. Johnson went on to say, "Additional forces will be needed later, and they will be sent as requested."

102. For the full press conference, see *PPPUS*, Lyndon B. Johnson, 1965, Book 2, 794–803; quotations on 795, 796, 801.

103. Goldstein, *Lessons in Disaster*, 197–98.

104. Ibid. According to Gordon Goldstein, who collaborated closely with Bundy on a set of memoirs that were not completed, Bundy often described Johnson as a compulsive liar in unguarded moments. In one interview, Bundy mused about Johnson, "Somewhere in Texas he learned that the truth was not good for you if you told it too freely" (200).

105. Berman, *Planning a Tragedy*, 146–47 [emphasis in original].

106. Logevall, *Choosing War*, 199.

107. On the retelling of events by the administration, see ibid., 196–97.

108. The Tonkin Gulf Resolution passed in the Senate with only two dissenting votes. The vote in the House was unanimous.

109. Edwin Moïse, *Tonkin Gulf and the Escalation of the Vietnam War* (Chapel Hill: University of North Carolina Press, 1996), 235. Moïse makes this statement in the context of a discussion of press coverage of the Tonkin Gulf incident. He argues that press coverage of Tonkin Gulf seemed to follow two rules. The first "was that the press should support our boys—support and praise the actions of the U.S. military." The second "was that the press should never accuse any US government spokesman of making an incorrect statement, even if it noticed that he had

made one." According to Moïse, "None of the press, not even the *New York Times*, showed any inclination to embarrass the government by pointing out errors or contradictions in government accounts of the events. If different sources provided flagrantly conflicting versions of events, both versions might be published, but neither news stories nor editorials pointed out the discrepancies" (234–35).

110. On the Desoto patrol, see ibid., chap. 3. On OPLAN 34A, see ibid., chap. 1.

111. Ibid., 228–29.

112. Telegram from the Department of State to the Embassy in Vietnam, August 3, 1964, *FRUS*, 1964–1968, Vol. 1: 271.

113. Quoted in Goldstein, *Lessons in Disaster*, 125.

114. Ibid., 123.

115. On McNamara's testimony, see Moïse, *Tonkin Gulf*, 86–89; McMaster, *Dereliction of Duty*, 133–35; Logevall, *Choosing War*, 203; Kaiser, *American Tragedy*, 336–37.

116. Porter, *Perils of Dominance*, 193.

117. That, at least, is the conclusion reached by Edwin Moïse, who has written the most extensive history of the Tonkin Gulf incident. "The weight of the evidence is overwhelming," according to Moïse, that "no attack occurred." *Tonkin Gulf*, 204.

118. Ibid., 143.

119. Ibid., 209; Logevall, *Choosing War*, 198. Before an attack had even been reported, Johnson had approached Bundy about taking a draft resolution to Congress and spoken with McNamara about identifying North Vietnamese targets for potential reprisal action; Goldstein, *Lessons in Disaster*, 125–26.

120. Porter, *Perils of Dominance*, 192–202. Further confusing the situation, only signals intelligence *supporting* the claim that the second attack had occurred was given to administration officials. Robert J. Hanyok, "Skunks, Bogies, Silent Hounds, and the Flying Fish: The Gulf of Tonkin Mystery, 2–4 August 1964," *Cryptologic Quarterly* 19, no. 4/ 20, no. 1 (2000/2001): 1–55.

121. Moïse, *Tonkin Gulf*, 144.

122. Eric Alterman, *When Presidents Lie: A History of Official Deception and its Consequences* (New York: Viking, 2004), 200. When McNamara pressured Johnson to respond to yet another Tonkin Gulf "incident" on September 18, 1964, Johnson chided him, "You just came in a few weeks ago and said that 'Damn, they are launching an attack on us—they are firing on us.' When we got through with all the firing we concluded maybe they hadn't fired at all." Quoted in Alterman, *When Presidents Lie*, 202.

123. On the issue of whether the Tonkin Gulf crisis was manufactured, see Logevall, *Choosing War*, 199–203.

124. Moïse, *Tonkin Gulf*, 225–26.

125. Logevall, *Choosing War*, 205.

126. Stone, *Elites for Peace*, 31–32.

127. Brewster and Fulbright are quoted in ibid., 28–29.

128. Moïse, *Tonkin Gulf*, 227; Logevall, *Choosing War*, 203–4.

129. Stone, *Elites for Peace*, 38. Wayne Morse (D-Oregon) was one of only two senators to vote against the Tonkin Gulf Resolution. "Hell, Wayne," a fellow lawmaker remarked to Morse, "you can't get in a fight with the president at a time when the flags are waving and we're about to go to a national convention." Quoted in Logevall, *Choosing War*, 205.

130. Logevall, *Choosing War*, 207. Moyar's take is that Johnson's feeble response to the Tonkin Gulf incident emboldened the North Vietnamese to escalate the insurgency in the South; *Triumph Forsaken*, 325.

131. Moïse, *Tonkin Gulf*, 253.

132. Logevall, *Choosing War*, 218–21; Moyar, *Triumph Forsaken*, 315–19, 326–28.

133. Logevall, *Choosing War*, 205–6.

134. Moïse, *Tonkin Gulf*, 246–47.

135. Telegram from the Embassy in Vietnam to the Department of State, January 6, 1965, *FRUS*, 1964–1968, Vol. 2: 9. Referenced in VanDeMark, *Into the Quagmire*, 51–52; Kaiser, *American Tragedy*, 386–89.

136. Memorandum from the President's Special Assistant for National Security Affairs (Bundy) to President Johnson, January 27, 1965, *FRUS*, 1964–1968, Vol. 2: 42.

137. On the "Fork in the Road" episode, see VanDeMark, *Into the Quagmire*, 58–59; McMaster, *Dereliction of Duty*, 212–14; Logevall, *Choosing War*, 317–19; Kaiser, *American Tragedy*, 392–93; Preston, *War Council*, 165–67; Goldstein, *Lessons in Disaster*, 152–54.

138. Memorandum for the Record, February 6, 1965, *FRUS*, 1964–1968, Vol. 2: 77.

139. For the full report and annex, see Memorandum from the President's Special Assistant for National Security Affairs (Bundy) to President Johnson, February 7, 1965, *FRUS*, 1964–1968, Vol. 2: 84. On the Pleiku attacks and the lead-up to Rolling Thunder, see VanDeMark, *Into the Quagmire*, chap. 4; McMaster, *Dereliction of Duty*, 214–16, chap. 11; Logevall, *Choosing War*, 324–32; Kaiser, *American Tragedy*, 398–408; Preston, *War Council*, pp. 167–90; Goldstein, *Lessons in Disaster*, 155–62.

140. The "streetcars" quotation can be found in Townsend Hoopes, *The Limits of Intervention* (New York: David McKay, 1969), 30.

141. Telegram from the Department of State to the Embassy in Vietnam, February 13, 1965, *FRUS*, 1964–1968, Vol. 2: 115.

142. At the end of his February 7 report, Bundy cautioned, "At its very best the struggle in Vietnam will be long. It seems to us important that this fundamental fact be made clear and our understanding of it be made clear to our own people and to the people of Vietnam. Too often in the past we have conveyed the impression that we expect an early solution when those who live with this war know that no early solution is possible. It is our own belief that the people of the United States have the necessary will to accept and execute a policy that rests upon the reality that there is no short cut to success in South Vietnam." Johnson, obviously, disagreed. Memorandum from the President's Special Assistant for National Security Affairs (Bundy) to President Johnson, February 7, 1965, *FRUS*, 1964–1968, Vol. 2: 84.

143. Summary Notes of the 547th Meeting of the National Security Council, February 8, 1965, *FRUS*, 1964–1968, Vol. 2: 87.

144. Herring, *America's Longest War*, 129.

145. For Westmoreland's request, see Telegram from the Commander, Military Assistance Command, Vietnam (Westmoreland) to the Commander in Chief, Pacific (Sharp), Saigon, February 23, 1965, *FRUS*, 1964–1968, Vol. 2: 155. For Taylor's dissent, see Telegram from the Embassy in Vietnam to the Joint Chiefs of Staff, Saigon, February 22, 1965, *FRUS*, 1964–1968, Vol. 2: 153. On the debate surrounding the deployment of the marines to Da Nang, see Herring, *America's Longest War*, 130–31; Berman, *Planning a Tragedy*, 52–54; VanDeMark, *Into the Quagmire*, 92–94; McMaster, *Dereliction of Duty*, 230–33; Goldstein, *Lessons in Disaster*, 162–64.

146. On the Harold Johnson mission, see Gibbons, *U.S. Government and the Vietnam War, pt. 3*, 158–66; McMaster, *Dereliction of Duty*, 245–49.

147. Memorandum from the Joint Chiefs of Staff to Secretary of Defense McNamara, March 20, 1965, *FRUS, 1964–1968*, Vol. 2: 208.

148. On the April 1 decisions, see VanDeMark, *Into the Quagmire*, 107–9; McMaster, *Dereliction of Duty*, 254–56; Kaiser, *American Tragedy*, 418; Goldstein, *Lessons in Disaster*, 169. On the afternoon of April 1, right before he agreed to the change of mission for the marines, Johnson was asked at an impromptu press conference whether "dramatic" proposals would be discussed at the White House meeting on Vietnam later that evening. Johnson answered, disingenuously, "I know

of no far-reaching strategy that is being suggested or promulgated." Quoted in VanDeMark, *Into the Quagmire*, 106–7.

149. Summary Notes of the 551st Meeting of the National Security Council, April 2, 1965, *FRUS,* 1964–1968, Vol. 2: 231.

150. Telegram from the Department of State to the Embassy in Vietnam, April 3, 1965, *FRUS,* 1964–1968, Vol. 2: 239.

151. National Security Action Memorandum No. 328, April 6, 1965, *FRUS,* 1964–1968, Vol. 2: 242.

152. McMaster, *Dereliction of Duty*, 263.

153. On Taylor's and McNamara's testimony, see Gibbons, *U.S. Government and the Vietnam War, pt. 3,* 212–16.

154. John W. Finney, "Johnson Permits U.S. Units to Fight if Saigon Asks Aid," *New York Times*, June 8, 1965. When asked about the leak in an interview some years later, McCloskey indicated his concern that the government was misleading the news media. He felt that his personal credibility and the institutional credibility of the State Department were on the line; Gibbons, *U.S. Government and the Vietnam War, pt. 3,* 278–79.

155. "Ground War in Asia," *New York Times*, June 9, 1965.

156. Reedy obliquely added, "General Westmoreland also has authority within the assigned mission to employ these troops in support of Vietnamese forces faced with aggressive attack . . . when, in his judgment, the general military situation urgently requires it." Quoted in John W. Finney, "U.S. Denies Shift on Troop Policy in Vietnam War," *New York Times*, June 9, 1965. See also VanDeMark, *Into the Quagmire*, 155–56; McMaster, *Dereliction of Duty*, 290–91.

157. Kaiser, *American Tragedy*, 442.

158. Slater, "Domino Theory and International Politics," 189.

159. Porter, *Perils of Dominance*, 242–43. Porter goes so far as to argue that Eisenhower did not buy into the domino theory when he originally formulated the idea. Rather, it was a tactic to convince the French, the British, the Soviets, and the Chinese that the United States would intervene in Indochina, so as to secure a favorable diplomatic settlement (234–36).

160. Ibid., 254–58.

161. Memorandum from the Board of National Estimates to the Director of Central Intelligence (McCone), June 9, 1964, *FRUS,* 1964–1968, Vol. 1: 209.

162. Porter, *Perils of Dominance*, 250. See also Rovner, *Fixing the Facts*, 55–56.

163. Memorandum from the Board of National Estimates to the Director of Central Intelligence (McCone), June 9, 1964, *FRUS,* 1964–1968, Vol. 1: 209.

164. Porter, *Perils of Dominance*, 249.

165. Rovner, *Fixing the Facts*, 58.

166. Rovner ascribes the administration's neglect of the BNE estimates to the relatively permissive domestic political context at the time. Johnson was not rallying support for war in spring and summer 1964, so he could afford to be casual toward intelligence dissent; ibid., 59–66.

167. In a follow-on estimate, on "Trends in the World Situation," Willard Matthias, a BNE analyst, did take direct aim at the psychological version of the domino theory. This estimate, too, was ignored; ibid., 56–58.

168. See Preston, *War Council*, 69–74. See also Mao Lin, "China and the Escalation of the Vietnam War: The First Years of the Johnson Administration," *Journal of Cold War Studies* 11, no. 2 (2009), 35–69.

169. In an influential article, Mueller finds that the military costs accepted by the Vietnamese communists were virtually unprecedented historically. He estimates that the communists suffered 500,000–600,000 battle deaths, or 2.5–3 percent of the prewar population. Only the main belligerents in the world wars rivaled this rate of loss, and they were fighting for their survival; "Search for the 'Breaking Point.'"

170. Jeffrey Record, *The Wrong War: Why We Lost in Vietnam* (Annapolis, MD: Naval Institute Press, 1998), chap. 2.

171. Jeffrey Record argues that the attrition strategy was doomed "because it rested on three false premises: that there was a communist breaking point within reach of US firepower; that the United States could acquire and maintain the initiative on the battlefield; and that attrition's progress could be accurately measured by keeping a reliable count of Vietnamese communists, both dead and alive." Ibid., 80. The military's preference for conventional warfighting goes some way toward explaining its dogged pursuit of an attrition strategy, but broader political pressures to limit casualties are also relevant. For a debate on the relative importance of these two factors, see Jonathan D. Caverley, "The Myth of Military Myopia: Democracy, Small Wars, and Vietnam," *International Security* 34, no. 3 (2009/2010): 119–57; James McAllister, "Who Lost Vietnam? Soldiers, Civilians, and U.S. Military Strategy," *International Security* 35, no. 3 (2010/2011): 95–123; Jonathan D. Caverley, "Explaining U.S. Military Strategy in Vietnam: Thinking Clearly about Causation," *International Security* 35, no. 3 (2010/2011): 124–43.

172. For an argument along these lines, see Andrew F. Krepinevich Jr., *The Army and Vietnam* (Baltimore: Johns Hopkins University Press, 1986). Krepinevich is representative of a counterinsurgency or "hearts-and-minds" perspective that says that the United States might have prevailed in Vietnam if it had focused more attention and resources on pacification rather than attrition. For the debate surrounding this perspective, see Hess, *Vietnam*, chap. 5.

173. Record, *Wrong War*, chap. 5. Record concludes, ultimately, that "a decisive U.S. military victory in Vietnam was probably unattainable except via measures—an invasion of North Vietnam or an unrestricted air attack on its population—that were never seriously considered by either civilian or military authorities" (xxi).

174. The Tet Offensive, which began on January 30, 1968, consisted of simultaneous attacks in major South Vietnamese cities timed to coincide with the traditional cease-fire surrounding the Tet holiday. The communists hoped that the offensive would spark a general uprising against the South Vietnamese government or, at the very least, force the Johnson administration to the negotiating table.

175. On the "order of battle" controversy, see Rovner, *Fixing the Facts*, 66–82.

176. The *crossover point* was the point at which communist forces were being captured and killed faster than they could be replaced. "Reaching the crossover point," explains Rovner, "would signal the beginning of the end for the North Vietnamese Army (NVA) and VC" (66).

177. Dominic D. P. Johnson and Dominic Tierney, *Failing to Win: Perceptions of Victory and Defeat in International Politics* (Cambridge, MA: Harvard University Press, 2006), 134. On the media's contribution to the Tet-as-defeat narrative, see Peter Braestrup, *Big Story: How the American Press and Television Reported and Interpreted the Crisis of Tet 1968 in Vietnam and Washington* (Boulder: Westview Press, 1977).

178. Melvin Small, *Johnson, Nixon, and the Doves* (New Brunswick, NJ: Rutgers University Press, 1988), chap. 5. In March 1968, approval of Johnson's handling of Vietnam collapsed to an all-time low of 26 percent; Johnson and Tierney, *Failing to Win*, 135.

179. As early as the 1966 election campaign, Republicans were making credibility a key focal point of their attacks on Johnson, with Gerald Ford quipping, "There's no longer a 'Credibility GAP'—it's become a Credibility CANYON!—and it's widening between the Johnson-Humphrey Administration and the American people with every week that goes by." Quoted in Johns, *Vietnam's Second Front*, 108–9.

180. Randall Woods argues that McNamara agreed to testify before the Senate Foreign Relations Committee to try to cleanse his reputation before he left the Pentagon for the World Bank. "From the beginning," Woods says, "it was clear that his intention was to manipulate the information at his command so as to prove decisively that the North Vietnamese had staged armed attacks on both August 2 and 4, even though he knew full well that there had been no second

assault" (477). This would explain why, after agreeing with Fulbright that neither would say any-thing to the press after the closed-door hearing, McNamara immediately released a twenty-one-page document "proving" conclusively that both the *Maddox* and *Turner Joy* had been attacked. Fulbright retaliated by accusing the Pentagon of locking up in a mental ward a navy commander who had volunteered to tell Congress what he knew of the Tonkin Gulf incident; Woods, *Fulbright*, 476–78.

181. Hearings before the Committee on Foreign Relations, Senate, 90th Congress, 2nd sess. (The Gulf of Tonkin, The 1964 Incidents), February 20, 1968, Washington, DC, 1968, p. 8. For an example of contemporary reporting on the hearings, see John W. Finney, "Fulbright Says Mc-Namara Deceives Public on Tonkin," *New York Times*, February 22, 1968, as well as the follow-on editorial, "Half Truths about Tonkin," *New York Times*, February 24, 1968.

182. Woods, *Fulbright*, 478–79.

183. Ibid., 479.

184. *PPPUS*, Lyndon B. Johnson, 1968–69, Book 1, 469–76.

4. Overselling the Iraq War

1. Lawrence Freedman, "War in Iraq: Selling the Threat," *Survival* 46, no. 2 (2004), 38. See also Robert Jervis, "War, Intelligence, and Honesty: A Review Essay," *Political Science Quarterly* 123, no. 4 (2008–2009), 659; Robert Jervis, *Why Intelligence Fails: Lessons from the Iranian Revolution and the Iraq War* (Ithaca: Cornell University Press, 2010), 124–26; Paul R. Pillar, *Intelligence and U.S. Foreign Policy: Iraq, 9/11, and Misguided Reform* (New York: Columbia University Press, 2011), 15.

2. For evidence that Iraq figured prominently in the deliberations immediately follow-ing the 9/11 attacks, see Bob Woodward, *Plan of Attack* (New York: Simon and Schuster, 2004), 24–27; Michael R. Gordon and Bernard E. Trainor, *Cobra II: The Inside Story of the Invasion and Occupation of Iraq* (New York: Vintage Books, 2007), 17–20; Terry H. Anderson, *Bush's Wars* (Oxford: Oxford University Press, 2011), 69–71, 75–76. It is important to note in this context that, although the Bush administration was open to a more aggressive Iraq policy upon taking office, there is little evidence that it was seriously contemplating war before 9/11; Woodward, *Plan of Attack*, chap. 1; Gordon and Trainor, *Cobra II*, 15–16; Anderson, *Bush's Wars*, 58–60. For a dissenting view, that there was movement toward war before 9/11, see Jane K. Cramer and Edward C. Duggan, "In Pursuit of Primacy: Why the United States Invaded Iraq," in *Why Did the United States Invade Iraq?* ed. Jane K. Cramer and A. Trevor Thrall (London: Routledge, 2012), esp. 213–20.

3. Anderson, *Bush's Wars*, 101.

4. The Downing Street memo was leaked to the London *Sunday Times* and published on May 1, 2005. It is reproduced in Mark Danner, *The Secret Way to War: The Downing Street Memo and the Iraq War's Buried History* (New York: New York Review of Books, 2006), 87–95. Also sug-gestive is a White House meeting that Richard Haass, the director of policy planning in the State Department, had with National Security Advisor Condoleezza Rice in early July 2002. When the subject turned to Iraq, Haass began to recite his reservations about a war. "Save your breath, Richard," Rice interrupted. "The president has already made up his mind on Iraq." Quoted in Richard N. Haass, *War of Necessity, War of Choice: A Memoir of Two Iraq Wars* (New York: Simon and Schuster, 2009), 4–5.

5. On the NIE on Iraq, see Woodward, *Plan of Attack*, 194–99; Gordon and Trainor, *Cobra II*, 146–49; Michael Isikoff and David Corn, *Hubris: The Inside Story of Spin, Scandal, and the Selling of the Iraq War* (New York: Three Rivers Press, 2007), 31–32, 42, 133–38; George Tenet, *At the Center of the Storm: The CIA during America's Time of Crisis* (New York: Harper Peren-nial, 2007), chap. 17; Anderson, *Bush's Wars*, 112; Pillar, *Intelligence and U.S. Foreign Policy*, 35–39;

Joshua Rovner, *Fixing the Facts: National Security and the Politics of Intelligence* (Ithaca: Cornell University Press, 2011), 152–54.

6. Referring to the "slam dunk" exchange, Tenet says in his memoirs, "Many people today believe that my use of the phrase 'slam dunk' was the seminal moment for steeling the president's determination to remove Saddam Hussein and to launch the Iraq war. It certainly makes for a memorable sound bite, but it is belied by the facts. Those two words and a meeting that took place in the Oval Office in December 2002 had nothing to do with the president's decision to send American troops into Iraq. That decision had already been made." *At the Center of the Storm*, chap. 19, quotation on 359. Also relevant are Freedman, "War in Iraq," 32; Woodward, *Plan of Attack*, 247–50; Anderson, *Bush's Wars*, 119–20; Rovner, *Fixing the Facts*, 155.

7. Appearing on *Meet the Press* in September 2006, Cheney reminded viewers: "George Tenet sat in the Oval Office and the president of the United States asked him directly, he said, 'George, how good is the case against Saddam on weapons of mass destruction?' [and] the director of the CIA said, 'It's a slam dunk, Mr. President, it's a slam dunk.' That was the intelligence that was provided to us at the time, and based upon which we made a choice." Quoted in Rovner, *Fixing Facts*, 155.

8. "'Lessons Learned' during Operation Enduring Freedom in Afghanistan and Operation Iraqi Freedom, and Ongoing Operations in the United States Central Command Region," Hearing before the Committee on Armed Services, United States Senate, July 9, 2003, Washington, DC, 2004, http://www.gpo.gov/fdsys/pkg/CHRG-108shrg96501/html/CHRG-108shrg96501.htm.

9. Douglas J. Feith, *War and Decision: Inside the Pentagon at the Dawn of the War on Terrorism* (New York: Harper, 2008), 520, 225 [emphasis in original]. Rice has also expressed regret over the overreliance of the Bush administration on intelligence "nuggets" in its selling of the war; Condoleezza Rice, *No Higher Honor: A Memoir of My Years in Washington* (New York: Crown Publishers, 2011), 195–99. As Robert Jervis points out, if Feith is correct that WMD stockpiles and ties to al Qaeda were not what were motivating the Bush administration to take action against Saddam Hussein, then "it lied to the American people about why they needed to go to war." "War, Intelligence, and Honesty," 673–75.

10. "Deputy Secretary Wolfowitz Interview with Sam Tannenhaus," *Vanity Fair*, May 9, 2003, http://www.defense.gov/transcripts/transcript.aspx?transcriptid=2594.

11. On WMDs as a least common denominator, see George Packer, *The Assassins' Gate: America in Iraq* (New York: Farrar, Straus and Giroux, 2005), 60. On WMDs as a consensus selling point, see Pillar, *Intelligence and U.S. Foreign Policy*, 30. Tenet cites the Wolfowitz interview in his memoirs, arguing, "The United States did not go to war in Iraq solely because of WMD. In my view, I doubt it was even the principal cause. Yet it was the public face that was put on it." *At the Center of the Storm*, 321.

12. Jeffrey Record, *Wanting War: Why the Bush Administration Invaded Iraq* (Washington, DC: Potomac Books, 2010), 85–86. Asking why the United States invaded Iraq, George Packer writes, "It still isn't possible to be sure—and this remains the most remarkable thing about the Iraq War." *Assassins' Gate*, 46.

13. Record dissects all these objectives in *Wanting War*, chap. 4. Also useful is Jane K. Cramer and A. Trevor Thrall, eds., *Why Did the United States Invade Iraq?* (London: Routledge, 2012).

14. There is a near-consensus that neoconservative influence was important in bringing on the Iraq War. When asked "Who influenced the decision to invade?" 83 percent of the expert respondents to a 2006 survey administered by Jane Cramer and Trevor Thrall cited "neoconservative advisors" as "very influential," just behind Vice President Richard Cheney (93 percent) and just ahead of Rumsfeld (79 percent) and Bush himself (74 percent); Jane K. Cramer and A. Trevor Thrall, "Introduction: Why Did the United States Invade Iraq?" in Cramer and Thrall,

Why Did the United States Invade Iraq?, 10. On the importance of the neoconservatives, see also Packer, *Assassins' Gate*, chaps. 1–2; John. J. Mearsheimer and Stephen M. Walt, *The Israel Lobby and U.S. Foreign Policy* (New York: Farrar, Straus and Giroux, 2007), chap. 8; Record, *Wanting War*, chap. 2. Trying to disrupt the consensus on neoconservative influence are Cramer and Duggan, "In Pursuit of Primacy," 210–25; Frank P. Harvey, *Explaining the Iraq War: Counterfactual Theory, Logic and Evidence* (Cambridge, UK: Cambridge University Press, 2012).

15. Robert Jervis, "Understanding the Bush Doctrine," *Political Science Quarterly* 118, no. 3 (2003), 386. On the Bush Doctrine, see also Jonathan Monten, "The Roots of the Bush Doctrine: Power, Nationalism, and Democracy Promotion in U.S. Strategy," *International Security* 29, no. 4 (2005), 112–56; Brian C. Schmidt and Michael C. Williams, "The Bush Doctrine and the Iraq War: Neoconservatives versus Realists," *Security Studies* 17, no. 2 (2008), 191–220.

16. Packer, *Assassins' Gate*, 36.

17. On Iraq as a preventive war, see Record, *Wanting War*, 98–100, See also Scott A. Silverstone, *Preventive War and American Democracy* (London: Routledge, 2007), 174–76. Putting the Bush administration preventive war policy in its historical context are John Lewis Gaddis, *Surprise, Security, and the American Experience* (Cambridge, MA: Harvard University Press, 2004); Marc Trachtenberg, "Preventive War and U.S. Foreign Policy," *Security Studies* 16, no. 1 (2007): 1–31. Putting the policy in its theoretical context is Alexandre Debs and Nuno P. Monteiro, "Known Unknowns: Power Shifts, Uncertainty, and War," *International Organization* 68, no. 1 (2014): 1–31.

18. White House, *The National Security Strategy of the United States of America*, Washington, DC, September 2002, 15, http://georgewbush-whitehouse.archives.gov/nsc/nss/2002/.

19. Cheney voiced the "1 percent doctrine" during a CIA briefing on potential collusion between Pakistani nuclear scientists and al Qaeda; Ron Suskind, *The One Percent Doctrine: Deep inside America's Pursuit of Its Enemies since 9/11* (New York: Simon and Schuster, 2006), 61–63.

20. This is the central thesis of Record's *Wanting War,* esp. 24–25 (quotation), 146–47. See also Cramer and Duggan, "In the Pursuit of Primacy," 230–38.

21. On the origins of the regime change consensus, see Russell A. Burgos, "Origins of Regime Change: 'Ideapolitik' on the Long Road to Baghdad, 1993–2000," *Security Studies* 17, no. 2 (2008): 221–56. During the 1990s and early 2000s, the debate among proponents of regime change was over whether an Iraqi exile army would suffice to bring Saddam down or whether a U.S.-led invasion would be necessary.

22. See Brent Scowcroft, "Don't Attack Saddam," *Wall Street Journal*, August 15, 2002, http://online.wsj.com/news/articles/SB1029371773228069195?mg=reno64-wsj&url=http%3A%2F%2Fonline.wsj.com%2Farticle%2FSB1029371773228069195.html; James A. Baker III, "The Right Way to Change a Regime," *New York Times*, August 25, 2002, http://www.nytimes.com/2002/08/25/opinion/the-right-way-to-change-a-regime.html. For more on the role that Scowcroft and Baker played in the prewar debate, see Woodward, *Plan of Attack*, 159–60; Jon Western, "The War over Iraq: Selling War to the American Public," *Security Studies* 14, no. 1 (2005): 120–22; Thomas E. Ricks, *Fiasco: The American Military Adventure in Iraq* (New York: Penguin Press, 2006), 46–49; Harvey, *Explaining the Iraq War*, 131–35.

23. On the August 5, 2002, meeting, see Woodward, *Plan of Attack*, 148–53; Gordon and Trainor, *Cobra II*, 80–83; Anderson, *Bush's Wars*, 103.

24. On Powell's Security Council presentation, see Woodward, *Plan of Attack*, 297–301, 309–12; Ricks, *Fiasco*, 90–94; Gordon and Trainor, *Cobra II*, 150 52; Isikoff and Corn, *Hubris*, 174 79, 185–90; Anderson, *Bush's Wars*, 122–23.

25. On civil-military relations during this period, see James Fallows, *Blind into Baghdad: America's War in Iraq* (New York: Vintage Books, 2006), 73–80; Ricks, *Fiasco*, 40–43, 68–74; Michael C. Desch, "Bush and the Generals," *Foreign Affairs* 86, no. 3 (2007): 97–108, http://www.

foreignaffairs.com/articles/62616/michael-c-desch/bush-and-the-generals; Risa A. Brooks, *Shaping Strategy: The Civil-Military Politics of Strategic Assessment* (Princeton: Princeton University Press, 2008), chap. 7.

26. Fallows, *Blind into Baghdad*, 77.

27. In the same testimony, Wolfowitz said, "It's hard to conceive that it would take more forces to provide stability in post-Saddam Iraq than it would take to conduct the war itself and to secure the surrender of Saddam's security forces and his army—hard to imagine." On the Shinseki-Wolfowitz exchange, see Packer, *Assassins' Gate*, 114–17; Fallows, *Blind into Baghdad*, 97–99; Ricks, *Fiasco*, 96–100; Isikoff and Corn, *Hubris*, 193–95.

28. Fallows, *Blind into Baghdad*, 99.

29. Packer, *Assassins' Gate*, 117.

30. The best source on the failings of the media in the run-up to the Iraq War remains Michael Massing, "Now They Tell Us," *New York Review of Books,* February 26, 2004, http://www.nybooks.com/articles/archives/2004/feb/26/now-they-tell-us/?pagination=false. Massing singles out the *New York Times* for being especially deferential to White House views.

31. Harvey, *Explaining the Iraq War*, 190.

32. Ricks, *Fiasco*, 89.

33. William G. Howell and Jon C. Pevehouse, *While Dangers Gather: Congressional Checks on Presidential War Powers* (Princeton: Princeton University Press, 2007), 156. Howell and Pevehouse find direct evidence for the indexing hypothesis in the Iraq case, demonstrating that the volume and content of news coverage, especially at the local level, closely tracked congressional activity (chap. 6). On the indexing hypothesis and Iraq, see also Ole R. Holsti, *American Public Opinion on the Iraq War* (Ann Arbor: University of Michigan Press, 2011), 163–65.

34. The realist argument was that, instead of attacking Iraq, the United States should contain it. See, for example, "War with Iraq Is Not in America's National Interest," the paid advertisement that over thirty security studies scholars—many of them realists—took out in the *New York Times* on September 26, 2002. On the debate between realists and neoconservatives over the Iraq War, see Schmidt and Williams, "Bush Doctrine and the Iraq War," 191–220. To simplify greatly, Schmidt and Williams argue that realists lost the debate over the Iraq War because their arguments did not resonate as deeply with Americans as those of neoconservatives.

35. Jane Kellett Cramer, "Militarized Patriotism: Why the U.S. Marketplace of Ideas Failed before the Iraq War," *Security Studies* 16, no. 3 (2007): 500–511.

36. On the Biden-Lugar-Hagel initiative, see also Isikoff and Corn, *Hubris*, 127–28.

37. Ricks, *Fiasco*, 61.

38. Cramer, "Militarized Patriotism," 509.

39. Ricks, *Fiasco*, 61; Isikoff and Corn, *Hubris*, 137; Tenet, *At the Center of the Storm*, 337; Pillar, *Intelligence and U.S. Foreign Policy*, 73.

40. Tom Daschle (D-South Dakota), the Senate majority leader, after announcing his support for the Iraq War Resolution, concluded his statement, "On Monday night in his speech to the Nation, the President said: The situation could hardly get worse for world security and the people of Iraq. Yes, it can. If the administration attempts to use the authority in this resolution without doing the work that is required before and after military action in Iraq, the situation there and elsewhere can indeed get worse. We could see more turmoil in the Persian Gulf, not less. We could see more bloodshed in the Middle East, not less. Americans could find themselves more vulnerable to terrorist attacks, not less. So I stress again, this resolution represents a beginning, not an end. If we are going to make America and the world safer, much more work needs to be done before the force authorized in this document is used." Senator Tom Daschle, "Authorization of the Use of United States Forces against Iraq," *Congressional Record* S10240–S10242, October 10, 2002.

41. Senator Joseph Biden, *Congressional Record* S10293, October 10, 2002.

42. Senator Hillary Clinton, *Congressional Record* S10289, October 10, 2002.

43. Silverstone, *Preventive War and American Democracy*, 180. The others were Kerry (D-Massachusetts), Hagel (R-Nebraska), Dodd (D-Connecticut), DeWine (R-Ohio), Kohl (D-Wisconsin), Dorgan (D-North Dakota), and Feinstein (D-California).

44. Robert C. Byrd, "Congress Must Resist the Rush to War," *New York Times*, October 10, 2002, http://www.nytimes.com/2002/10/10/opinion/congress-must-resist-the-rush-to-war.html. See also Senator Byrd, *Congressional Record* S10235–S10236, October 10, 2002. On Byrd's futile attempt to shame his fellow senators into opposition, see Ricks, *Fiasco*, 62–63, 88.

45. Ronald R. Krebs and Jennifer K. Lobasz, "Fixing the Meaning of 9/11: Hegemony, Coercion, and the Road to War in Iraq," *Security Studies* 16, no. 3 (2007), 445n. 137. Scott Silverstone shows that what little congressional opposition there was to the Iraq War was concentrated among political liberals; *Preventive War and American Democracy*, 179–81.

46. Amy Gershkoff and Shana Kushner, "Shaping Public Opinion: The 9/11-Iraq Connection in the Bush Administration's Rhetoric," *Perspectives on Politics* 3. no. 3 (2005): 525–37.

47. Throughout the 1990s, survey after survey showed that a majority of Americans was open to the use of force to unseat Saddam Hussein; Western, "The War over Iraq," 112; Silverstone, *Preventive War and American Democracy*, 185–87; Holsti, *American Public Opinion*, 133.

48. Gary C. Jacobson, *A Divider, Not a Uniter: George W. Bush and the American People* (New York: Pearson Longman, 2007), 96. See also Scott L. Althaus and Devon M. Largio, "When Osama Became Saddam: Origins and Consequences of the Change in America's Public Enemy #1," *PS: Political Science and Politics*, no. 4 (October 2004): 795–99.

49. Douglas C. Foyle, "Leading the Public to War? The Influence of American Public Opinion on the Bush Administration's Decision to Go to War in Iraq," *International Journal of Public Opinion Research* 16, no. 3 (2004), 273.

50. Foyle, "Leading the Public to War?" 269, 288.

51. Jacobson, *Divider, Not a Uniter,* 109–10. On the public's preference for a multilateral approach to Iraq, see also Holsti, *American Public Opinion*, 36–38; Harvey, *Explaining the Iraq War*, 182–85.

52. On partisan differences over Iraq, see Jacobson, *Divider, Not a Uniter*, 113–18. See also A. Trevor Thrall, "A Bear in the Woods? Threat Framing and the Marketplace of Values," *Security Studies* 16, no. 3 (2007): 479–83; Adam J. Berinsky, *In Time of War: Understanding American Public Opinion from World War II to Iraq* (Chicago: University of Chicago Press, 2009), 100–111; Holsti, *American Public Opinion*, chap. 3. Berinsky notes that "the magnitude of the partisan differences over the Iraq War is unparalleled in the history of opinion polling." *In Time of War,* 218.

53. Steven Kull, Clay Ramsay, and Evan Lewis, "Misperceptions, the Media, and the Iraq War," *Political Science Quarterly* 118, no. 4 (2003–2004): 586–88.

54. Evan Braden Montgomery, "Counterfeit Diplomacy and Mobilization in Democracies," *Security Studies* 22, no. 1 (2013): 33–67.

55. Danner, *Secret Way to War*, 11–12. See also Jane M. O. Sharp, "Tony Blair Nurtures the Special Relationship," in Cramer and Duggan, *Why Did the United States Invade Iraq?* 177.

56. Danner, *Secret Way to War*, 12.

57. On August 26, 2002, Cheney told a gathering of the Veterans of Foreign Wars, "Saddam has perfected the game of shoot and retreat, and is very skilled in the art of denial and deception. A return of inspectors would provide no assurance whatsoever of his compliance with UN resolutions. On the contrary, there is a great danger that it would provide false comfort that Saddam was somehow back in his box." White House, "Vice President Speaks at VFW 103rd National Convention," August 26, 2002, http://georgewbush-whitehouse.archives.gov/news/releases/2002/08/20020826.html.

58. Cheney, quoted in Woodward, *Plan of Attack*, 157.

59. On the debate within the Bush administration over whether and how to approach the United Nations, see Woodward, *Plan of Attack*, chaps. 15–17; Alexander Thompson, *Channels of Power: The UN Security Council and U.S. Statecraft in Iraq* (Ithaca: Cornell University Press, 2009), 137–40; Kelly McHugh, "Bush, Blair, and the War in Iraq: Alliance Politics and the Limits of Influence," *Political Science Quarterly* 125, no. 3 (2010): 477–81.

60. Thompson, *Channels of Power*, 171; on the politics surrounding the inspections process and a second resolution, see 143–54.

61. See Harvey, *Explaining the Iraq War*, 129. Se also Gordon and Trainor, *Cobra II*, 149. It is hard to believe that Democrats sincerely held this view, given all the indicators that Bush was intent on regime change regardless of the outcome of the UN process.

62. As Danner has argued, "The inspectors' failure to find weapons in Iraq was taken to discredit the worth of the inspections, rather than to cast doubt on the administration's contention that Saddam possessed large stockpiles of weapons of mass destruction." *Secret Way to War*, 22.

63. As Kelly McHugh has put it, "Essentially, the diplomatic process was always designed to culminate in war." "Bush, Blair, and the War in Iraq," 486. See also Woodward, *Plan of Attack*, 222; Danner, *Secret Way of War*, 17; Thompson, *Channels of Power*, 142; Record, *Wanting War*, 75–76.

64. Quoted in Woodward, *Plan of Attack*, 234.

65. Don Van Natta Jr., "Bush Was Set on Path to War, Memo by British Adviser Says," *New York Times*, March 27, 2006, http://www.nytimes.com/2006/03/27/international/europe/27memo.html?pagewanted=all&_r=2&.

66. On Saddam's mind-set in the run-up to war, see Kevin M. Woods, with Michael R. Pease, Mark E. Stout, Williamson Murray, and James G. Lacey, *Iraqi Perspectives Report: A View of Operation Iraqi Freedom from Saddam's Senior Leadership* (Norfolk, VA: US Joint Forces Command, March 2006). See also Amatzia Baram, "Deterrence Lessons from Iraq: Rationality Is Not the Only Key to Containment," *Foreign Affairs* 91, no. 4 (2012), 87–89, http://www.foreignaffairs.com/articles/137693/amatzia-baram/deterrence-lessons-from-iraq; Harvey, *Explaining the Iraq War*, chap. 8.

67. *Politicization* can be defined broadly as leaders giving inaccurate accounts about intelligence to garner political support or defined narrowly as leaders putting pressure on the intelligence community to tell them what they want to hear. There is a near-consensus that politicization, defined broadly, was prevalent in the Iraq case, but there is more disagreement about the role that political pressure played in shaping intelligence assessments of the Iraq threat. Jervis, in particular, discounts the importance of political pressure; the reason for the intelligence failure, he argues, was that the inference that Saddam had WMDs was more plausible than any of the alternatives; *Why Intelligence Fails*, 131–36, 146–50. Analyses that emphasize both types of politicization include Chaim Kaufmann, "Threat Inflation and the Failure of the Marketplace of Ideas: The Selling of the Iraq War," *International Security* 29, no. 1 (2004): 37–41; Pillar, *Intelligence and U.S. Foreign Policy*, chap. 6; Rovner, *Fixing the Facts*, chap. 7.

68. George W. Bush, "Address before a Joint Session of the Congress on the State of the Union," January 28, 2003, http://www.presidency.ucsb.edu/ws/index.php?pid=29645&st=&st1=.

69. See Joseph Cirincione, Jessica T. Mathews, George Perkovich, with Alexis Orton, *WMD in Iraq: Evidence and Implications* (Washington, D.C.: Carnegie Endowment for International Peace, 2004), http://carnegieendowment.org/files/Iraq3FullText.pdf p. 43; Kaufmann, "Threat Inflation," 16–19. See especially *Report on Whether Public Statements Regarding Iraq by U.S. Government Officials Were Substantiated by Intelligence Information*, Senate Select Committee on Intelligence, Senate Report 110-345 (June 5, 2008), 71, 82, http://www.intelligence.senate.gov/pdfs/110345.pdf.

70. NIE 2002–16HC, *Iraq's Continuing Programs for Weapons of Mass Destruction*, October 2002, 8, http://www2.gwu.edu/~nsarchiv/NSAEBB/NSAEBB129/nie.pdf (redacted version).

71. Quoted in Isikoff and Corn, *Hubris*, 102. On the PCTEG and the Atta-in-Prague story, see chap. 6. See also Pillar, *Intelligence and U.S. Foreign Policy*, 45–49. Powell was suspicious enough of the intelligence coming out of the PCTEG, including the Atta-in-Prague story, that he refused to include it in his address to the UN Security Council.

72. This chapter focuses more on how the Bush administration dealt with the nuclear weapons issue than with other forms of WMDs such as biological and chemical weapons. This is both because the disparity between administration statements and the underlying intelligence was greater on the nuclear weapons issue and because it was more crucial to the overall case for war.

73. White House, "Vice President Speaks at VFW 103rd National Convention," August 26, 2002, http://georgewbush-whitehouse.archives.gov/news/releases/2002/08/20020826.html. Tenet says that Cheney's speech "went well beyond" what intelligence analysis could support; *At the Center of the Storm*, 315. For his part, Haass "thought the vice president's speech badly overstated the Iraqi threat." *War of Necessity, War of Choice*, 218.

74. George W. Bush, "Address to the Nation on Iraq from Cincinnati, Ohio," October 7, 2002, http://www.presidency.ucsb.edu/ws/index.php?pid=73139&st=&st1=.

75. George W. Bush, "Address before a Joint Session of the Congress on the State of the Union," January 28, 2003, http://www.presidency.ucsb.edu/ws/index.php?pid=29645&st=&st1=.

76. The conclusion reached by the Senate Select Committee on Intelligence in its report on the subject was that "Statements by the President, Vice President, Secretary of State and the National Security Advisor regarding a possible Iraqi nuclear weapons program were generally substantiated by intelligence community estimates, but did not convey the substantial disagreements that existed in the intelligence community." *Report on Whether Public Statements*, 15.

77. NIE 2002–16HC, *Iraq's Continuing Programs*, 8–9.

78. Ibid., 5–6.

79. Quoted in Isikoff and Corn, *Hubris*, 40. When they were readmitted to Iraq in late 2002, inspectors from the International Atomic Energy Agency (IAEA) rushed to the Iraqi 81 mm rocket production facility and found 13,000 complete rockets—all made from the same aluminum tubes that the Bush administration had been claiming were for centrifuges (165).

80. NIE 2002–16HC, *Iraq's Continuing Programs*, 6. On the aluminum tubes controversy, see Isikoff and Corn, *Hubris*, 33–41, 165–66; Jervis, *Why Intelligence Fails*, 142–44; Rovner, *Fixing the Facts*, 145.

81. Isikoff and Corn, *Hubris*, 90–91.

82. Anderson, *Bush's Wars*, 97.

83. Rovner, *Fixing the Facts*, 183.

84. Quoted in Anderson, *Bush's Wars*, 97–98.

85. David E. Sanger and James Risen, "C.I.A. Chief Takes Blame in Assertion on Iraqi Uranium," *New York Times*, July 12, 2003, http://www.nytimes.com/2003/07/12/world/after-the-war-intelligence-cia-chief-takes-blame-in-assertion-on-iraqi-uranium.html.

86. For Tenet's take on the yellowcake uranium episode, see *At the Center of the Storm*, chap. 24.

87. Isikoff and Corn, *Hubris*, 201–4.

88. For rebuttals of the notion that Saddam was undeterrable, see John J. Mearsheimer and Stephen M. Walt, "An Unnecessary War," *Foreign Policy* 134 (2003): 50–59, http://www.foreignpolicy.com/articles/2003/01/01/an_unnecessary_war; Robert L. Jervis, "The Confrontation between Iraq and the US: Implications for the Theory and Practice of Deterrence," *European Journal of International Relations* 9, no. 2 (2003): 315–37; Kaufmann, "Threat Inflation," 9–16.

89. George W. Bush, "Address to the Nation on Iraq," March 17, 2003, http://www.presidency. ucsb.edu/ws/index.php?pid=63713&st=&st1=.

90. Record, *Wanting War*, chap. 3.

91. Rovner, *Fixing the Facts*, 177–81. Leffler is adamant, based on a survey of memoirs, that the Bush administration went to war with Iraq to neutralize the perceived threat posed by the nexus of WMDs and terrorism. At the same time, he concedes that Bush, Cheney, Rice, Rumsfeld, and Powell distorted intelligence to mobilize public sentiment in favor of war; Melvyn P. Leffler, "The Foreign Policies of the George W. Bush Administration: Memoirs, History, Legacy," *Diplomatic History* 37, no. 2 (2013), esp. 201–3.

92. Dan Reiter, "Democracy, Deception, and Entry into War," *Security Studies* 21, no. 4 (2012), 595, 602–3.

93. Kaufmann, "Threat Inflation," 32–46.

94. Ronald R. Krebs, "Selling the Market Short? The Marketplace of Ideas and the Iraq War," *International Security* 29, no. 4 (2005), 198–99.

95. Krebs and Lobasz, "Fixing the Meaning of 9/11."

96. Cramer, "Militarized Patriotism."

97. Kenneth A. Schultz, *Democracy and Coercive Diplomacy* (Cambridge, UK: Cambridge University Press, 2001), 68. For additional examples, see Howell and Pevehouse, *While Dangers Gather*, chaps. 1, 5.

98. On the "Afghan model," see Richard B. Andres, Craig Wills, and Thomas E. Griffith Jr., "Winning with Allies: The Strategic Value of the Afghan Model," *International Security* 30, no. 3 (2005/2006): 124–160; Stephen D. Biddle, "Allies, Airpower, and Modern Warfare: The Afghan Model in Afghanistan and Iraq," *International Security* 30, no. 3 (2005/2006): 161–76.

99. See Gordon and Trainor, *Cobra II*, 59–61. See also Record, *Wanting War*, 124–32, on Rumsfeld's larger "transformation" agenda at the Pentagon.

100. Woodward, *Plan of Attack*, 326. The best source on military planning for Operation Iraqi Freedom is Gordon and Trainor, *Cobra II*.

101. On planning for postwar Iraq, see Packer, *Assassins' Gate*, chap. 4; Nora Bensahel, "Mission Not Accomplished: What Went Wrong with Iraqi Reconstruction," *Journal of Strategic Studies* 29, no. 3 (2006): 454–62; James Fallows, *Blind into Baghdad*, 43–106; Gordon and Trainor, *Cobra II*, chap. 8; Isikoff and Corn, *Hubris*, chap. 11; Ricks, *Fiasco*, esp. 78–80, 109–11; Jervis, "War, Intelligence, and Honesty," 663–69; Aaron Rapport, "The Long and Short of It: Cognitive Constraints on Leaders' Assessments of 'Postwar' Iraq," *International Security* 37, no. 3 (2012/2013):133–71. For an account that emphasizes the failure to implement the postwar planning that was done, as opposed to the paucity of planning itself, see Stephen Benedict Dyson, "What Really Happened in Planning for Postwar Iraq?" *Political Science Quarterly* 128, no. 3 (2013): 455–88.

102. Packer, *Assassins' Gate*, 147. In summer 2002, Cheney assured Dick Armey, the House majority leader, "They're going to welcome us. It will be like the American army going through the streets of Paris. They're sitting there ready to form a new government. The people will be so happy with their freedoms that we'll probably back ourselves out of there within a month or two." Record, *Wanting War*, 81.

103. Fallows, *Blind into Baghdad*, 46–47. See also Rapport, "Long and Short of It," 163–64.

104. The NIC report is reproduced in *Report on Prewar Intelligence Assessments about Postwar Iraq*, Senate Select Committee on Intelligence, Senate Report 110-76, May 25, 2007, app. B, http://www.intelligence.senate.gov/11076.pdf. For more on the report by the intelligence official who oversaw its drafting, see Pillar, *Intelligence and U.S. Foreign Policy*, 55–59.

105. Isikoff and Corn, *Hubris*, 412. See also Fallows, *Blind into Baghdad*, 61; Jervis, "War, Intelligence, and Honesty," 665; Pillar, *Intelligence and U.S. Foreign Policy*, 54–55.

106. Alison Mitchell, "Democrats, Wary of War in Iraq, Also Worry about Battling Bush," *New York Times*, September 14, 2002, http://www.nytimes.com/2002/09/14/us/threats-responses-democrats-democrats-wary-war-iraq-also-worry-about-battling.html?pagewanted=all&src=pm.

107. See Isikoff and Corn, *Hubris*, 21–23. See also Western, "War over Iraq," 129.

108. This is according to Senator Byrd, in Ricks, *Fiasco*, 62.

109. Quoted in Isikoff and Corn, *Hubris*, 138.

110. In their speeches on the House and Senate floor, congressional Republicans presented, on average, 4.1 different arguments for the use of force and just 0.1 arguments against; Howell and Pevehouse, *While Dangers Gather*, 177.

111. Silverstone, *Preventive War and American Democracy*, 179.

112. Gary R. Hess, "Presidents and the Congressional War Resolutions of 1991 and 2002," *Political Science Quarterly* 121, no. 1 (2006), 102.

113. Ibid., 95.

114. Joel Achenbach, "The Experts, in Retreat; after-the-Fact Explanations for the Gloomy Predictions," *Washington Post*, February 28, 1991.

115. Hess, "Presidents and the Congressional War Resolutions," 97, 101.

116. Stephen Biddle, *Military Power: Explaining Victory and Defeat in Modern Battle* (Princeton: Princeton University Press, 2004), 1.

117. Ibid., 133.

118. Hess, "Presidents and the Congressional War Resolutions," 108.

119. "The President and his key communications advisers," Feith speculates, "apparently decided that the failure to find WMD stockpiles was such an embarrassment that the President should not even try to explain it or put it in context. Rather, the Administration tried to change the subject." "This change in rhetoric aggravated the damage to the Administration's credibility," Feith argues. "It made the President appear to be shifting his ground—changing the rationale for the war—without forthrightly explaining the change." *War and Decision*, 477.

120. On the public's growing disenchantment with the Iraq War, see Holsti, *American Public Opinion*, chap. 2, esp. figs. 2.1–2.4. Gelpi, Feaver, and Reifler argue that public support for the war did not collapse entirely because some optimism remained that a decent outcome could be achieved in Iraq; Christopher Gelpi, Peter D. Feaver, and Jason Reifler, *Paying the Human Costs of War: American Public Opinion and Casualties in Military Conflicts* (Princeton: Princeton University Press, 2009).

121. *The Commission on the Intelligence Capabilities of the United States Regarding Weapons of Mass Destruction*, Report to the President of the United States, March 31, 2005, http://govinfo.library.unt.edu/wmd/report/wmd_report.pdf. Neither the Silberman-Robb Commission nor the Senate Select Committee on Intelligence in its July 2004 report on prewar intelligence (http://www.intelligence.senate.gov/108301.pdf) addressed the issue of how the Bush administration used intelligence in its sales campaign for the war. This was left to a follow-on report by the Senate Select Committee on Intelligence (http://www.intelligence.senate.gov/pdfs/110345.pdf), which was not released until June 2008, after control of the committee had changed hands in that year's election. On the political biases of the various official investigations into prewar intelligence failures, see Robert Jervis, "Reports, Politics, and Intelligence Failures: The Case of Iraq," *Journal of Strategic Studies* 29, no. 1 (2006): 3–52.

122. Cramer and Thrall, "Why Did the United States Invade Iraq?" 5.

123. The polling results were culled from Polling Report's Iraq page, http://www.pollingreport.com/iraq.htm (accessed June 13, 2013).

124. John Mueller, "The Iraq Syndrome," *Foreign Affairs* 84 (2005): 44–54, http://www.foreignaffairs.com/articles/61196/john-mueller/the-iraq-syndrome. See also John Mueller, "The Iraq Syndrome Revisited," *Foreign Affairs* 90 (2011), http://www.foreignaffairs.com/articles/67681/

john-mueller/the-iraq-syndrome-revisited; Mueller, "Iraq Syndrome Redux," *Foreign Affairs* 93 (2014), http://www.foreignaffairs.com/articles/141578/john-mueller/iraq-syndrome-redux.

125. Thom Shanker, "Warning against Wars like Iraq and Afghanistan," *New York Times*, February 25, 2011, http://www.nytimes.com/2011/02/26/world/26gates.html?_r=1&.

126. See, for example, David E. Sanger, *Confront and Conceal: Obama's Secret Wars and Surprising Use of American Power* (New York: Crown Publishers, 2012).

Conclusion

1. Dan Reiter, "Democracy, Deception, and Entry into War," *Security Studies* 21, no. 4 (2012), 596. Reiter goes on to say later, "On the democratic side, there are few examples of governments entering wars on the basis of deliberate deception" (604).

2. Keir A. Lieber, "The New History of World War I and What It Means for International Relations Theory," *International Security* 32, no. 2 (2007), 155.

3. See, for example, the contributions to Steven E. Miller, Sean M. Lynn-Jones, and Stephen Van Evera, eds., *Military Strategy and the Origins of the First World War*, Rev. ed. (Princeton: Princeton University Press, 1991).

4. See Stephen Van Evera, *Causes of War: Power and the Roots of Conflict* (Ithaca: Cornell University Press, 1999), 150–51, 230–31; Dale C. Copeland, *The Origins of Major War* (Ithaca: Cornell University Press, 2000), chap. 4; Lieber, "New History of World War I," 185–87.

5. Copeland, *Origins of Major War*, 105–13.

6. Christopher Layne, "Kant or Cant: The Myth of the Democratic Peace," *International Security* 19, no. 2 (1994), 41–44.

7. See Copeland, *Origins of Major War*, 80. See also Dan Reiter, "Exploding the Powder Keg Myth: Preemptive Wars Almost Never Happen," *International Security* 20, no. 2 (1995), 20.

8. Michael C. Desch, *Power and Military Effectiveness: The Fallacy of Democratic Triumphalism* (Baltimore: Johns Hopkins University Press, 2008), 97.

9. Ibid., 102–3.

10. See Michael C. Desch, "Democracy and Victory: Very Selective Effects," in *Democracy and Victory*, H-Diplo/ISSF Roundtable 2, no. 12 (2011), 49–52; See also Jack S. Levy and Joseph R. Gochal, "Democracy and Preventive War: Israel and the 1956 Sinai Campaign," *Security Studies* 11, no. 2 (2001/2002), 37–38.

11. See Desch, "Democracy and Victory," 56–60. See also Miriam Fendius Elman, "Israel's Invasion of Lebanon, 1982: Regime Change and War Decisions," in *Paths to Peace: Is Democracy the Answer?* ed. Miriam Fendius Elman (Cambridge, MA: MIT Press, 1997), 321–25. What distinguishes the 1982 Lebanon War from the other cases discussed in this book is the extent to which Sharon deceived the remainder of the Israeli government as well as the public about his plans.

12. Joshua Rovner, *Fixing the Facts: National Security and the Politics of Intelligence* (Ithaca: Cornell University Press, 2011), 198.

13. Ibid., 188–89. Making the same point is Robert Jervis, *Why Intelligence Fails: Lessons from the Iranian Revolution and the Iraq War* (Ithaca: Cornell University Press, 2010), 158–59.

14. Evan Braden Montgomery, "Counterfeit Diplomacy and Mobilization in Democracies," *Security Studies* 22, no. 1 (2013), 51.

15. Ibid., 58–64.

16. Austin Carson, "Facing Off and Saving Face: Covert Intervention and Escalation Management in the Korean War," *International Organization*, forthcoming.

17. See also Steven Casey, "White House Publicity Operations during the Korean War, June 1950–June 1951," *Presidential Studies Quarterly* 35, no. 4 (December 2005), 691–717; Casey, *Selling the Korean War: Propaganda, Politics, and Public Opinion in the United States, 1950–1953* (Oxford: Oxford University Press, 2008), esp. chap. 1.

18. According to Zhang, "Soviet pilots flew 63,229 sorties. . . . They fought 1,683 combat missions and claimed the destruction of 1,309 UN aircraft." Xiaoming Zhang, *Red Wings over the Yalu: China, the Soviet Union, and the Air War in Korea* (College Station: Texas A&M University Press, 2002), 202.

19. Jon Halliday, "Air Operations in Korea: The Soviet Side of the Story," in *A Revolutionary War: Korea and the Transformation of the Postwar World,* ed. William J. Williams (Chicago: Imprint Publications, 1993), 160.

20. Another potential example of deception in the cause of peace is the secret diplomacy that brought the Cuban Missile Crisis to an end. As is now well known, members of the Kennedy administration made in private a number of key concessions that in public they vehemently denied making. Jonathan Brown and Anthony Marcum argue that democratic leaders should be more capable than their nondemocratic counterparts of making private concessions. The logic is that "large-coalition leaders possess a greater ability to hide policy choices from their supporters." Jonathan N. Brown and Anthony S. Marcum, "Avoiding Audience Costs: Domestic Political Accountability and Concessions in Crisis Diplomacy," *Security Studies* 20, no. 2 (2011), 141–70, quotation on 143. On secret diplomacy between adversaries, see also Keren Yarhi-Milo, "Tying Hands behind Closed Doors: The Logic and Practice of Secret Reassurance," *Security Studies* 22, no. 3 (2013): 405–35.

21. Rosato, for example, goes too far in arguing that "pacific publics and antiwar groups rarely constrain policymakers' decisions for war." Sebastian Rosato, "The Flawed Logic of Democratic Peace Theory," *American Political Science Review* 97, no. 4 (2003), 593.

22. Reiter argues that "autocracies engage in deception related to war initiation more frequently than do democracies." "Democracy, Deception, and Entry into War," 604. Such a conclusion is premature. Establishing it would require a fuller comparison of the prewar politics in autocracies and democracies than has yet been undertaken.

23. If democracies do have an information advantage over their competitors when it comes to selecting into wars, its source seems to lie more at the elite than at the mass level. One possibility is that democracies get better advice from a professional and meritocratic officer corps. This argument holds only if nondemocratic militaries are generally afflicted with cronyism and incompetence. Risa Brooks concludes, however, that the quality of civil-military relations varies independently of regime type, which means that democracies do not have a uniform edge over nondemocracies when it comes to strategic assessment; Risa A. Brooks, *Shaping Strategy: The Civil-Military Politics of Strategic Assessment* (Princeton: Princeton University Press, 2008).

24. For the criteria underlying this distinction, see Sebastian Rosato and John Schuessler, "A Realist Foreign Policy for the United States," *Perspectives on Politics* 9, no. 4 (2011): 803–819.

25. "All lies, unlike all men, are not created equal," as Cannon has put it. Carl M. Cannon, "Untruth and Consequences," *Atlantic,* January/February 2007, 58, http://www.theatlantic.com/magazine/archive/2007/01/untruth-and-consequences/305561/.

26. John Mearsheimer, "Imperial by Design," *National Interest,* no. 111 (2011), 18–19, http://nationalinterest.org/article/imperial-by-design-4576.

27. John J. Mearsheimer, *Why Leaders Lie: The Truth about Lying in International Politics* (Oxford: Oxford University Press, 2011), 102. See also John Mearsheimer, "America Unhinged," *National Interest,* no. 129 (2014), 25–26, http://nationalinterest.org/article/america-unhinged-9639.

28. For blueprints along these lines, see Eugene Gholz, Daryl G. Press, and Harvey M. Sapolsky, "Come Home, America: The Strategy of Restraint in the Face of Temptation," *International Security* 21, no. 4 (1997): 5–48; Stephen M. Walt, *Taming American Power: The Global Response to U.S. Primacy* (New York: W. W. Norton, 2005), chap. 5; Christopher Layne, *Peace of Illusions: American Grand Strategy from 1940 to the Present* (Ithaca: Cornell University Press, 2006), chap. 8; Barry R. Posen, "Pull Back: The Case for a Less Activist Foreign Policy," *Foreign Affairs* 92 (2013):

116–28, http://www.foreignaffairs.com/articles/138466/barry-r-posen/pull-back; Barry R. Posen, *Restraint: A New Foundation for U.S. Grand Strategy* (Ithaca: Cornell University Press, 2014).

29. I thank Robert Jervis for pressing me to grapple with this issue.

30. See Elizabeth N. Saunders, "War and the Inner Circle: Democratic Elites and the Politics of Using Force," *Security Studies*, forthcoming.

31. Warren F. Kimball, "Franklin D. Roosevelt and World War II," *Presidential Studies Quarterly* 34, no. 1 (2004), 98.

Index